More Winegums From The Telegram

A second helping of essays and stuff

More Winegums from The Telegram

A regular online essayist for five years, Johnny Monroe in his alter-ego guise of 'Petunia Winegum' has managed to provoke thought, debate and discussion by documenting events of the day with a satirical, critical eye and the odd side-splitting turn-of-phrase. His good fortune is to be writing in an era stripped of certainties, a turbulent, Stygian interregnum in which no waspish wordsmith worth his salt can bemoan the absence of inspiration or dearth of source material.

From the combative cockpit of cyberspace to the printed page, here is the second volume of Johnny Monroe's collected essays from the 'Winegum Telegram' blog – covering everything from the political to the pop cultural whilst refusing to recognise either side of the divide as exclusive copyright-holders of the moral high-ground. Outside the tent pissing-in, Monroe's detached perspective allows for a clearer picture of the most unpredictable (and occasionally mind-boggling) period in living memory than can be found on Fleet Street, and this collection widens the net from Brexit Britain to Trump's America, Kim Jong-un's North Korea, and other similarly tranquil dots on the map.

Divided into five distinctive chapters, this second volume again highlights the advantages of the author having the freedom to set his own remit. From affectionate obituaries for both the household name and the cult figure to vitriolic studies of the human misery arising from the abuse industry – not to mention shining an unflattering light on the double-standards and hysterical hypocrisy of Identity Politics – volume two maintains the height of the bar set by volume one and then edges it a little higher.

Reproducing reportage chronicling the past three highly eventful years, 'More Winegums from The Telegram' is a series of subjective time capsules capturing the mood of the moment in which they were written – and few of those moments were dull...

1
Pop Life (and death)
Overtures and obituaries

David Bowie is dead. Still doesn't sound right, does it? Standing at the crossing this morning, waiting for the red man to be superseded by the green man, a student girl in her late teens stood on the other side of the road, bright scarlet hair; and there, in an instant, barely a minute after locking the front door, I see the influence of David Bowie as one of Ziggy's grandchildren faced me across the traffic. She may or may not know, I thought, but without him she wouldn't be there.

Flashback to 1974, wandering around the aisles in the novel new Asda superstore, leaving my parents to attend to the weekly shop as I seek out the comic racks; en route, I find myself drawn like a little iron filing to the magnet nestled in the record racks, and I come face-to-face with *that* face – side-by-side are 'Aladdin Sane' and 'Diamond Dogs', works of art in an age when the LP sleeve was the contemporary canvas. Accustomed to painted faces via 'Top of the Pops' regulars such as Roy Wood of Wizzard, Steve Priest from the Sweet and the rest of the Glam court jesters, I nevertheless knew this was something on another level; the radio hits were already being absorbed – 'The Jean Genie', 'Life on Mars', 'Rebel Rebel', even the much-maligned 'Laughing Gnome', all sung in that strange neo-cockney voice that could range from high-pitched scream to low-pitched growl – as the otherworldly spectre hovering over a culture I was too young to participate in was unable to stand still. By the time I had begun spending my pocket-money on seven-inch singles, he was in drag to promote 'Boys Keep Swinging' as a prologue to anticipating the coming wave of pretty things poised to conquer the charts that came via 'Ashes to Ashes'.

Aged 15, I experienced the colossal commercial monster of 'Let's Dance' in a year when Bowie's influence on mainstream pop was at its zenith as Duran Duran, Spandau Ballet and Culture Club were living out their adolescent Bowie fantasies on the world stage. His biggest period of sustained success for a decade inspired the canny cash-in of his former record label RCA, who reissued all of his 70s albums at an affordable price; I had an entire career ready and waiting for me to dive into and by doing so, I passed through a door that changed me forever and for the better. I wouldn't be alone. The Punks, the New Romantics, and their bastard offspring the Goths, were all in his debt.

In 1983, I was mining a legacy that only stretched back fourteen years, yet there was enough richness in there to span a century. From acoustic folk to full-blown Metal, from Art School Glam to Plastic Soul, from synthesized soundscapes to endless isolated sub-genres that were never limited by labels, the variety was staggering. The restless artistic spirit rewards the devotee with an abundance of options and renders those who cling to a hit formula for life one-trick ponies who eventually subside into irrelevance. With Bowie, there was even an additional icing on the cake that proved just as influential for closet extroverts: for each musical about-turn, there was an accompanying visual one too.

The founder of the Biba fashion house, Barbara Hulanicki, once observed that British wartime and post-war rationing had left an entire generation malnourished, enabling them to mature into stick-thin clothes hangers ideal for the androgynous peacockery that Swinging London defined in the 60s and David Bowie remodelled in the 70s. Although he was born eighteen months after VE Day, Bowie grew up in a nation taking its time to recover from the conflict; both his older brother's recurring mental illness that eventually led to his suicide and the stifling suburban conformity that the Jones family relocated to from dirty urban Brixton were factors that formulated his impatient oeuvre and contributed to his steady evolution from long-haired R&B ingénue to cosmic Leper Messiah, sprinkling stardust over a generation that had missed the 60s and cried out for their own heroes, escapist pied-pipers leading them out of the candlelit gloom of early 70s Britain to a divinely decadent parallel universe. Bowie, like his contemporaries Marc Bolan, Rod Stewart and Elton John, had been whispering Open Sesame for years, yet it took the abdication of The Beatles and the cold chill of a drastically different decade to create the climate that could facilitate the great breakthrough.

The second half of the twentieth century witnessed a pop culture supernova that the first sixteen years of this century have cowered in the shadow of. If the band that exemplify the supremacy of that supernova are The Beatles, the only comparable solo act in terms of a body of work whose influence stretches way beyond the parameters of its art-form is Bowie. Like Marilyn Monroe, Rudolph Nureyev or even George Best, Bowie was unique – an artist in a field of one, often imitated, never equalled. After all, these special people only come in ones and when they're gone they aren't replaced, for broken moulds, as with Humpty Dumpty, cannot be put back together again.

But we have the work; it's still here even though its creator has gone, and it'll still be here when we're all gone too. Time may well flex like a whore and fall wanking to the floor, but he won't erase that magic preserved on plastic. David Bowie is dead, but David Bowie simultaneously lives. And he always will.

One more untimely death came last week, albeit one that rather slipped under the mainstream radar – that of 53-year-old Colin Vearncombe, who used the stage-name Black; best remembered for his 1987 international hit, 'Wonderful Life', Vearncombe was one of many 1980s musicians who had cut their musical teeth via the DIY ethic of Punk, yet eschewed a three-chord straitjacket to embrace an eclectic (and occasionally esoteric) potpourri of sounds. At the beginning of the 80s, a generation emerged that blended the visceral energy of Punk with an appreciation of classic melodious pop and an appetite for experimentation.

Enduring characters such as Julian Cope, Ian McCulloch, Billy Mackenzie, Kevin Rowland, Robert Smith, Roddy Frame, Edwyn Collins and Morrissey were promoted as an alternative to the synthesizer-based New Pop that rose to chart prominence in 1981/82, yet were all part of the same fresh wave of talent that characterised the opening three or four years of the decade. Nobody can deny that the likes of The Human League or Depeche Mode were just as adept at producing pop the milkman could whistle as their guitar-slinging opponents; they merely utilised hi-tech technology as the vehicle for their melodies and found themselves becoming part of the 'Top of the Pops' wallpaper in the process.

Although heavily influenced by Kraftwerk, Bowie and Roxy Music, the Synth Pop acts were very much in the here and now in terms of sound and vision, whereas the guitar alternative favoured floppy-haired 60s chic and the jangly aural trademark of The Byrds. At the same time, that in itself is a too-neat summary of their differences.

Both strands of early 80s pop shared a yearning to boldly go where no pop stars had gone before – if top 10 records as contrasting in style as 'Ghosts' by Japan, 'Reward' by The Teardrop Explodes, 'Party Fears Two' by The Associates, 'Torch' by Soft Cell, 'The Cutter' by Echo and the Bunnymen, 'Living on The Ceiling' by Blancmange, 'Kings of the Wild Frontier' by Adam and the Ants, 'Rip it Up' by Orange Juice, 'Mad World' by Tears for Fears and 'Come on Eileen' by Dexy's Midnight Runners had anything in common, it was their determined aim to sound unlike anything that had preceded them and to sound unlike anything else alongside them in the charts. In this, they succeeded. They may have had one eye on their formative influences, but the other was firmly looking forward.

The refreshing willingness of this generation to follow their adventurous instincts could lead to an album as strange and original as 'Sulk' by The Associates or one as grandiosely romantic as 'The Lexicon of Love' by ABC; it could produce a hit single as bizarre as 'John Wayne is Big Leggy' by Haysi Fantayzee or a pop star as weird and wonderful as Boy George.

During this creatively fruitful era, 'Smash Hits' was as important to the moment as the NME had been to the moment of ten years earlier; glossy, colourful and yet simultaneously possessing a richness of witty, incisive writing, the fortnightly magazine launched in 1978 is retrospectively branded as an archetypal all style/no substance product of the so-called shallow 80s, but it was a good as anything promoting music on the newsstands in 1981-84 and forced the old 'inkies' to reluctantly up their game when their circulations began to plummet.

When the most commercially ambitious representatives of the crop found their innovative utilisation of the promo video gained them a foothold in America thanks to the arrival of MTV, the Second British Invasion of the USA was underway, resulting in a now-unimaginable situation such as that which occurred one week in 1983 when 20 of the Billboard top 40 singles were by British acts, including 7 of the top 10; this even exceeded the American chart domination by British acts in the mid-60s. The impact of UK pop upon US culture wasn't lost on a trio of American artists who were busily taking notes – Prince, Madonna and Michael Jackson – all of whom capitalised on the craze and sold a few coals to Newcastle as they did so.

Ironically, it was this generation's eagerness to keep up with technology that would prove to be their undoing; the clunky samples on mid-80s hits such as 'Wood Beez' by Scritti Politti and 'A View to a Kill' by Duran Duran reflect the move away from melody-based fare which was then prevalent in early Hip Hop. Within a couple of years, one isolated vocal lifted from an old soul record, trimmed down to a solitary sampled phrase and repeated over and over again would be enough to pass for melody when welded to an electronic beat; equally, the backlash behemoth of stadium rock, either from the likes of U2 or the American Glam Metal bands, left pure pop in the hands of production team Stock, Aitken & Waterman and their interchangeable boys and girls next-door. Mainstream melody had been reduced to the level of nursery rhymes and synths had been reduced to the level of deliberately monotonous repetition

Don't get me wrong; I certainly enjoyed the Rave scene when it happened and even that eventually spawned some radically energetic chart-toppers from The Prodigy and The Chemical Brothers; but as I look back now on the first half of the 80s, currently sprouting anew on BBC4's rerun through 1981 'Top of the Pops', I can see (and hear) how variety really was the spice of life and nobody sounded like anyone else. These were pop stars on their own terms, bereft of stylists and Svengalis and allergic to the crassness of the TV talent show; their genesis in the shadow of Punk instilled a passion for taking risks and rejecting the kind of uniform careerism that now passes for pop. We didn't know how lucky we were.

IDIOTEQUE
18 February 2016

Not being especially child-friendly, a couple of perennials on 'Desert Island Discs' always make me want to retch. One is when the guest selects a piece of music on which one of their children either plays or sings; the other is when they pick a tune their children like, usually by some contemporary pop act. 'This is what the kids insist we have to listen to on long drives in the car' etc. A few weeks ago, the latter category came up and something by Ed Sheeran disrupted the Sunday morning vibes. Bloody awful, it was too – the soulless sound of a purpose-built performer purposely built to play a purpose-built arena.

Unsurprisingly, the ginger Berni Flint is up for a Brit or two next week, as are (equally predictably) coffee table queen Adele and the terminally soporific Coldplay. There's young blood in the shape of James Bay, who shares at least one thing with his more established contenders in that he has absolutely nothing to say. Chris Martin might do a lot for *charadee* – and likes to talk about it, weirdly enough; but his political stance, for what it is, is pure Live Aid, throwing his weight behind worthy causes ala Bono and never short of advertising what a 'decent bloke' he is for doing so. None of the acts on the Brits roll of honour were ever what could be called 'left-field' and have been shamelessly content to kiss corporate buttocks from the off.

Left-field is an old term used by music critics to describe acts in opposition to the mainstream; you don't hear it used to so much now, but thirty-five years ago it had more than one meaning. If a wilful attempt to break loose of rock 'n' roll's Blues roots and 1950s three-chord straitjacket was the musical characteristic of the post-punk generation at the crossroads between the 70s and 80s, a political element also marks them out as retrospectively unique. Unlike the misguided alliance between socially-conscious, musically-pedestrian pop stars and the Labour Party that was Red Wedge in the middle of the 80s, there was a fiercely intelligent edge to the politically-aware musicians that preceded them, one largely derived from the Marxist rhetoric prevalent on the university campuses where many of these bands were formed. Well-read and in it for more than vacuous status symbols, they peppered their lyrics with references to obscure literary and historical figures of a radical and revolutionary bent and avoided the clumsy plebeian posturing of The Clash.

It seems refreshingly bizarre now that so many of the acts that typify the glossy pop of the 80s hadn't come to the mainstream platform via a showbiz Svengali figure, but had begun the journey to their unlikely destination via a route that hasn't been traversed since. Adam Ant may have been largely apolitical, but his early pre-success records displayed knowledge of the Marquis de Sade and other kinky icons that were hardly guaranteed to appeal to a mainstream audience. Scritti Politti, best known for shiny mid-80s hits, had chosen their name as an Anglo-Saxon variation of Italian for 'political writings', inspired by Marxist theorist Antonio Gramsci. The Passions, responsible for perhaps the greatest one-hit wonder of 1981, 'I'm in Love with A German Film

Star', were led by a singer who had spent part of her adolescence in a Marxist commune.

Altered Images, best remembered for bouncy smashes such as 'Happy Birthday', had a distinct Banshees/Slits vibe to their first single, 'Dead Pop Stars', and Clare Grogan has subsequently affirmed the band members were politically conscious as a given. People tend to forget how political allegiances then were as important as which mobile phone or video game you prefer is today; and those who emerged from the left-field back then really *were* on the left, albeit a vague, romantic ideal of the left that was traditionally the province of champagne socialists. This would be no surprise in literature or the theatre, but pop music? Regardless of their politics, what strikes one now is that these guys were actually quite *smart,* perhaps the least archetypal dumb rock 'n' rollers ever to pick up guitars.

Bands that didn't make the breakthrough into the top ten, such as The Pop Group or The Gang of Four, abandoned the unadventurous musical limitations of Punk's first wave and developed a distinctly jagged, white funk that meant listeners could tap their toes to songs about subjects that were as far removed from the euphoric hedonism of Disco as it was possible to imagine. The influence of the post-punk avant-garde also filtered into the music press via the new journalists that had received the same education and lingered in the NME up until the Rave era at the end of the 80s. Devoting front covers to the experience of school-leavers forced to endure the Youth Opportunities Scheme or even teenage suicides suggested as a consequence of Thatcherite policies were commonplace practices where the NME was concerned at the time and nobody thought it odd. Any left-field musician being interviewed by the music press in the first half of the 80s was more likely to discuss Rimbaud than listing their top ten

'Classic Rock' albums. It's hard to imagine that happening today, especially with the appalling free version of the NME that resembles a giveaway lifestyle mag produced in-store by Starbucks, simply begging to be put out of its misery.

Unless we're talking Bucks Fizz or Shakin' Stevens, divisions between pop and 'serious music' weren't as evident as they were to become in the 90s; even Bananarama had their first single produced by Sex Pistols drummer Paul Cook. There was less reliance on pigeon-holing and acts could have a foot in both camps, appearing on TOTP one week and the OGWT the next, appearing on the front cover of the NME one week and the front cover of 'Smash Hits' the next. Something similar had happened at the beginning of the 70s, when acts from the hippy underground like Atomic Rooster, Curved Air and Hawkwind scored surprise hit singles, but it didn't last then and it didn't last in the 80s either. It partially resurfaced in the likes of The Manic Street Preachers and Radiohead; but being 'clever' isn't *cool* now. The notion of pop music as anything other than a lowbrow branch of the entertainment industry is essentially redundant in 2016.

The current crop think TV talent shows are a legit route to recognition - and if they didn't begin on one, they end up being a judge on one; they think it's perfectly fine to enter the Big Brother House once they've churned out a few hits; they think nothing of endorsing products. As much as I would've loved Brian Eno advertising Cresta in 1973, the thought is so ludicrous that it could only ever appear in the pages of 'Viz'. An assembled line-up of nominees coming together to pay 'tribute' to Bowie is threatened for this year's Brit Awards ceremony; this horrific prospect is akin to 'The One Show' devoting a full edition to an in-depth analysis of the works of Sylvia Plath.

Spike Milligan once said his epitaph would read – 'Wrote The Goons, died'; it's an inevitability that when someone whose working life created something that has impacted upon the consciousness of the general public in the most benign manner, the rest of the creator's life (and their afterlife) will be lived in the shadow of his or her creation. The Beatles as a musical unit effectively covered around thirteen years of Paul McCartney's seventy-four on the planet, yet it is those thirteen for which he will be forever remembered. And so it is with Tony Warren, whose death at the age of 79 was announced today.

Warren was an actor from childhood, though had been a novelist for the majority of his adult life; however, the obituaries will be headed 'Coronation Street creator dies'. 'Coronation Street' was something that occupied Warren's time at the turn of the 1960s – over fifty years ago; his involvement with the programme essentially covered the first 13 episodes and then other writers such as Harry Kershaw were brought in by Granada to allegedly lift the writing burden from the man whose imagination the entire concept sprang from. Warren felt his input was being minimised by the same people who were against the programme in the beginning and now had an overnight sensation on their hands; control of his baby was wrestled away from him, though he continued to write occasional scripts for it up until the late 1970s. In recent years, his services as a consultant had been called upon by a younger generation of writers and producers who had grown up with Warren's brainchild and he received belated recognition as the father of the institution.

Tony Warren was born three years before the outbreak of the Second World War, and like most children whose earliest memories emanate from the home front he was raised in a matriarchal community. He confessed his happiest times were hiding under the kitchen table merely to listen to the conversations carried out by a tough breed of women who had already lived through one global conflict as well as the Great Depression; there was also the fact that they had been raised in a hard environment of virtually Dickensian poverty, residing in bug and vermin-ridden houses bereft of running water and mired in appalling sanitation, forever burying babies at a time when there was no NHS to save them. Their response was not to buckle under, but to knuckle down. One way of dealing with such a gritty existence was gallows humour, something that was evident in the myriad of curious phrases that dripped from the lips of the extended female family surrounding Warren in his formative years. These were seared onto Warren's memory and resurfaced when he abandoned speaking the words of others and began to write his own.

It's debatable whether someone who created some of the most iconic female characters in British popular culture owed those creations to his childhood experiences or the fact that he himself was distanced from the macho male psyche especially prevalent in the North of England by virtue of his homosexuality at a time when a prison sentence was a perennial concern. In truth, it was probably a combination of the two. Drifting towards the theatre as a safe haven, Warren turned to the new medium of television when Granada was established as the North's outlet for the expanding ITV network in 1956; acting in some of Granada's early productions, he reckoned he could do a better job of concocting scripts than those whose woeful efforts he was being forced to endure and his contributions were readily accepted. However, it seemed to Warren that Granada's regional remit was being overlooked when it came to the drama the station produced and he began to delve into his upbringing when the idea of a series based in the reality of what the company fancifully called 'Granadaland' entered his thoughts.

'Florizel Street' was a hard sell as the 50s morphed into the 60s. Despite the revolution taking place in British theatre, literature and then cinema, with 'Look Back in Anger', 'Saturday Night and Sunday Morning', 'A Taste of Honey', 'A Kind of Loving' and numerous others, television was resistant to allowing the lives of its largely working-class audience onto screens dominated by middle-class actors, presenters and subject matters. Successive rejections from the Granada bigwigs as Warren polished and honed his story of a street like the ones he could see from the windows of his office at the citadel that was supposed to reflect its surroundings only served to intensify his determination. To be fair, the reluctance of his bosses to commit themselves to Warren's radical concept needs to be placed in context; there had been nothing comparable to what Warren envisaged on British TV, and it was seen as a huge gamble that could leave Granada with egg on their faces.

Gradually gaining the invaluable support of drama producer Harry Elton, Warren's labour of love was cautiously given the go-ahead in 1960 and the task of casting the characters began. Regional rep and radio were trawled for the right actors to fit the parts, many of whom had been journeymen thespians for decades and had little experience of television. Doris Speed, cast as landlady of the pub at the end of Warren's fictitious street, was semi-retired from acting; Violet Carson, a relatively late choice for resident battleaxe Ena Sharples, had more or less abandoned acting after a degree of modest wartime fame on the wireless; Pat Phoenix, cast as colourful tart-with-a-heart Elsie Tanner, had worked at Joan Littlewood's Theatre Workshop in London and foresaw a future eking out a living playing small parts on stage and in the odd B-movie; only William Roache, cast as the street's intellectual angry young man Ken Barlow, had ambitions to become a big star, viewing his part as a stepping-stone to greater glory. In an infant medium trying its hand at a novel new drama of a kind that had never been produced before, it was no wonder few of the original cast saw further ahead than the 13 initial episodes Granada had commissioned.

When the first episode of what was renamed 'Coronation Street' (one of Warren's few compromises) aired on 9 December 1960, it's hard to conceive of the seismic impact it made on viewers from the distance of over 55 years later. A TV nation that was accustomed to television talking down to it like a benevolent colonial governor addressing the natives was shocked and excited to see archetypes they instantly recognised on-screen. Every working-class neighbourhood in the country had an Ena Sharples, an Elsie Tanner, an Annie Walker, an Albert Tatlock, a Minnie Caldwell and a Leonard Swindley. Yes, 'Coronation Street' was so rooted in a particular Northern culture that the odour of bread-and-dripping could almost be sniffed in the room when it was broadcast; but the characters possessed traits that could be found anywhere in the country wherever there was a close-knit community living in each other's pockets, and the show was networked in a matter of weeks, shooting to the top of the ratings in record time.

The BBC woke up from its rather smug slumber in the wake of this new sensation and was encouraged to bring a little realism into its own staid TV output, resulting in the commissioning of other groundbreaking series such as 'Z-

Cars', 'Steptoe and Son' and 'The Wednesday Play'. The importance of 'Coronation Street' should be disregarded at one's peril. Simply getting it onscreen in the first place – a testament to Tony Warren's grit and determination – stands as perhaps the single greatest achievement in the history of British broadcasting. His obituaries may be prefixed with 'Coronation Street creator', but there's really no greater epitaph that could grace his tombstone. Rest in peace, and thank you, Tony.

THE TOTAL FOOTBALLER
24 March 2016

There will always be the debate – Stanley Matthews or George Best? Pele or Maradona? For me, the man who played the beautiful game with greater artistry than anyone ever to slip into a pair of studded boots was Johan Cruyff, whose death from lung cancer at the age of 68 has been announced. The outspoken and opinionated Dutchman displayed an undoubted arrogance and absence of modesty both on and off the pitch because he knew he was the best; and he was. Although he made his professional debut as a 17-year-old in 1964, domestic football in Holland had only recently emerged from its amateur age and the Netherlands had never made any notable impact at either club or international level. Cruyff's club, whose books he had been on from the age of ten, was Ajax of Amsterdam. When former Ajax player Rinus Michels returned to the club as coach, he saw in Cruyff a player around whom he could build a team playing a style of football that would eventually turn Ajax into the world's greatest club side.

Ajax first became a name to reckon with when reaching the 1969 European Cup Final; though they lost to AC Milan, there were clear signs that a little tinkering here and there

21

could take the team onto the next level. Bringing a crop of remarkably talented youngsters such as Johan Neeskens, Johnny Rep, Barrie Hulshoff, Ruud Krol, Gerrie Muhren and Arie Haan into the side, Michels, with Cruyff as his eyes and ears on the pitch, developed what was christened 'Total Football'; this system required all outfield players to be equally adept up front and in defence, a fluid, rotating form of play that was expertly orchestrated by Cruyff, who acted as a veritable puppet-master, pulling the strings of the team and directing events as a virtual footballing auteur. Due to an act of serendipitous superstition, Cruyff wore No.14 on his shirt at both club and international level (at a time when teams were exclusively numbered 1-11), as though his unique talents couldn't be contained within the numerical strictures of the game. The style of football was special; the team were special; and he was special.

The Total Football system swept all competition aside in the early 1970s. Ajax won three consecutive European Cups in 1971, '72 and '73 – a feat that had only previously been achieved by the great Real Madrid side of the late 50s. On the domestic front, Ajax were almost unbeatable. In the 1971-72 season, they won the domestic treble as well as their second European Cup and the Intercontinental Cup, a contest between the top teams in Europe and South America in which the brutal approach to the game typified by the latter couldn't contrast greater with that of the Dutch. Come the 1974 World Cup in West Germany, the time had arrived to showcase Total Football on the international stage.

Although Rinus Michels had by this time relocated to Barcelona (with Cruyff joining him there after Ajax's third consecutive European Cup win), he took control of the Dutch national side for the 1974 World Cup tournament and filled the team with players he'd brought to fruition at Ajax.

Holland illuminated that summer; World Cups traditionally draw in viewers who don't follow domestic soccer but become bedazzled by the event, and watching Cruyff in full flow at the peak of his powers transformed him and Total Football into a global phenomena. That Dutch team resembled rock stars and remain the coolest-looking group of players the World Cup has ever seen. Watching Cruyff was like watching Nureyev; he had the same God-given grace in his feet and it seemed only right that he should lift the new FIFA World Cup trophy in the Final. Unfortunately, the all-conquering Dutchmen came up against the host nation.

The significance of Holland taking on West Germany in Munich just thirty years after the Netherlands had been subjugated by the German jackboot cannot be underestimated. Many members of that Dutch side had lost family members under the Nazi regime and it would be hard to deny the arrogance that often comes with greatness was evident for more than mere football reasons in the Final. Cruyff showed he meant business straight from the kick-off, cutting a swathe through the West German defence and being brought down in the penalty area. With barely a minute gone, Holland were awarded a penalty which Neeskens scored; they were 1-0 up with West Germany yet to touch the ball. Rather than building on that early lead, the Dutch chose to humiliate the Germans on their own soil, using their breathtaking talent to toy with and taunt what was undoubtedly a great German side, one containing the likes of Beckenbauer, Muller, and Breitner. This time, however, Dutch arrogance backfired and sabotaged what should have been the nation's crowning glory as the Germans clawed their way back into the game, taking a 2-1 lead at half-time that remained the score when the ref blew the whistle after 90 minutes. Holland's greatest team had failed at the final hurdle. It was the swansong for Total Football.

Cruyff chose not to participate in the 1978 World Cup in Argentina, perhaps stung by the memory of Independiente, the Argentine team that had kicked Ajax off the pitch in the 1972 Intercontinental Cup. He cited disapproval of the military junta then running Argentina as his main reason for pulling out, which seems a remarkable stance to take from today's money-grabbing football perspective. How many international soccer superstars will decline to go to Russia for the 2018 World Cup on political grounds, I wonder?

Despite his voluntary retirement from the national side in 1977, Cruyff's domestic career continued until 1984, when he ironically ended his twenty-year journey at Ajax's bitter rivals Feyenoord. As soon as he hung-up his boots, he entered management and proved to be as successful on the touchline as he had been on the pitch, coaching Ajax, Barcelona and the Catalonian national side, despite the latter remaining unrecognised by FIFA. For most watchers of the game, however, it was his role conducting the footballing orchestra of both Ajax and the Dutch national team in the early 70s that left us with the quintessential memories of Johan Cruyff, gone at just 68, but never to be forgotten.

RETURN TO BRENDA
21 April 2016

A royal record is poised to be broken, though unlike the publicity afforded Queen Elizabeth II's overtaking of Queen Victoria last September, this one 'officially' doesn't count and probably won't get much in the way of coverage. Brenda may turn 90 today, solidifying her position as the oldest sovereign Britain has ever had; but if she makes it to May 11, she will have surpassed the titular reign of James III, the reign that never was. History knows him as The Old Pretender, but the King across the Water was never crowned, his birth as a

Catholic heir leading to the Glorious Revolution of 1688. To those loyal to the Jacobite cause, James Francis Edward Stuart was always recognised as the legitimate King of England, Scotland and Ireland, and as such reigned in a parallel universe for 64 years.

James succeeded his dethroned father James II aged just 13. By contrast, Brenda was 25 when she ascended to the throne in 1952, seven years older than Victoria had been when she became queen in 1837. But her maternal genes are made of strong stuff; the Queen Mother was over 100 when she died, lest we forget, so it's not beyond the realm of possibility that there could even be an unprecedented Platinum Jubilee on the horizon. I don't suppose anyone anticipated this when Princess Elizabeth was informed of her father's death whilst on a royal tour of Kenya. George VI had reigned for just sixteen years. In fact, anyone over, say, fifty-three the day we entered what was trumpeted as the New Elizabethan Age would have already seen five different monarchs occupying the throne; by contrast, to have been born just before the reign of Elizabeth II began, one would now be within a year or two of retirement age.

The longer the reign, the more potential for change in the wider society, and it could be argued the changes that have taken place since 1952 are on a par with those that took place during the Victorian Age. When Victoria became queen upon the death of her uncle William IV, she was the only legitimate living child sired by any of her grandfather George III's notoriously rakish sons. She was born into a transitional era that had seen both the end of Napoleonic domination of Europe and the beginnings of the Industrial Revolution, with the pendulum of power swinging away from France towards Britain. The woman who ended up being associated with a strain of prudish Puritanism was actually a product of the

Regency and was in possession of all the hedonistic frivolity that went with it during her spell as Europe's most envied marital prize. It was strait-laced husband Albert (the son of a philandering rake himself) and his determination not to repeat his father's mistakes that redesigned the image of a battered brand and turned the royal household from a hotbed of disreputable debauchery to the nation's moral barometer.

With Victoria as the figurehead, Britain spread its imperial wings and was ruling over almost a quarter of the world's population by the time of her death aged 81. Its navy acted as the maritime world police and its language, culture and industry circumnavigated the globe. After Bonaparte, Victoria became one of the first internationally recognisable public figures, with her iconic properties as the reincarnation of Britannia the nineteenth century's equivalent of the Che Guevara poster that used to be an obligatory addition to the bedroom walls of every campus dormitory. When she celebrated her 1897 Diamond Jubilee, the event was marked everywhere from Calcutta to Cape Town, from Sydney to Singapore, and from Montreal to Malta.

During Victoria's reign, transport went from horsepower to steam power and then the internal combustion engine. Advances in industry built railways and laid cables under the ocean to open up a new lines of communication, whilst advances in science and medicine saved lives and (in the case of Darwin) rewrote the history of mankind; social reformers attempted to do something about the kind of poverty we'd now associate with the Third World; the working-class was given a voice with the formation of trade unions and extension of the voting franchise; demands for women's rights became organised; and the flourishing of the Arts in particular helped establish Britain as the cultural capital of the world. Dickens, Thackeray, the Brontës, Eliot, Gaskell, Trollope, Hardy, Lear,

Carroll and Wilde all produced their literary masterpieces on Victoria's watch; the Pre-Raphaelites rocked the galleries and Elgar embarked upon his distinguished musical journey, whilst photography and then moving pictures brought us one step closer to the twentieth century. The formation of police forces and improvements in street lighting via gas and, eventually, electricity made the streets safer, the Gothic Revival gave dramatic new architectural skylines to the towns and cities in which those streets were situated, and rising literacy levels, not to mention civic museums, libraries and swimming baths as well as the codification and new professionalism of sports such as cricket, tennis, golf, association football and both strains of rugby aided in the intellectual and physical improvement of Victoria's subjects. When she finally passed away in January 1901, the country that mourned her was very different to what it had been in 1819.

And what of the country inherited by Victoria's great-great-granddaughter half-a-century later? The slow recovery from the ravages of war was still a work-in-progress with many of the new queen's subjects living in housing that had been condemned as unfit for human habitation decades before, the class system had been temporarily fractured by conflict and was attempting to revert to its pre-war distinctions, television had yet to supplant radio or the cinema as the medium of the masses, corporal and capital punishment were still enforced, National Service continued to interrupt male civilian lives, homosexuality and abortion remained illegal acts punishable with prison sentences, illegitimate birth was a social stigma, mass immigration from the colonies hadn't yet altered what was a predominantly white society, and the nation's Prime Minister, Churchill, was approaching eighty. Sixty-four years later, the same monarch presides over a different country in a different century.

The year of Elizabeth II's Coronation saw Crick and Watson discover the structure of DNA, an early sign that the new queen was about to begin her reign on the cusp of changes that would radically transform the monochrome kingdom in ways comparable to those that Elizabeth's great-great-grandmother had overseen. These changes are perhaps more evident and within living memory, so don't necessary need to be recited like the ones that occurred during Victoria's reign; but even those of us whose lifetimes haven't yet spanned fifty years have witnessed dramatic alterations to everyday life that in many cases would have been pure sci-fi in 1952. The technology that enables me to write this piece as well as enabling you to read it, wherever on the planet you happen to be, is just one.

Whatever one's opinion of her or the institution of monarchy in general, Elizabeth II's place in the history books is already ensured, with the next landmark on the list being just three weeks away. It would therefore be somewhat churlish not to wish her a happy birthday on yet another day in which we've all seen her face again – even if that was only due to pulling change from our wallets and purses.

PRINCE CHARMING
22 April 2016

I didn't think I'd have to do this just 48 hours after giving honourable mention to Victoria Wood, but this year doesn't give me much choice. So, let's go back to 1988, eh? The history books will tell you everyone under 30 was digesting E for breakfast and spending all day and night raving away in a derelict warehouse. Of course, that was 1988 for some, but very much a minority, just as the Roxy club had played host to a minority in 1977 and the UFO club had done likewise in 1967. In 1988 I was still entombed in a bedroom at my mother's house, surrounded by own mini-gallery of pop cultural icons; most were of a generation before my time, as by this late stage the 80s had petered out into a dreary wasteland with Goths at one end and Stock Aitken and Waterman at the other, and not a lot to get excited about in the middle.

One notable and fairly unique exception was a man who still embodied all that had been great about pop's past, a man who absorbed the spirit of everyone from Little Richard and Sly Stone to Stevie Wonder and Marc Bolan, a man whose nude portrait dominated the wall my bed was shoved against. I only mention this in that the giant poster of the 'Lovesexy' sleeve I had somehow acquired from its display at either the nearest HMV or Virgin (I can't remember which now) proved to be a talking point when my windows were being replaced by a bunch of archetypal gruff Yorkshire workmen.

'Dunt it make ye feel sick?' asked one of them when confronted by an image of glorious androgyny that was beyond his own experience. 'Dunt it make ye feel sick, though, seeing Prince wi' nowt on?' I just laughed; I should have said, 'As a matter of fact, I wank myself to sleep looking at that every night', but figured it wouldn't have gone down well; besides, I just wanted the new bloody windows putting in so I could have my room back ASAP. I loved the fact, however, that a contemporary figure rather than someone whose best work was twenty years behind him had provoked a bit of mini-outrage that showed the generation gap was still clinging on for dear life.

That same year, I attended the best live show I've ever been witness to by far when my mate Paul and I saw Prince in the flesh (though not quite as abundant as on the 'Lovesexy' sleeve) at Wembley Arena. We'd become Big Gig-goers over the past twelve months, seeing Bowie twice and Dylan once; this brief phase would climax a couple of years later when we'd see the Stones, but when we caught the coach down to the capital that summer, it was the only time we ever saw someone who was at the peak of his powers. Unlike the other legends whose concerts we attended, when Prince played songs from his new album, we wanted to hear them as much as the old stuff; he was still 'present tense', and if his previous LP, 'Sign 'O' the Times' had been his 'What's Going On', 'Lovesexy' was his 'Let's Get it On'. We knew we were seeing something that was rooted in the here and now when we spotted Patricia Morrison from The Sisters of Mercy stood outside the venue as though she was waiting for Andrew Eldritch to turn up with the tickets.

Once within the hallowed walls of the Arena, we realised somebody was sat in the shit seats we'd been allocated half-a-mile away from the stage; we then embarked upon a game of musical chairs that eventually took us into the sacred press enclosure when the security guards were too mesmerised by the show to notice our presence. We had the best bloody view in the house as Prince gyrated on a giant bed with one of his impossibly sexy dancers midway through another contemporary classic – and he hadn't yet reached the stage of his career when his set-list could contain any duff numbers. He was playing his greatest hits and not one of them stretched back further than five years.

Unfortunately, there was an intermission that brought the house-lights up and our lack of press passes meant we had to find somewhere else to sit that wasn't quite as close. But we'd had a good half-hour with the man himself within touching distance; at that moment in time, there was no other performer under 30 in possession of the genuine otherworldly star quality that had been spread evenly amongst Prince's predecessors. He was out there on his own and he revelled in ruling the world. As a performer, he remained pretty damn peerless for the rest of his life; but as a recording artist, I think he had peaked. His next project was the disappointing soundtrack for the first 'Batman' movie the following year, and bar a few great singles in the early 90s, he never again came close to the heights he'd scaled on vinyl in the 80s.

He'd always operated in his own universe, but the disappearance of the entertaining element of the 80s that died a death at Live Aid left the field clear for Prince to fill the void and he grabbed it with such gusto that no one else came close. It took Madonna until the end of the decade before she approached his greatness on record, and who should she collaborate with on one of the tracks on 'Like a Prayer' but the little genius from Minneapolis himself. While she went on to produce her finest album ten years later, Prince concentrated on doing his own thing; if the record-buying public wanted it, fair enough; if they didn't, he didn't care; he carried on doing it regardless.

Every online obituary will recite his achievements in detail, but this isn't a list; it's merely me recalling how important he was to me and many others starved of stars at a point in pop culture history that seemed bad at the time, yet seems positively golden by today's standards. Self-contained singer-songwriters who labour under the misapprehension that their trivial middle-class angst is a source of fascination to others beyond their own narcissistic navel-gazing are ten-a-penny these days; but none of them can also get funky, dress like a dandy, ooze sex appeal to both sexes and do it all with such flamboyant witty panache as the man who has inexplicably left the stage at 57. Of course we won't see his like again; we won't see the likes of anyone who makes music with more depth than a bloody ringtone anymore. The rules of the game have changed and with every light extinguished, the firmament moves one step closer to total blackout.

SARTORIAL EFFLUENCE
26 May 2016

It's an old saying, but it rings true – clothes maketh the man. I believe they maketh the woman as well. Whether we like it or not, first impressions are often made by the way in which an individual is 'turned-out', and sartorial choices can speak volumes as to what kind of individual we are encountering. These first impressions can also stretch to those we don't even encounter in person.

I was recently watching one of the extras on the DVD of a cult movie, featuring footage from a BFI-type event wherein the director of the film in question attended a special screening of it and answered questions from the audience. I'm sure you're familiar with the set-up. As per usual, there was a guy with a microphone doing a little interview prior to hands being raised in the auditorium, and as the segment progressed I found myself becoming more irritated by him – not so much the evident absence of interviewing skills that is customary for the amateurs chosen for such a duty, but by the contrast between the dress sense of him and his counterpart on stage. The old director, well into his seventies, was a dapper gent who had clearly made the effort, whereas the interviewer looked like he was attending a gig by a Death Metal band – unshaven, clad in black baggy T-shirt and well-worn jeans. He may as well have travelled to the event straight from the sofa after dozing off with a half-scoffed pizza settled on his beer-gut the night before. No attempt at entering into the spirit of things, just the standard slob chic that now appears to be the default setting for so many men under fifty.

The history books tell us the hippies are to blame, that their emphasis on 'letting it all hang out' and dispensing with the straitjacket of the suit has led us to where we are now. This theory tends to overlook the fact that the initial hippies (at least on this side of the pond) morphed out of the Carnaby Street Dandy; photographs from the late 60s prove these were no scruffy hobos. Victorian velvet frock-coats and Regency ruffles were compulsory; only in the early 70s did a more tramp-like variation on the theme appear, most obviously in the likes of Jethro Tull's Ian Anderson. At the same time, however, mainstream fashion retained its peacock aspects and presented the male of the species with a dazzling dressing-up box that even those too old to have participated in the Swinging 60s (i.e. Jon Pertwee and Peter Wyngarde) took full advantage of.

For me, it stems more from the Rave/Madchester era of the late 80s/early 90s, a deliberately slovenly style that was in part a reaction to the suited and booted Yuppie and the most public pop culture promoters of the look such as Rick Astley. Britpop may have boasted a certain debonair eccentricity via Jarvis Cocker and (on occasion) Damon Albarn, but its core audience members were largely disciples of the Stone Roses 'jeans, T-shirt and sneakers' ensemble, an unimaginative uniform that has subsequently become the standard acceptable male wardrobe.

There is also the 'sportswear' look, which is equally responsible for the decline in dress. This grew out of football fans following English clubs during their all-conquering European sojourns in the early 80s, picking up Italian designer products en route and developing the 'casual' look as a consequence. They always looked like thuggish versions of Val Doonican to me, but this style gradually bled into the mainstream and eventually resulted in clothes originally designed for sports arenas evolving into accepted street gear. The most odious of this to me is the tracksuit bottom, the ultimate slob statement, usually worn by people who are the least athletic types one could ever imagine. Sod banning the burqa; ban the bottoms!

Teenagers, I believe, can be cut a little slack. I myself had a proto-Grunge look in the middle of the 80; photos of Kurt Cobain from the same period – and he was born the same year as me – show I wasn't alone, despite my parents' best attempts to convince me I was a one-off freak. Teenage studied scruffiness is nothing more than a traditional reaction geared to get up the noses of mater and pater and they do (or should) grow out of it. Any female adolescent is also contending with the narrow role models she's bombarded with on a constant loop, all those designer dolls endorsing girlie stereotypes that any woman with anything about her would instinctively rebel against. This, however, is no excuse for the most recent female street style that is simply unforgivable. I'm talking, of course, about wearing bedroom outfits outdoors – dressing gowns and pyjama bottoms. I applaud schools and supermarkets that have barred such monstrosities from their premises. What does it say about someone if they can't even be bothered changing the sweaty rags they've slept in when they venture beyond the doorstep? Unless you're an old dear stricken with dementia, a slipper is not designed for the pavement.

There has been much talk of the Metrosexual male of late – the well-groomed semi-Dandy who actually takes the time to present himself to the world at his best. Metrosexual males may exist, but they tend to be small in number as well as mocked in that predictable knee-jerk manner so characteristic of the man who regards any aesthetic effort to look good as a sign of effeminacy. I do my bit, usually in financially-deprived circumstances; but not having the ready cash to buy the clothes I'd like means I improvise and have developed my own personal look that requires the kind of preparation before facing the world akin to an actor taking to the stage in full costume. Penury is no excuse for the slovenly. Everyone can look good if they want to. It's just that society is now telling them they don't need to.

SOMETHING IN THE AIR
19 July 2016

The title of this post is lifted from the 1969 chart-topper by one-hit wonders Thunderclap Newman, a song that seems to encapsulate within its grooves a moment at the end of the 1960s when the tumultuous events of 1968 hadn't entirely exterminated the optimistic spirit of '67. Though very much a project sponsored by the same state that was simultaneously slaughtering peasants in Vietnam, the momentous achievement of putting a man on the moon suggested the general cultural zeitgeist remained forward-looking and convinced better days were just around the corner. John Lennon expressed as much when profiled in an ATV mini-series aired in December '69 called 'Man of the Decade'; the belief may have been misplaced or naive, but it was genuine and heartfelt. A generation born in a collective air-raid believed a different way of doing things was possible. Imagine no heaven, no countries, no possessions.

It certainly feels as though something is again in the air in 2016, though the odours of that something are not of incense, peppermints or even napalm; I can't really put my finger on it, but there are a lot of people I know who seem to be wading through a dense, noxious fog as dense and noxious as that which permeated every nook and cranny and rookery of Dickens' London in the memorable opening of 'Bleak

35

House'. Granted, many are experiencing personal crises that aren't necessarily specific to 2016, ones that could have happened at any moment in history, in any turbulent chapter of this planet's story as much as in any so-called Golden Age forever recalled with nostalgic reverence. They could have taken place in 1916 or 1966, and the world outside their window wouldn't have played any discernible role. But all of the internal events that are affecting the lives of loved ones right now appear to be synchronised with external events to an unsettling degree. Perhaps that's the impact of the age of 24/7 social media; perhaps not.

A close friend who is finding life exceedingly heavy going at the moment said to me last week that 'everything seems to have gone wrong since Bowie died'. I thought of the vinyl label of Bowie's 1973 LP 'Aladdin Sane'; the song from which the album took its title is listed as 'Aladdin Sane (1913-1938-197?)'. The information contained within the brackets marks the two years prior to the twentieth century's twin global conflicts and clearly taps into the paranoia of the time by suggesting a year in the 1970s will serve the same calm-before-the storm purpose. True, it could merely have been Bowie playing with that paranoia for artistic effect or simply reflecting his own nihilistic worldview that he took onto another apocalyptic level with 1974's 'Diamond Dogs'. But 'Aladdin Sane' was released just a few months before the bleak economic meltdown of the Three Day Week, an era marked by rumours of right-wing military coups instigated by MI5 and/or retired colonial colonels with private armies on one hand and left-wing communist coups instigated by Moscow on the other.

What appears to be in the air today is not so black and white, but a multi-layered mosaic of malodorous uncertainty. It is the murder of Jo Cox as well as the ongoing massacres in the US;

it is the litany of unexpected celebrity deaths as well as the terrorist atrocities on the Continent; it is the failed Turkish *coup d'état* as well as Brexit; it is Donald Trump as well as austerity; it is Syria as well as curbs on free speech; it is incompetence and corruption in public services as well as refugees drowning at sea. Possibly because of the way in which we are able to instantly access news, to quickly switch from one horror story to another or to be bombarded by them on Facebook and Twitter even when we're not seeking them out, they seem bigger and uglier than they ever would have seemed in the past, when limited television news bulletins and 24 hours-later newspapers exerted breathing space between each horrendous headline. It's a theory, anyway.

Were that the root cause of events in which we have no direct involvement seeping into our individual neuroses and exacerbating them, fair enough; but I wonder why so many seem to be struggling in the first place? If we compare the comforts we can call upon to the real hardships endured by our grandparents or great-grandparents, we haven't got a leg to stand on when it comes to complaints. The dazzling variety of choice, whether in relation to electronic goods, TV channels, food, clothing or virtually every luxury item that constitutes an acquisitive society should suffice, yet endless choice itself can actually be quite overwhelming and incapable of filling the inexplicable inner vacuum that our forefathers seemed capable of filling without any of our fripperies.

I suppose age could play a part as well; most of my friends are over 40; I myself am careering towards 50. But recent surveys suggest the kind of social isolation that appears quite commonplace within my own demographic is as high amongst teenagers. And it's a vicious circle. Something awful in the news drags us down when we're already feeling low because we've just received some stupid bill that we can't afford to pay, making us vulnerable sitting targets for the next horrific news event as well as the next dispiriting demand on our limited finances; it can get to the point where the internal and external are practically interchangeable as sources of anxiety and helplessness. I think a sense of helplessness is crucial too: we don't have the money required to pay the bill and we can't do anything to alter whatever depressing news story has invaded our private space via the mass media. Both feel as though they are ultimately out of our control.

I don't know what the solution is. Watch less TV news and don't regularly buy a paper? I started doing that about a decade ago, but I wasn't online back then. It's so much harder to avoid the big stories now. They eventually find your address. And, if you're feeling lousy to begin with, these big bad wolves will huff and they'll puff and they'll blow your house down. But one little pig did survive, of course; so maybe we should simply build with bricks and we'll get through it.

IN PRAISE OF SILENT PARTNERS
29 July 2016

1998 on paper doesn't seem that long ago; but 1998 was the year an 18-year-old footballer called Michael Owen scored a wonder goal for England against Argentina in the World Cup; he's now retired from playing and is struggling to replicate his talent on the pitch by droning into the pundit's microphone. Tony Blair was twelve months into his decade as Prime Minister and was still largely enjoying a honeymoon period, playing his part in the Good Friday Agreement; he's now almost universally condemned as a warmonger, doomed to wander from one obscure after-dinner speech to another while the western world craves his head on a plate. DVDs were introduced to the UK in 1998 – as were ASBOs; Bill Clinton was still US President – and 9/11 was three years away. And the house I shared was overrun with mice. Seems like a long time ago to me.

In 1998, the girl I lived with intervened in our rodent problem and delivered a stray cat to the house, something I thought madness due to the fact we had a dog. I'd underestimated the dog's good nature and the cat's knack for putting him in his place. The first night this feline recruit spent under our roof, I strolled into the kitchen, switched on the light, and she looked up at me with a mouse hanging out of her mouth. And so the very function that domesticated the cat in the human household proved as durable as ever. Mice, sparrows and (on one memorably gruesome occasion) pigeons had been warned.

That dogs and cats should remain the most popular of pets is no surprise considering the respective talents these once wild animals showed could be of service to us homo-sapiens if we invited them into our homes, whether helping us to hunt down our food or ridding us of vermin. This mutually beneficent partnership was entered into from the earliest organised communities, and while some of the roles these animals performed may have been watered down due to changing social environment in more recent times, it is still a partnership we instinctively crave, and one that both parties derive immense enjoyment and comfort from. The cat that entered *my* world as a stray mouser eighteen years ago accompanied me on every change of address thereafter (three in total) and finally left my world this week. The impact of her sudden removal from that world has rendered it a far emptier place than it was.

Up until this week, I would have said I've lived alone since 1999, though I now know that's not true. It's only coming home to an empty flat for the first time in twenty years that's made me realise I had housemates all along. The relationship one has with a cat or a dog is obviously different to that which one has with a fellow human being, but no less rich for it; they may not be able to answer you back, but a rewarding game of telepathic chess develops over time, to the point where you can anticipate their next move and they can anticipate yours. Actual conversation may be one-way traffic, but I now see that one chatters away regardless; it is the silencing of that chatter that jars so much today. There are so many daily sayings I will no longer utter, let alone the silly singing of songs and altering the words to include the cat's name. Moreover, I will never hear her miaow again either.

There's a moving moment at the end of 'The Dam Busters', when the camera pans across the canteen at the RAF base from where the pilots dropping Barnes Wallis's bouncing bombs are launched and we see the empty tables, signifying those airmen who never returned from the mission. Yet, there's an equally moving moment earlier in the film when Richard Todd's character has received the news his beloved dog (whose name we're not allowed to say now, of course) has been killed by a hit and run driver. He holds the dog's collar in his hand and glances across at his office door, which bears the paw-marks of those occasions when the dog has scratched it to notify him that it's time for a walk. That's what hits you when your four-legged companion has gone, all those little and poignant forensic insignias scattered around the house. Confronted by a vacant basket, an unsoiled litter tray, an untouched water bowl and surfaces strewn with her discarded hair, it feels as though she's just popped out and she'll be back in a minute. But she won't.

Having shared my space with a dog for twelve years and a cat for eighteen (ten of them having the pair competing for my affection like a pair of sibling rivals), I know the distinct differences between the two species and also know the characteristics they share. Just as cat owners have to contend with the stereotypes – ageing lesbian spinster etc. – they also have to contend with the misinformation about cats themselves. Yes, they are more independent minded than their canine equivalents and less demanding in terms of what they require of us; but they are no less affectionate, nor (in the case of a house-cat, as mine was for fifteen years) no less dependent on us to ensure they're fed and their litter is changed when it's soiled. It's not much to ask, really; and what we get in return far outweighs the necessity to organise one's daily routine around their needs.

My cat was fiercely possessive of me, welding herself to my lap whenever a visitor called, sending out the message as to ownership, just in case. Perhaps that was her way of recognising that, without her, I probably wouldn't be here. At my lowest ebb in my darkest hours, it was always the thought of her being abandoned that ultimately kept me going. I could abandon everyone else, but not her. The cat made me laugh when I didn't feel like laughing via some daft, seemingly meaningless gesture; the undoubted eccentricities cats exhibit in their occasionally odd behaviour is very much in synch with my own outlook. Also, she was extremely teddy bear-like and became even more receptive to cuddles as she grew older; no longer able to leap great heights – including onto my shoulder, one of her favourite youthful destinations – and needing me to lift her up and down, she relied on my assistance even more and expressed her gratitude accordingly. She was so pivotal to the harmony of the household that it no longer feels like home anymore; it seems wrong that she's no longer here to share it with me.

She was so robust in health for so long that watching the years catch up with her in the last couple of months of her life was heartbreaking; I never even had cause to take her to the vets until the very last day, when I had the most unenviable of responsibilities thrust upon me. The disparity between human and animal years is often commented on as unfair, something I wouldn't dispute; but the cycle of life is played out before you with a pet in a way it isn't with a person; one sees the seven ages from start to finish and adapts one's relationship as a consequence, from parent to sidekick to carer – to paraphrase Rupert Everett's lovely description in his memoirs, when referencing his changing role for his dog. Only later does one recognise the privilege in being privy to that cycle; it really is an honour. And confronted by a wider world that appears to grow increasingly ugly with each passing day, there is so much to miss and so, so much to mourn now that my beautiful silent partner has gone.

THINK OF A NUMBER
21 August 2016

When the world was a far bigger (not to say more mysterious) place than it is today, information on a subject that didn't receive mass media coverage was often acquired from some dusty volume in the local library – if you were lucky. Some subjects, it appeared, remained uncovered and unnoticed. Take what could be found on the outer limits of the wireless. Before the colonisation of the family home by FM units incorporated into swanky hi-fi sound systems, the humble portable radio had several options at the flick of a switch that FM ultimately downgraded.

There was medium-wave, which was the option of the masses – home to all four national BBC radio stations, not to mention the local BBC ones, wherever you happened to be in the country, and the ILR alternative. There was long-wave, primarily the choice of the cricket devotee tuning into 'Test Match Special', as well as providing the BBC with split slots when glamorous new FM began to reserve the popular programmes for itself. And then there was the enigmatic poor relation, shortwave. I was always intrigued by shortwave because its presence on the airwaves made no sense. Medium-wave, long-wave and FM schedules were listed in the Radio Times – nothing on shortwave was. It seemed to be a repository for the odd, the eccentric and the quirky; and, needless to say, I found it fascinating.

I remember early family holidays on the Continent, furtively moving the dial around the radio that had come along for the ride, trying to pick up Radio 1 or anything broadcasting in English; I usually located the World Service at various times, but it was prone to drifting in and out of hearing as though the transmitter was fixed to a pendulum. The snap, crackle and pop of the reception, the atmospheric SOS of the Morse code messages that could be discerned in the distance, and the strange stew of foreign tongues that babbled for a handful of seconds before disappearing again created a uniquely alluring and anarchic audio mosaic that seemingly had no structure whatsoever. Even when music was stumbled upon, it was usually in French or German and had more than a touch of the Eurovision about it.

Those wonderful old radios had the names of stations printed in a little panel on the front, where turning the dial moved what resembled the clapometer from 'Opportunity Knocks', gliding in and out of the stations listed without them ever actually being situated where the panel claimed. Nevertheless, the names themselves were in possession of a curious, archaic exotic quality that is utterly redundant today. FM rendered them redundant to a degree, and relegated the old family radio to my bedroom, where I had free rein to explore the parallel universe of shortwave. It was during this period that I began to come across some sounds that were disturbingly weird even by shortwave standards.

I wasn't to know then that shortwave's ability to broadcast across far greater distances than any other radio frequencies meant that I was picking up stuff from thousands of miles away, though what sounded to me like distorted Russian voices certainly suggested I was hearing something emanating from the wrong side of the Iron Curtain. I began to notice these voices regularly, usually in the early evening; sometimes they sounded more Chinese than Russian, but always they had a detached and chilly element to them that evoked all kinds of spy movie clichés, particularly as the Cold War was still in full swing. They were often infiltrated by what my imagination pictured as flying radioactive jellyfish falling from the sky and landing on the earth's surface – well that was the image that entered my head whenever the voices were interrupted by an alien sound I had no reference point for. On other occasions, what I can only describe as Tom & Jerry incidental music being performed by a Krautrock band would break up the voices. At the time, I had no idea I was listening to 'Jamming'; but at the time I had no idea what I was listening to at all.

The voices were almost robotic; even if I'd been able to speak the lingo, I suspect I'd have struggled to decipher what was being said. One thing I could make out, however, was that numbers were being recited and repeated with unwavering monotony night-after-night. I thought I was the only person on the planet tuning into this bizarre medley of spoken word gibberish, and though I often recorded some of it onto a cassette, I couldn't imagine anyone else doing likewise.

Fast forward a couple of decades and I now know I most certainly wasn't alone. Thanks to the internet, I discovered the sounds I'd been tuning into were unofficially recognised as Numbers Stations, the means by which secret service agencies communicated with their spies in the field behind enemy lines. No government has ever publicly admitted they exist, but there is now a plethora of information and background out there on this clandestine phenomenon. And while many of the old ones have subsequently vanished from the airwaves, an outfit called The Conet Project have released several CDs of recordings over the last ten-fifteen years, many of which are far creepier than anything I heard when I used to tune in.

If some of us not involved in the spying game have just cause to sometimes suspect we're being monitored by anonymous nosy parkers, the Numbers Stations can be viewed as symbolic of a more innocent age, an age when only those operating in an arena one entered into with full knowledge of its dangers could expect to be exposed to the all-seeing eye of the secret state.

THE MAN WHO WROTE THE RULEBOOK
19 March 2017

In November 1972, a novelty hit sat atop the charts and 'Top of the Pops' proceeded with caution. In his introduction to the video clip, Jimmy Savile reminded viewers the song was about a bell and nothing else; to emphasise this during the performance, the programme's producer mixed in footage of Rolf Harris sketching bizarre bell-themed self-portraits. Everybody watching and everybody who had made the record an unlikely No.1 knew that the song's title, 'My Ding-a-Ling', was a euphemism for a penis; the fact it had topped the charts presented radio and TV with a problem, but forty-five years on the ironic legacy of this particular piece of BBC

45

ingenuity is that the TOTP presentation of the performance is now off-limits for completely different reasons. The moral barometer has swung in another direction, and Chuck Berry's smutty ditty is not the cause of retrospective panic. I'm sure Chuck would have found the whole business hilarious.

The performance of 'My Ding-a-Ling' used on TOTP was lifted from Berry's recent appearance on BBC2's ground-breaking 'In Concert' series; the programme had been designed as a thirty-minute showcase for some of the era's prominent singer-songwriters, with the likes of Neil Young, Joni Mitchell, James Taylor, Carole King and Don McLean receiving rare TV exposure that gave them more breathing space than the hit-machine conveyor belt of most music shows. In hindsight, Chuck Berry seems an incongruous gate-crasher into this sedate patchouli oil-scented refuge from showbiz glitz, yet confronted by a cross-legged audience, he wins them over and wakes them up by encouraging their participation in 'My Ding-a-Ling'; they can't resist it. The man oozes charisma and the cheeky schoolboy smirk that spreads across his face come each *double-entendre* is pure Benny Hill.

Of course, 'My Ding-a-Ling' may have been the only time the name Chuck Berry hit the No.1 spot, but it hardly serves as the most accurate obituary for a man whose passing at the grand old age of 90 will be marked across the media this weekend. His sole chart-topper came at a moment when the music he'd pioneered almost twenty years earlier was undergoing a popular revival after being shoved off the radar by the cultural revolution of the 60s. The same year 'My Ding-a-Ling' topped the charts he'd shared the bill with fellow bad-boy survivors Little Richard and Jerry Lee Lewis at Wembley Stadium in the landmark 'London Rock 'n' Roll

Show'. Watching the DVD of this event is fascinating and I heartily recommend it.

The audience is a mix of long-haired Hell's Angels-biker types (still in their twenties) and their 50s Rocker predecessors, the kind of ageing Teddy Boys I remember from my childhood; most are pushing forty, yet their haircuts haven't altered since the mid-50s; the seismic shifts in the pop landscape of the previous decade seem to have passed these guys by. In 1972, they were still partying like it was 1957, though it's interesting to note a blink-and-you'll-miss-him cameo from none other than Malcolm McLaren, manning a stall from which he's flogging goods sold in his original Let it Rock boutique. At one gig, you have the immortal innovators without whom the 60s could never have happened, but you also have the presence of someone who would eventually shape the 70s.

It's virtually impossible to overstate the importance of Chuck Berry. The blistering chainsaw guitar that sliced through the slick tuxedo crooning club of the 1950s and illuminates the incendiary Rock 'n' Roll anthems his reputation was built upon still splits the musical atom sixty years on. That guitar is the starting pistol for Hank Marvin, George Harrison, Keith Richards, Jeff Beck, Jimmy Page, Jimi Hendrix and every axe warrior to have strut his stuff before a stack of Marshall amps ever since. The electric guitar itself was in its infancy when Charles Edward Anderson Berry first took to the stage, largely in the hands of veteran Bluesmen whose audience was as segregated as everything else in the Deep South; an ambitious Berry soon began composing his own songs and played them in a frenetic speeded-up Blues style that gradually crossed the racial divide in a part of America that suddenly had a generation whose appetite for change wasn't coloured by the prejudices of their parents.

Berry's songs made him a lyrical cartographer, mapping out the landscape of fast cars and loose women that rebranded America as the turbo-charged, Technicolor Sodom and Gomorrah that proved especially attractive to the war babies coming of age on the monochrome side of the Atlantic. But Berry was no detached observer; by living his lyrics, he also pioneered the outlaw myth of the Rock 'n' Roll guitarist. He'd already served time as a juvenile delinquent in the US equivalent of Borstal before anyone had heard of him, but once he'd established himself both as a live and recording act his talent for trouble earned him three years behind bars after transporting a 14 year-old girl across state lines; he served another sentence in 1979 for tax evasion.

Like the other cast members of Rock 'n' Roll's opening act (bar Elvis), Chuck Berry never enjoyed the sustained commercial success and immense riches that those he directly inspired have continued to mine. By the 80s, he occupied the same 'living legend' nostalgia circuit that kept Sinatra in business, recycling signature tunes penned decades earlier in a permanent road-show that nevertheless paid the bills. He was still performing just three years ago, well into his eighties.

John Lennon once remarked that if Rock 'n' Roll was ever to be given another name, it may as well be renamed Chuck Berry. It's hard to dispute Lennon's logic; he knew, as did every other adolescent wannabe to graduate from British bomb-site to US baseball stadium, that the debt owed to the duck-walking gunslinger with the six-stringed revolver was immeasurable.

THE BASH STREET KING
27 April 2017

Unless you're in the know, chances are the name Leo Baxendale means nothing to you. However, if you're over at least 30, you'll be more than familiar with the characters this unsung National Treasure gave us – The Bash Street Kids, Minnie the Minx, Little Plum, and Grimly Feendish, to name a few. It's been announced that Baxendale has died at the age of 86 and – subsequent innovators such as Alan Moore and the '2000AD' generation aside – it's hard to think of anyone who revolutionised British comics more than this remarkably gifted draughtsman from Preston.

Beginning before the Second World War, both The Dandy and The Beano were firmly part of the British cultural furniture by the time Baxendale became a regular contributor to the latter in 1952. The introduction of Dennis the Menace the year before had given Britain's schoolboys a new anti-hero that enabled them to live out their revenge fantasies on authority figures such as parents and teachers by proxy. Tapping into this new spirit of cartoon anarchy that served to inject some much-needed colour into monochrome Austerity Britain for anyone under the age of around 13, Baxendale added to the list of naughty schoolboys with an entire class of them, The Bash Street Kids.

With Desperate Dan the cowboy star of The Dandy, Baxendale decided to showcase the other side for The Beano by creating Red Indian character Little Plum as well as The Three Bears. Both strips ran for over thirty years, long after their creator had left the comic, whereas The Bash Street Kids continue to run riot in their preserved 50s playground to this very day, as does the other character whose creation he will forever be associated with, Minnie the Minx.

Clearly a female equivalent of Dennis the Menace, Baxendale's tomboy (first appearing in 1953) even wore the same red-and-black hooped jersey Dennis had virtually trademarked. However, whilst her male counterpart can be placed in a long tradition of unruly little boys such as William Brown (AKA 'Just William'), there were few precedents in either literature or comics for Minnie. Yes, there were the wild pupils of St Trinian's, though they were posh girls at a boarding school; Minnie was a working-class heroine when the idea of a girl from 'the lower orders' being as mischievous and badly-behaved as a boy was very much frowned upon. She instantly provided female readers with their own role model that parents were destined to disapprove of; the fact she also happened to be ginger gave hope to redheads everywhere. Like Dennis, her wicked deeds may have ended with the obligatory slipper on the backside, but readers at the time were aware that's how all wicked deeds concluded, so her ultimate failure didn't matter; what mattered was that she had the guts to have a go.

Dundee-based DC Thomson, publishers of The Dandy and The Beano as well as a host of other popular titles, were notoriously reluctant to give credit to the artists illuminating the pages of their publications; the serf-like approach they had to the men whose creations and artwork sold millions of copies (in 1950, the weekly circulation of The Beano alone was estimated at 1,974,072) irked Baxendale and he left the company after a decade in 1962, moving to DC Thomson rivals Odhams Press. Whilst there, he helped create Wham!, a gloriously insane comic that allowed his vivid imagination to run riot and one that introduced one of his most memorable creations, Grimly Feendish.

If you've ever seen the animated movie 'Despicable Me', the influence of Feendish is unmistakable. A fat bald villain clad in black, Feendish's army for achieving world domination included bats, spiders and various fictitious creatures that made him a cult horror figure so potent to 60s children that when some of them grew up and formed The Damned, they even wrote a hit single about him. Unfortunately, the high production cost of Wham! and its sister titles pushed Odhams into financial difficulties and the company was absorbed into IPC, whose titles showcased most of Baxendale's new work in the 70s as well as introducing that decade's comic readership (myself included) to the likes of Grimly Feendish.

Still smarting from his treatment by DC Thomson and the fact that the strips he created remained amongst the most popular in the company's comic stable, Baxendale took the company to court in the 80s in order to gain the rights to his creations. This legal battle spanned seven years, eventually settled out of court with an arrangement that apparently suited both parties. The fact that Baxendale was prepared to take on the authority of Thomson seemed to echo the attitude of Minnie the Minx and The Bash Street Kids towards their own authority figures, perhaps showing there was more than a touch of the creations in the creator.

Whereas the 1960s may have opened the door to irreverence that in turn heralded the death of deference, without the foundations laid in the previous decade we wouldn't have had 'Beyond the Fringe' or John Lennon asking the people in the expensive seats at the Royal Variety Performance to rattle their jewellery. Whilst the likes of Spike Milligan and The Goons are rightly recognised as hugely significant pioneers in helping to manufacture this atmosphere, credit is also due to the men whose madcap characters enlivened the comics read by kids who went on to play their own part in the 60s cultural revolution.

Leo Baxendale stands at the head of these neglected innovators; that it's still possible to follow the adventures of Minnie the Minx and The Bash Street Kids in the twenty-first century is testament to their enduring appeal and to the man who made them. RIP.

BACK TO THE TEACHER
25 May 2017

Okay, so it's been a bloody grim week so far, and as a means of combating the worst elements of the twenty-first century, I've been retreating into the selective embrace of the past in the shape of programmes for schools and colleges produced in the 1970s. Thanks to YouTube, over the last 48 hours I've sat through 40-odd year-old editions of 'Look and Read', 'Words and Pictures', 'How We Used to Live' *et al*. If I dip into my desk drawer and pull out a copy of the Radio Times from the same era (the copy in question dated 31 August-6 September 1974), the centre pages provide the most striking contrast between television then and television now, for they contain a four-page guide to that autumn's educational schedule across BBC TV and radio.

And the variety on offer in this schedule is all the more eye-opening because these series are all primarily aimed at adults; there isn't even room for cataloguing the myriad of programmes produced for schools during this period. Got kids? Watch 'Parents and Children' on BBC1; like football? Listen to 'Behind the Goals' on Radio 3; just qualified as a social-worker? Watch 'Developments in Social Work' on BBC2; interested in 'news-making, decision-making and forms of loyalty'? Watch 'Focus' on BBC1 – and that's not the flute-based, yodelling Dutch prog-rock band, despite 'House of the King' being used as the theme tune to numerous educational programmes in the 1970s.

52

You can learn to speak German, Spanish, Russian and Welsh, learn to become a mountaineer, rugby player and gardener, learn how to understand economics, the National Health and local government, not to mention 'systematic thinking in action'! Arts, sciences, languages, the community, home and leisure, work and industry, teaching – all fall under the umbrella of public service broadcasting in 1974. Despite his reservations over the one-eyed monster, no doubt Lord Reith would have been proud his original remit remained relatively intact.

Today, what used to be viewed as television down-time is filled during the day with cheap and cheerful antiques/cookery/house-buying and selling/quiz show formulas and late at night with rolling news, interactive game shows and repeats of daytime fodder with a man in the corner of the screen aptly gesticulating his way through 'The Jeremy Kyle Show'. In retrospect, it's amazing how a TV landscape that switched-off around midnight seemed to cram more into its limited broadcasting hours than one that never sleeps. The adult education programmes described above could usually be found hidden away last thing at night or presented together in a large chunk on a Sunday morning, sandwiched between a religious service and farming news; space in the listings may have been at a precious premium, but the schedulers always found a space to educate and inform as well as entertain.

Then of course, there were the twilight hours that were occupied by hirsute men in spectacles with little or no evident experience in front of a camera – the Open University. Who could forget that eerie, unnerving jingle jolting the armchair snoozer back to life far more effectively than a car alarm would do today? And who could forget programmes for schools and colleges? For anyone who was of school age in the 60s, 70s or 80s, they were amongst the few breathers from the classroom tedium on offer. What a ritual that was, being ushered into the library and watching the teacher wheel-in a huge telly, waiting for what felt like an aeon for the machine to warm-up, and then being greeted by some unsettling Radiophonic Workshop ditty accompanying a pulsating diamond or a circle of disappearing dots before the actual programme began.

It's worth bearing in mind just how many hours were given over to schools broadcasts as well. An average BBC1 week during term-time would begin around 9.38am and would sign-off not long after midday; following a dinner-break for the test card, the news, 'Pebble Mill at One' and 'Watch with Mother', schools TV would open its gates again for another hour or so at the precise time of 2.2pm. That's not even including BBC schools broadcasts on the radio, when the VHF wavelength on Radio 4 would be used exclusively for them between 10.00 in the morning and 3.00 in the afternoon.

We should also remember that ITV – yes! *ITV!* – played its part in the television education of the nation's children as well. Even though commercial considerations freed them from a less rigid public service commitment than the Beeb, their weekday schedule ran from 9.30-12.00 and produced some of the most memorable schools programmes of them all. There was even an advertising armistice during these transmissions.

Calculate just how much of pre-24 hour TV on both sides of the British broadcasting divide was given over to educational programming and it'd be pretty impressive. It's indisputable that many were cheaply-made on shoestring budgets, especially the Open University broadcasts; and some were uniquely dull in a manner that elevated visual boredom to a level that now seems quite radical, on a par with the worst Warhol movies or a contemporary art installation But I'd still be more bored sitting through an edition of 'This Morning' than an episode of Granada's austere schools science show, 'Experiment'.

Noble ventures are not something one would now really associate with British television. Most 21st century TV execs would probably regard 'Comic Relief' or 'Children in Need' as such, and in their own way, they are. But annual or bi-annual telethons, when the normal schedule is set aside for one night only to accommodate a good deed, are different to the noble venture that was educational television. It was a product of a period in which the people who ran television regarded it as a tool of communication that amounted to more than a ratings-chasing commercial cash-cow or a daytime sedative. Much like the internet is today, TV then was viewed as a multi-purpose medium capable of all that life can afford.

So, where did it go? Firstly, the advent of the VCR hailed the death-knell of schools programming in its traditional slot; secondly, in the mid-80s BBC TV schools programmes were shunted over to BBC2 in preparation for the launch of daytime BBC1 and the arrival of cosy sofa chinwags about child abuse and the menstrual cycle. Not long after, ITV transferred their schools schedule to Channel 4 in order that Richard and Judy could do likewise, paving the way for menopausal gobshites and underclass-baiting bullies. It is ironic that a slot once reserved for mind-expansion is now reserved for the gradual erosion of the brain cells, and after-dark telly today is no less retarded. It does seem a shame that the increase in broadcasting hours doesn't seem capable of embracing the same breadth of broadcasting available when less was more.

Before hyperactive twenty-somethings, uncles used to be the model – lacking the stern authority of father-figures, managing to earn respect with lingering juvenile slapstick silliness; when I was the child watching, uncles were everywhere. Derek Griffiths and Brian Cant on 'Play School' and 'Play Away'; Tony Hart on 'Vision On'; Johnny Morris on 'Animal Magic'; Roy Castle on 'Record Breakers'; yes...Rolf Harris; and then there were John Noakes and Peter Purves on 'Blue Peter'. With the news that Noakes has passed away at the age of 83, having mercifully evaded the pernicious net of malicious revisionism that hangs over his television era, those of my generation cannot help but recall how much he meant to us at the time.

John Noakes joined 'Blue Peter' as a very young-looking 30-year-old when his far-from spectacular acting career was floundering. Becoming the third member of the team in 1965, he was quite unlike anyone to have appeared on children's TV previously. Christopher Trace and Valerie Singleton were very much in a 50s parental mould – RP-speaking, frightfully middle-class and sensible; they represented the norm. Noakes was Northern and didn't hide his Yorkshire accent, for one thing; and he never talked down to the audience, communicating with them in their own language. It never looked as if Noakes' mother took a comb to his hair, so he was definitely 'one of us'.

John Noakes was also child-like in his anarchic recklessness, quickly earning a reputation as something of an amateur daredevil that saw him put in situations that would today provoke a cardiac arrest in most Health and Safety Officers. He climbed up one of the chimneys at Fulham Power Station, up Nelson's Column, up the mast 127 feet above the deck of HMS Ganges; he skydived with the RAF; and had a lucky escape when tobogganing at 90mph. There was a fearlessness to him that seemed to echo the tree-climbing zest for life his core viewing public were encouraged to believe they would one day grow out of. He clearly hadn't grown out of it, so there was hope for all of us.

It later emerged that Noakes' popularity with the young audience was something of an irritant to his on-screen sidekick Peter Purves. Not that the two men didn't get on – far from it; but it seems Purves resented having to play 'the straight man' to Noakes' comedy character; perhaps that's why Purves went for the cool dude look, straight out of Carnaby Street. It was then up to Valerie Singleton to play the responsible parent to an unruly rascal and a coiffured dandy, keeping the boys in order. Singleton was the studio representative of the show's backstage editor Biddy Baxter, whose strict headmistress persona often clashed with Noakes' instinctive rebel. But the off-screen tensions benefitted the programme, as Noakes became (and remains) the longest-serving presenter in its history, clocking-in at 12 years 6 months.

One of the more ingenious ideas 'Blue Peter' came up with was to introduce dogs and cats as surrogate pets for those children watching whose parents wouldn't allow them to keep either (me included). It was also an astute move in that animals are one of the best ways in for children to learn about the cycle of life in that they die after a few short years. Petra and Jason were the original dog and cat members of the line-up and when the series decided to keep one of Petra's puppies Patch as the second canine star of the show, Noakes was entrusted to look after him. The first lesson of the life cycle came for 'Blue Peter' viewers in 1971 when Patch suddenly died after catching a rare disease during location filming. A few months later, his replacement appeared and a legendary double-act was born in the process, John Noakes and Shep.

The Border collie appeared to be the perfect best friend for a man like John Noakes; he was just as silly and loveable as Noakes himself. In fact, the two were so inseparable that they even gained their own spin-off series, 'Go with Noakes', in which John and Shep went on their travels around the country, usually indulging in the more energetic rural pursuits. By the mid-70s, John Noakes was one of the most famous faces on British television and it was all-but impossible to imagine 'Blue Peter' without him. However, that moment came in June 1978, barely three months after Peter Purves had also walked; for the children watching, both 'Blue Peter' and children's television would never be quite the same again.

The clash between Noakes and Biddy Baxter wasn't eased by his departure; although Shep was technically 'BBC property', Noakes was told he could take Shep with him when he left the programme as long as he didn't capitalise on their celebrity by advertising products on ITV. Noakes agreed and then promptly did a dog food commercial with a Shep lookalike, infuriating Baxter. The ill-feeling lasted a long time, with Noakes refusing to participate in any of the programme's anniversary reunions until Baxter had herself retired. The feud was a shame in that both contributed hugely to the success of the show and made it one of the jewels in the BBC's children's crown during a genuine golden age.

In the years after his 'Blue Peter' career ended, Noakes appeared occasionally on TV, presenting a regional series called 'Country Calendar' for Yorkshire Television in the early 80s and then largely popping up as a guest blast from the past here and there. His public bitterness about his 'Blue

Peter' years was, to those of us for whom he was a hero, a bit like finding out your dad had been having an affair throughout his marriage to your mum. It sours the memory a little, but can't take away the warmth that memory continues to generate. Patch and Shep were my dogs, Jason was my cat, and John Noakes was my daft uncle. Just as they all were to everyone else my age. RIP.

STATION TO STATION (1)
23 September 2017

A week from today will mark half-a-century since the day the nation's stations received the most comprehensive facelift in their history; and, lest we forget, fifty years ago we only had three national radio stations. Yes, there were the pirates, though they – bar Caroline – were poised to sail away into the sunset; officially, the country had just the Light Programme, the Home Service and the Third Programme. There were no local BBC stations, and the Independent Local Radio network was still six years away. Once the Marine Broadcasting Offences Act sank the pirate ships, listeners were left with Luxembourg and its erratic reception if they sought an alternative to the BBC's wireless output.

If one is to credit pirate radio with one thing it really should be giving the kiss of life to an ailing medium. From being very much the poor relation before the war, television had gathered pace with the arrival of ITV in 1955 and by the early 60s had usurped radio as the people's choice. In response, all the BBC's creative energies were directed towards TV and radio was left to its own devices, with only the Third Programme receiving special treatment courtesy of its high standing in the artistic community. Listening figures were plummeting and it didn't help that, with Britain the epicentre of a pop revolution conquering the globe, BBC radio's

59

concession to the revolution was limited to the likes of 'Saturday Club' and 'Pick of the Pops'.

Belated recognition that the BBC needed to reflect the changing climate on the airwaves led to plans being hatched for a new addition to the existing trio of national stations. But it wasn't simply a case of the Beeb replicating what the pirates had done so successfully since 1964; Musicians Union rules over needle time meant the in-house BBC orchestras that provided so much of the light 'mood music' that had soundtracked the daily chores of the housewife for a couple of decades were not going to be disbanded overnight. A BBC idea of a pirate radio station risked being the aural equivalent of a pipe-smoking, cardigan-clad dad dancing around the living room to The Jimi Hendrix Experience or the Light Programme in a kaftan. Live music was going to be as much a staple of what became Radio 1 as spinning discs, though the fact this ruling eventually gave birth to the legendary Peel Sessions was pure serendipity.

With the new law enforcing the illegality of the pirates, the entire staff of DJs that had become household names to anyone under 25 were about to be made redundant; by happy coincidence, a new employer was looking for a workforce with their precise qualifications. So it was that the cream of the pirate crop sat alongside a handful of veteran broadcasting stalwarts to pose for a photo that used to be re-staged every ten years until the participants started dying or ended up in prison. Radio 1 had recruited almost all the pirate DJs, and when the new station went on air with Caroline's Tony Blackburn on 30 September 1967 – preceded by heavy promotion in the Radio Times and its 'swinging' front cover for the week – the pirate model sufficed for the first ninety minutes. The second programme on Radio 1 was 'Junior Choice' with Leslie Crowther.

The wavelength sharing between Radio 1 and its new sibling Radio 2 was scattered throughout that opening day and this continued to be the case for more or less the whole first decade of the station. The recurring term 'As Radio 2' in the Radio Times listings for Radio 1 was a regular feature that meant any hip 'n' groovy listener either had to endure Light Programme leftovers for a couple of hours in the middle of the schedule or simply switch off. Mind you, it's worth remembering that DJs we all associate with Radio 2 – such as Terry Wogan and Jimmy Young – were part of the Radio 1 line-up in the beginning.

The schizophrenic nature of the station, viewed by many as a pale imitation of the pirates at best and little short of a charlatan at worst, helped prompt 1969's landmark in-house report, 'Broadcasting in the Seventies', that sought to rectify the problems. By the early 70s, however, a generation too young to remember the pirates had taken to the station as it gradually grew into the familiar form those of us old enough can still recall, and listening figures reflected this.

The 'star' DJs such as Tony Blackburn, Jimmy Savile, Noel Edmonds, Dave Lee Travis, Kenny Everett and 'Emperor' Rosko were all familiar faces as presenters of 'Top of the Pops', and the mutual appreciation society between BBC TV's leading music show and Radio 1 benefitted both. In the 70s, the Radio 1 DJs were almost as famous as the pop stars whose careers they had the power to make or break - opening supermarkets, judging wet T-shirt contests, and drawing huge crowds when making prats of themselves on stage during the annual summer institution of the Radio 1 Roadshow. This was the heyday of the 'Smashie and Nicey' incarnation of Radio 1, though it also spanned the 80s; regardless of personnel changes, the mid-Atlantic accent, the bomber jacket and the cheesy persona had already been established as a mould, whether inhabited by Simon Bates or Bruno Brookes.

By the time of Harry Enfield and Paul Whitehouse's painfully accurate parody, the BBC was concerned that a radio station supposedly aimed at an audience in its teens and twenties had retained listeners of a much older age range that hadn't followed the traditional migratory route to Radio 2. The call went out to Matthew Bannister and what followed was a traumatic period in which Radio 1 didn't seem to know what it was (or who it was for) anymore. The old school were shown the door, and after the crash-and-burn era of Chris Evans, a semblance of stability returned to the station as it entered the 21st century.

I haven't listened to Radio 1 for a good decade, so I can't comment on its current state of health with any authority. Last time I tuned in, Chris Moyles was still the host of the breakfast show and Jo Whiley was still espousing all she regarded as 'cool' mid-morning. I stopped listening not necessarily because I found the music being played increasingly irritating, but because I simply couldn't stand the prattling DJs. At the same time, I recognise this has always been a regular factor for the listener where Radio 1 is concerned, and probably always will be.

STATION-TO-STATION (2)
25 September 2017

Being a notoriously dour Scotsman, Lord Reith's famous proclamation that the BBC's role was to inform, educate and entertain meant that the last of that trio wouldn't have got much of a look in had Reith's tenure as DG lasted way beyond 1938. His austere Presbyterian idea of entertainment would have driven a war-weary listening audience away from the BBC in their droves during the 1950s; they'd already turned to Radio Luxembourg for a lighter evening in front of the wireless before the war, and chances are they'd have continued to do so had not Reith's successors at the helm reorganised the Beeb's network when hostilities ceased in 1945.

Taking over from the General Forces Programme, the Light Programme debuted on the airwaves just two months after VE Day and quickly established itself as the most popular of the BBC stations for the next couple of decades. Whenever a documentary requires a piece of music to accompany footage of the 50s and wants to evoke a certain Home Counties 'cosiness', chances are the piece of music in question is the theme tune from a Light Programme mainstay such as 'Housewives' Choice', 'Workers' Playtime' or 'Listen with Mother'. It's also worth noting radio institutions like 'The Archers', 'Woman's Hour' and 'Pick of the Pops' formed part of the Light Programme's line-up along with a rash of memorable comedies such as 'Hancock's Half Hour' and 'Round the Horne'. And then there was the music – fittingly light with soupy strings and melodies so unobtrusively polite they almost asked for permission to rent the airwaves. By the mid-60s, however, the music was the problem.

With the Beeb belatedly attempting to swing along with the rest of the 60s, the rebirth of radio on 30 September 1967 saw the teen pop offerings of the Light Programme shift over to the new Radio 1; what of Radio 2, though? How would it differ from the station it succeeded? Not that much, really, which I suppose was part of the strategy to hold onto the Light listeners. Amongst the offerings on Radio 2's first day (a Saturday) were Pete Murray, Kenneth Horne, Max Jaffa, the BBC Midland Light Orchestra, Sidney Davey and his

Orchestra – Light Programme veterans all. It seemed the only real change was the name.

Come Monday morning, though 'Housewives' Choice', 'Music Box' and 'Music While You Work' had all vanished and the station shared the shows of Jimmy Young, Simon Dee and Pete Brady with Radio 1, 'Mrs Dale's Diary' (now 'The Dales') clung on, as did 'Woman's Hour' - albeit considerably longer than 'The Dales'. Musically, the presence of the Central Band of the Royal Air Force, Frank Chacksfield, and the wonderfully-named Reginald Leopold and the Palm Court Orchestra suggested familiar fare. Dotted through the schedule of the first Radio 2 week were other stalwarts of the Light such as 'Family Favourites', 'Sing Something Simple', 'Top of the Form', 'The Navy Lark', 'Any Questions?', 'Friday Night is Music Night', and plenty of sport, which remained a fixture of Radio 2 until the launch of Five Live in the early 90s.

There was a good deal of channel crossing between Radio 2 and Radio 4 in terms of genres and repeats in the early days, as there had been between the Light Programme and the Home Service; there was a distinct lack of identity where both stations were concerned, something that led to 'Broadcasting in the Seventies', the BBC's far-reaching 1969 review of its radio output. As a result of the changes recommended in the report, the four networks began to morph into recognisably individual entities from the early 70s onwards. When Radio 1 transferred Jimmy Young and Terry Wogan to Radio 2 around the same time, the classic morning schedule had finally taken shape.

Although a few quizzes and comedies lingered on 2, along with a solitary soap ('Waggoners' Walk'), my own childhood memory of the station is of its playlist, largely derived from staying at my grandparents' house in the 70s. For me, it presented a curious alternative to the pop diet of Radio 1 so familiar at home and served as an introduction to Easy Listening, Jazz, Big Bands and the song stylists of the pre-Rock n Roll era, none more so than Sinatra. By the late 70s, a combination of Simon Bates and Punk (awkward bedfellows, to say the least) had seen my dad switch his listening allegiance from 1 to 2, something the soccer coverage on the latter helped.

Aside from Wogan and Young, the voice I associate most with childhood exposure to Radio 2 is that of the superb football commentator, the late great Peter Jones; at a time when football coverage on TV was at a minimum unimaginable to today's Sky subscribers, radio provided an essential service, and the theme tunes to 'Sport on 2' and 'Sports Report' respectively still evoke the old spirit of Saturdays for me as much as the sight of Tom Baker's hat-&-scarf ensemble. When VHF – as FM radio was always called then – first appeared in our household, the wavelength was shared between 1 and 2, so any listen to a Radio 1 documentary in my teens was generally followed by a Radio 2 Jazz or Folk show.

The old joke about Radio 2, that it was a retirement home for Radio 1 DJs, is as relevant now as it ever was. Chris Evans, Jo Whiley, Zoe Ball, Sara Cox, Trevor Nelson and Simon Mayo were all still on Radio 1 twenty years ago, whereas they now comfortably slot in alongside ex-Radio 1 stars of a far older vintage such as Bob Harris, Johnnie Walker, Tony Blackburn, Paul Gambaccini and Steve Wright. However, the daytime playlist is usually geared towards listeners suddenly feeling nostalgic about their 20s for the first time, something that tends to creep in when people hit their 40s; therefore, the station's presenters and musical selection reflect this for each generation. One thing Radio 2 has continued to do far more successfully than Radio 1 is to gently lower the average age of its audience every couple of decades.

In recent years, the blend of old and older broadcasters has helped make Radio 2 the nation's most listened-to station and it appears to have finally shed its pipe & slippers image in the process. There does seem to be a worrying reliance on TV personalities presenting programmes, with Graham Norton, Paul O'Grady, Dermot O'Leary, Claudia Winkleman, Clare Balding, Craig Charles, Vanessa Feltz, Liza Tarbuck and the Partridge-esque Jeremy Vine all making the journey from television to radio; but former Radio 2 presenters who now reside in that great Broadcasting House in the sky, such as Terry Wogan and David Jacobs, also had a foot in both camps. And Radio 2 can still boast the archetypal broadcaster with a great face for radio, the indestructible Ken Bruce.

STATION-TO-STATION (3)
26 September 2017

Those of you who take note of the time of day these posts are dispatched will by now have gathered I'm prone to burning the midnight oil; living in a household where neighbours are a thin wall away, however, requires a degree of tact in terms of background sounds. The usual routine has always been to leave the World Service on come the Radio 4 closedown at 1.00am, though the volume is so low that what the voices are saying is generally inaudible. Of late, I've been switching over to Radio 3 to soundtrack my jottings in the wee small hours instead. As an alternative, it's refreshingly soothing, comprising piano pieces in the Erik Satie mould, string quartets or choral music. They're loud enough to absorb, but quiet enough not to disrupt anyone else's slumber; I only wish my recently departed 'Club DJ' neighbour had considered a similar course of post-midnight audio action.

As a child, Radio 3 was the national radio station I knew the least about; Radio 4 was almost as alien to my ears, though I do remember my dad regularly listening to 'Brain of Britain', from which he no doubt sourced questions and answers for the pub quizzes he organised. In old-school terms, Radio 1 was for the terminal working-classes; Radio 2 was for the working-classes whose social mobility scooters had steered them away from the backyard privy; Radio 4 was for the middle-classes; and Radio 3 was for...well, who? The aristocracy? Pipe-smoking dons in tweed jackets? It had an enigmatic mystery to me because I never heard it, though no doubt its previous incarnation as the Third Programme would have been just as mysterious to ears weaned on Tony Blackburn.

It's a measure of how much of a special case the Third Programme was that when BBC Radio underwent its great rebranding shake-up on 30 September 1967 and added Radio 1 to the long-standing trio of stations it was really only the daytime Music Programme, occupying the Third's frequency since 1965, that became Radio 3. In the evening, it was business as usual with the Third continuing to provide cultural riches as well as Network Three's educational 'Study Session'; the station also retained its Sports Service strand on an afternoon (which included 'Test Match Special'). As far as Radio 3 after dark was concerned, however, the impression given was that the station remained a highbrow night-school behind the various doors of which were numerous means of self-improvement; it was still the worthiest of broadcasting endeavours.

There had been more opposition to tinkering with the Third than accompanied the facelift of the BBC's other two radio stations in 1967; it was viewed by many as an artistic oasis that deserved preservation. Even the 'hit' classical music composers like old Ludwig Van and Mozart were more familiar on the Home Service than on the Third, which revelled in the esoteric and uncommercial; there were also fears the station would lose its high proportion of spoken word programming when rebranded as Radio 3. Concerns that Radio 3 would effectively become Classic FM a quarter-of-a-century early were perhaps responsible for the compromise that kept the Third intact for another two-and-a-half years. However, the impact of 1969's 'Broadcasting in the Seventies' report finally saw the Third vanish from the schedules in April 1970 and a full-time Radio 3 at last.

The station did gain 'Choral Evensong' from Radio 4 in 1970, with Radio 3 being a more fitting home for a series that has been on air since 1926; in return, political coverage became the exclusive province of Radio 4; any spoken word broadcasts on 3 would henceforth focus solely on the Arts, including plays and poetry. Many had worried the latter would be lost, as the Third Programme had been a major platform for contemporary poetry – virtually the only one in the field of radio. Periodical panic over Radio 3's future wasn't helped by the fact that the BBC's monopoly of the airwaves was coming to an end; but there were few signs the ILR network (which spread across the country from 1973 onwards) intended to compete with Radio 3; as a consequence, its unique status seemed secure.

The station was an early beneficiary of VHF stereo broadcasting, something its playlist could have been designed for; its extensive coverage of the Proms and other major classical music events also often went hand-in-hand with simultaneous broadcasts on BBC2, which at the time was the nearest BBC TV had to an in-vision Radio 3. To the casual radio listener, the Third Programme may have had the reputation of being unfathomably intellectual, but Radio 3 retained the 'elitist' tag in the popular imagination simply by virtue of specialising in genres of music that wouldn't threaten to gatecrash 'Top of the Pops'. It's worth noting, though, that Prog Rock would occasionally surface on the Radio 3 schedules in the 70s, paving the way for widening the musical scope that eventually encompassed 'World Music'. Jazz has also been a key component from the beginning, as it had been in the latter days of the Third.

The arguments for and against the continued existence of a radio station with a relatively small (albeit passionate) listening audience are the same as those that surrounded Radio 3's predecessor. One former managing director of BBC Radio had described the station as 'a private playground for elitists to indulge in cerebral masturbation' during its early years, while those to whom Radio 3 remains the same artistic oasis as the Third was before it are quick to protest whenever a new controller of the station implements 'controversial' changes, such as the arrival of Paul Gambaccini as a presenter in 1995; his presence was regarded by some as a populist move to prevent migration to Classic FM.

As we all – well, most of us – contribute towards the funding of the BBC, I think it only right some of that licence fee is diverted into niche broadcasting that doesn't have the audience of a 'Strictly' or a 'Bake-Off'. If we all pay in, we should all have our own tastes catered for, even if the tastes of the many naturally count for more in respect of how the money is dished out than the tastes of the few. The Third Programme or Radio 3 was never destined to be a ratings winner, but so what? Some things in broadcasting (and life) count for more.

STATION-TO-STATION (4)
30 September 2017

The final moments of the BBC Home Service took place during the final moments of Friday 29 September 1967; David Dunhill, the announcer, made reference to the soon-to-be Radio 1 DJ (and soon-to-be disgraced) Chris Denning having just appeared on BBC2's 'Late Night Line-Up' wearing a T-shirt bearing the words 'Death to the Home Service', yet Dunhill assured listeners that the process of rechristening the following day would be akin to being 'like a bride on the eve of her wedding; we go on being the same person, we hope; but we'll never again have the same name'. It was a fittingly cosy analogy and one that seemed entirely in keeping with the image the Home Service had in the public imagination – one that typified everything antiquated and irrelevant about BBC radio to the generation tuning in to the pirates.

It wasn't merely the addition of Radio 1 to the mix and the rebranding of the established three stations that spelt the death-knell for the Home Service; the imminent onset of BBC local radio would also rob it of one of its traditional functions. With the outbreak of the Second World War, the BBC had merged its National Programme and Regional Programme radio stations and the result of the marriage was the Home Service, based in London but peppered throughout the day with regional opt-outs from either Birmingham, Manchester, Bristol, Cardiff, Glasgow or Belfast – depending where you were listening. This hallmark of the station survived the birth of Radio 4 until the countrywide spread of local radio made it redundant; the last such opt-out on Radio 4 was in Devon and Cornwall as late as 1982.

After the war, the reorganisation of the BBC's radio network that saw the arrival of the Light Programme removed many entertainment shows from the Home Service, though the station continued to host the likes of 'ITMA' as well as 'The Goons'. In fact, for all its reputation as a carrier of serious news programming, the Home never entirely lost its entertainment elements, with adventure serial 'Dick Barton' especially appealing to young listeners who had their own show in 'Children's Hour'; sitcoms such as the long-running 'All Gas and Gaiters' and 'The Men from The Ministry' even lasted into the station's incarnation as Radio 4. Factual mainstays that could also be classed as entertainment like 'Gardeners' Question Time' and 'Desert Island Discs' survived the transition too and are still with us, as are news and current affairs institutions such as 'Today in Parliament', 'The World at One', 'From Our Own Correspondent' and, of course, 'Today'.

As we have already seen with Radio 2 and Radio 3, many of the changes that occurred when the BBC stations were renamed were essentially superficial. For one thing, daytime Radio 4 was lumbered with its most unwanted inheritance from the Home Service during its early years, BBC schools broadcasting. Glancing through the musty pages of a Radio Times issue from November 1969, just two years into Radio 4, the station's morning and afternoon schedule has schools programming from 9.20am till noon, then following 'Listen with Mother' at 2.00 there's a further hour of it – an arrangement that's all-but inconceivable to a modern-day R4 listener. This state of affairs frustrated more than one Radio 4 controller, though the schools service ironically provided my main contact with the station in the 70s.

By the beginning of the 1973/74 term, schools (as well as adult education programmes) had switched to Radio 4's VHF wavelength; at a time when most in long pants were still listening on Medium Wave, it freed-up the schedules at last and facilitated the transfer of 'Woman's Hour' from Radio 2 to what seemed to be its natural home. The next big change came in November 1978, when all four national stations shifted around the dial; Radio 4 swapped places with Radio 2, moving from Medium to Long Wave. The change also marked the beginning of 4 as a truly national station with the end of all-but a tiny few regional variations and the debut of the late lamented 'UK Theme' to open proceedings every morning; meanwhile, the Shipping Forecast sailed into a more conducive harbour at the same time.

It had taken a decade for Radio 4 to emerge from the long shadow cast by its predecessor, but it appeared to have finally managed it; by the 80s, more listeners were beginning to tune in to FM, which accelerated the relocation of schools broadcasting to the new Radio 5 in 1990. Perhaps the last lingering legacy of the Home Service remit had been dispensed with at last. The FM and LW versions of Radio 4 only temporarily go their separate ways today with 'Test Match Special' and 'Daily Service'.

For my generation, and the generations after, names like the Home Service, the Light Programme and the Third Programme have a quaint, monochrome magic to them, belonging as they do to a lost, post-war 50s world that disappeared before our time. Radios 1, 2, 3 and 4, on the other hand, have always sounded contemporary. All four stations predate me by just a couple of months, so it's no wonder. Of the four, I cannot deny Radio 4 is my preference and has been for around a decade, though I acknowledge it can be far from perfect.

There's a tendency to over-egg the 'right-on' pudding on occasions; equally, whenever those hideous words 'The Kardashians' threaten to gatecrash the environs of 'Woman's Hour' or 'Front Row', I switch to Radio 3. Radio 4 produces many superb programmes on pop culture (Saturday evening's 'Archive on 4', for example), but there are already enough – *more* than enough – media mouthpieces for the afterbirths of Reality TV without R4 following suit. It's supposed to provide an alternative with a brain rather than half of one.

After Radio 2, Radio 4 is the most listened-to station in the country, which is impressive considering what a radical counterpoint it can be to the overabundance of what the Americans refer to as Top 40 stations. The thought that the erudite interlude of 'In Our Time' can attract more listeners than some waffling wanker on Crass FM – the sort of white noise that serves as the in-car soundtrack of taxi-drivers – gives one hope that all is not lost. Fifty years old today, Radios 1, 2, 3 and 4 appear to have provided a cradle-to (not quite) grave listening experience for my entire lifetime; and that lifetime would have very been different without them. Many happy returns.

MUSICAL YOUTH
8 October 2017

A paragraph from the previous post provoked this one, and if you haven't read it, where have you been? Anyway, let's go back 30 years. Actually, I'd rather not; if 2017 is pretty grim, I can't say I rated 1987 much at the time either and it doesn't acquire a nostalgic glow the further away I travel from it. The stuff I cared about then – general popular culture and pop music in particular – was, in my opinion, rubbish; there were a couple of contemporary exceptions, but I was a scholar of what is now referred to as 'Classic Rock'. I also extended my appreciation of the recent past to then-unfashionable 70s pop such as Abba and The Bee Gees, acts who had yet to receive the kitsch makeover the next generation would give them. The arrogance of youth told me I could do better than what the present was offering me as a record-buyer.

My mate Paul played the guitar; I wrote the lyrics. Between us, we moulded them into melodies which I sang; Paul provided the riffs. He and I shared a wavelength neither of us shared with anyone else; Paul was the first friend I'd had who looked like he could've been in the Stones rather than Curiosity Killed The Cat, and we sparred off one another in our attempts to resemble rock stars. He was as much of an outsider in his part of town as I was in mine, and we'd both experienced run-ins with 'the beer monsters'; city centre streets may have been low on knife crime and acid attacks in the 80s, but you still had to watch yourself. It was easier when there were two of you.

We'd spend virtually every weekday ensconced in Paul's bedroom at his mum's house, listening to a range of LPs from the extensive record collection he'd amassed during his brief stint in 9-to-5 Land. We studied and absorbed the masters; it was our university. Eventually, I'd produce my exercise book crammed with lyrics, he'd tune up his acoustic guitar, and we'd devote the next few hours to putting a song together; if it was any good, we'd record it on his ghetto blaster and improve it the following day before moving onto the next one. We were hungry to make our mark, and though we may have been dreaming the dreams many music-obsessed young men dream, we were prepared to put the work in.

After several months of assembling a songbook, we decided to locate other musicians, and there was no shortage of venues to visit where we could check them out. Unfortunately, it took time to find like-minds; commitment was hard to come across. Rehearsal space wasn't, but as Paul and me were both signing-on, it could be a stretch to pay for it. A room above a pub with an unsavoury reputation as the hostelry of choice for football hooligans was the one we eventually settled on because it was the one we could afford. By then, we'd acquired a bass-player and drummer, though it had taken well over a year of searching and numerous disappointments before we got there.

Our first gig was on the bill of an all-day event featuring dozens of local bands, staged in one of the many pubs that packed the punters in by hosting live music. In a dense fog of fags, and fuelled by booze that was probably less than a quid a glass, we took to the stage, collectively crapping ourselves. We had the usual repertoire of crowd-pleasing standards, such as 'Teenage Kicks', but primarily showcased our own material. We were rather under-rehearsed, but went on in the late afternoon, by which time the well-sozzled audience greeted every act with enthusiasm. I can't honestly remember how many numbers we played; I mainly remember wearing a second-hand psychedelic jacket, which a lady complimented me on – the first such compliment a lady had ever paid me. It wasn't a bad day.

We recorded a demo tape – tape being the operative word, as the songs went straight from reel-to-reel acetate to cassette; the recording studio cost what must have been a small fortune to us then, and we had to record and mix four songs with the clock rapidly ticking towards the end of the time we could pay for. We didn't sound bad, and it's undoubtedly invigorating when you hear yourself in top-notch quality sound for the first time. The end result received reviews in regional fanzines and was optimistically dispatched along the tried-and-tested route that led to John Peel and the music industry. We played a few more gigs: one as support to another local band in another pub, one on our own (in another pub), and one on the bill of another all-day event – this time in a pub car-park. That gig turned out to be our last.

We had the impossible task of following a folk duo singing a song called 'F**k Off, Yuppie Scum' to the tune of 'Knees-Up, Mother Brown'; but we were such a shambles on the final performance that I actually apologised to the audience who were too pissed in the summer sun to even notice. We hadn't rehearsed in weeks. The drummer was still at school and this was just a hobby to him; the bass-player enjoyed jamming but had no real interest in being a professional; and Paul was smoking a lot of dope, perhaps to cope with the fact we were going nowhere after all the work he and I had put into it. Our friendship survived, but our musical partnership didn't. We never shared the same vision thereafter; I got into the nascent Dance scene, whereas he preferred chilling out to 'Astral Weeks'. We'd had high hopes, but we'd crashed and we'd burned.

Paul and I had probably squandered twelve months searching for other musicians because we were so determined to do it the traditional way we revered. Today, we wouldn't need them; we'd have the technology to create a 'virtual' band and we could record on bedroom PCs without having to bankrupt ourselves for studio time, uploading our endeavours online to a worldwide audience. We wouldn't have to bombard record companies or the music press because neither exists anymore; but we'd struggle to play live because the gig circuit has gone along with the pubs that were vital to it. We also wouldn't have the dole to subsidise our musical education and we wouldn't have the money to invest in instruments.

They weren't great days. They were frustrating and disappointing. We gave our all to something that eluded us, and whilst it genuinely doesn't bother me now that we didn't make it, it always seems a shame that all the dynamic verve and energy we exuded was drained from us in such in a depressingly crushing manner - though we weren't the first and we weren't the last either. Les McQueen from 'The League of Gentlemen' (guitarist with Crème Brulée, a 70s band that never made it) would look back by saying 'It's a shit business; I'm glad I'm out of it'; but I don't regret doing it. Everyone should give it a go and then gracefully exit the stage when it all goes tits up. It's an experience that prepares you for the rest of your life.

THE LOST WORLD
10 November 2017

I was talking to a friend the other night about my brief stint as a Big Gig-goer in the late 80s. I saw Bowie twice, as well as Dylan, the Stones and Prince once each within a three-year period and I did it all whilst signing-on, suggesting the ticket prices (not to mention the obligatory coach travel costs) weren't that extortionate. The stubs from said gigs are probably gathering dust in my mum's loft, so I'm unable to announce here and now how much I was charged for the privilege of being squeezed into Roker Park, Maine Road, Wembley Arena and the NEC; but a cursory glance at vintage ticket stubs from the same era on eBay suggests that even when the change in the cost of living is taken into account, the gap between wages (or dole) and ticket prices wasn't that great a gulf.

It goes without saying that those were the days when touring was a handy sideline rather than the prime source of earning for musicians; like being able to turn up at your local football club on match-day without having to take out a loan beforehand, it was possible to see your musical heroes in the flesh for an affordable amount. The simple reason was that record sales financed their tax-exiles back then; even though there wasn't much difference between the price of seeing them live and the price of their new album, the album would sell to more people than could attend a tour, thus negating the need to hike up ticket prices to a point where they'd be beyond the reach of fans short on ready cash. Not so now, in this post-Napster world.

Other the Ronnie Biggs model (which is itself redundant now the drugs market brings in a far higher income than an old-school blag), Rock 'n' Roll and football were *the* tried and tested working-class escape routes, as well as passionate pursuits for those who couldn't sing a tune or kick a ball. The audience projected its own aspirations onto the performer, who had come from the same place, and believed it was possible to do likewise. The view from the terraces on a Saturday afternoon was similarly imbued with possibilities, especially for those youngsters hemmed into 'the boy's pen'.

There was considerable media coverage when England's U17 team won their equivalent of the World Cup a couple of weeks back, though few members of that starting eleven will make it off the bench at Premier League clubs crammed with overseas signings. And unless a boy or girl from nowhere is prepared to suffer the indignity and humiliation of being a Cowell marionette, the only kids who can afford guitars, basses and drums today are the posh ones – which would explain why none of them have anything to say. Classic working-class pastimes have effectively priced out the working-class. But, hey, we've got Smartphones, X-Factor and microwave meals – what more do we need, eh?

Even the theatre was once an escape; some of our most iconic actors of the 60s and 70s came from humble backgrounds, but getting into drama school without the fear of being saddled with a lifelong debt and then honing their skills on the regional rep circuit is a lost world in 2017. The slashing of local council budgets that previously funded after-school drama classes and theatre workshops runs parallel with Government emphasis on the arts as a 'luxury' in state education (not much point reciting Shakespeare soliloquies when you're cold-calling, I suppose). By contrast, the arts remain a fixture on the public school syllabus, which would explain why the majority of today's under-40 household name thespians are Old Etonians. Their parents could afford to finance such 'luxury'.

Considering the last time the economic climate was probably this grim was in the recession-struck early 1980s, it's worth remembering what that period produced in terms of art reflecting life; and memorable music aside, it's been interesting to recently reunite with a one-off TV series of the era that has unexpectedly surfaced on DVD. And, no, it's not 'Boys from The Blackstuff'.

'Johnny Jarvis' aired just the once on BBC1 at the back-end of 1983, and at the time of its broadcast was a must-see at my high-school. Appearing at the tail-end of the gritty social realism characteristic of 'Play for Today', this six-parter accurately documented the scrap-heap we Easter Leavers were poised to be tossed onto. The title character was played by Mark Farmer – a familiar juvenile lead at the time via his stint on 'Grange Hill', and who sadly passed away last year. Jarvis is the focus of his best friend, the bookish outsider Alan Lipton; Jarvis is a borderline 'David Watts' character to Lipton, both envied and idolised. But whilst Jarvis is dutifully subservient to the system once he leaves school, his subservience amounts to nothing when the firm he's apprenticed to goes under before he fully qualifies as a skilled tradesman.

Lipton opts out and finds his voice with a guitar, starting a band he continues to write for after he forgoes the spotlight, leaving fame to his ex-bandmates whilst he settles for fortune. The steady progress of Lipton's musical endeavours as the series spans 1977-1983 is a vivid demonstration of how such a thing was then possible from the starting point of a council flat; Jarvis's struggles to make a living in the traditional heavy industries that were dying on their arses under Thatcherism are equally prescient for the era, and watching the programme after a 34-year gap really brought home to me how much has changed.

It not only reminded me of how those coming from nothing were able to articulate their experiences and could make themselves heard doing so. It also made me realise how those experiences wouldn't be dramatised by mainstream television today. There is no working-class representation now unless we're talking stereotypical chavvy thugs in gangs or victims of sexual abuse; and those playing such parts probably learnt their lines in end-of-term productions on the stages of Harrow or Roedean, anyway. Sixty years ago, Arthur Seaton said 'Don't let the bastards grind you down'; well, they *have* ground us down and they've got us where they want us – complicit in our own lethargy. Never mind the bollocks – here's the Bake Off.

WHAT BECAME OF THE PEOPLE WE USED TO BE?
22 November 2017

It's a weird sensation, but there's often no more sober a reminder of one's own mortality as when the death is announced of a famous face whose countenance is inexorably bound up with dim and distant formative years. Over the past 24 hours, two such deaths have been announced and both make me feel unaccountably sad. I never met either in person, but actor Rodney Bewes and pop star David Cassidy were in the room when I was opening my eyes. The former was one half of a sitcom duo, whereas the other was the luminous pin-up of the moment. Just turned five, 'Whatever Happened to the Likely Lads?' and 'The Partridge Family' were twin telly treats; one was rooted in a Northern English reality I recognised, whilst the other was a Californian fantasy that nevertheless sold an alluring illusion, one that said a bunch of kids could be in a successful band with their mother yet still lead ordinary suburban lives. Well, why not?

Both Rodney Bewes and his 'Likely Lads' co-star James Bolam had made their initial marks as big-screen sidekicks to one of the rising stars of early 60s 'Kitchen Sink' cinema, Tom Courtenay – Bewes in 'Billy Liar' and Bolam in 'The Loneliness of the Long Distance Runner'. In 1964, the pair came together in the first attempt to transplant the vogue for the North to the small screen for comic effect; the success of 'Steptoe and Son' had legitimised the sitcom as a vehicle for serious actors rather than music-hall comedians, and 'The Likely Lads', launched along with BBC2, was a refreshing break in the new channel's otherwise highbrow schedule. Penned by Dick Clement and Ian La Frenais, 'The Likely Lads' was the first outing for a writing partnership that went on to define comedic portrayals of male friendship, as demonstrated in later successes such as 'Porridge' and 'Auf Wiedersehen Pet'.

Sequels years after the event are usually cynical affairs manufactured to exploit sentimental longing for the past and are about as effective in recapturing lost magic as high-school reunions. However, 'Whatever Happened to the Likely Lads?', which first aired in 1973, actually surpasses the original series by carrying Bob and Terry into their uncertain (and far more interesting) thirties.

James Bolam's Terry returns home from an overseas sojourn in the Army with a fresh chip on his shoulder, having missed the Swinging end of the 60s and arriving back in Ted Heath's Three-Day Week Britain. He strolls bewildered through a landscape in which the close-knit back-to-back communities have been swept away by concrete tower-blocks. And with them have gone the characters constituting Terry's carefree youth, now subdued by marriages and mortgages. Even worse, Rodney Bewes' Bob has moved up the social scale, engaged to middle-class Thelma and living on a new housing estate, leaving his single life (and background) behind, much to Terry's chagrin.

'Whatever Happened to the Likely Lads?' is as potent a study of the crossroads between youth and middle-age as any TV drama has managed, let alone sitcom. The sacrifice of adolescent hopes and aspirations on the altar of a system that will dispense material rewards yet still dump those who submit to it in the cultural vacuum of the suburbs is handled with humour and humanity. Terry is an inverted snob, clinging to his beer and football whilst Bob tries to better himself with wine and badminton clubs, reflecting a now-lost world of social mobility and the belief that things can only get better. For Bob and Terry's generation, things *could* get better; but it depended how far one was prepared to compromise. I can imagine Bob ending up as a divorcee with an ulcer after putting the work in, whereas Terry seems the type to eventually win a fortune on the Lottery after bumming around for decades.

When Bob and Terry were engaged in their class war, a graduate of a US TV ensemble piece had already progressed to solo status in the singles charts. A product of an American acting dynasty, David Cassidy made his name towards the end of his teens playing the whiter-than-white Keith Partridge alongside his real-life stepmother Shirley Jones and the impossibly beautiful Susan Dey. 'The Partridge Family' capitalised on the earlier success of 'The Monkees' by blending sitcom and pop, the main difference being that Cassidy was the only member of Mrs Partridge's mixed brood with any musical ability. His was the sole Partridge voice on any of the Partridge Family hits, and his launch as a pop idol in his own right was inevitable.

At a time when home-grown pop stars were dabbling with a decadent dressing-up box, David Cassidy and his bedroom wall rival Donny Osmond appealed to the British pubescent female craving for the cute, the cuddly and the unthreatening. Both were more successful here than in the States, inspiring the kind of hysterical reaction unseen since Beatlemania; but whereas Donny Osmond was genuinely clean-cut, David Cassidy soon became irked by his image and attempted to trash it by appearing half-naked on the front cover of 'Rolling Stone' and ripping 'The Partridge Family' to pieces in the accompanying interview.

His US career stalled thereafter, so he concentrated his efforts on the far more receptive UK. However, his career here climaxed in tragic fashion when a 14-year-old fan was crushed to death during a concert at the old White City Stadium in 1974. Cassidy withdrew from the stage as a result and his recording career gradually declined as he returned to full-time acting.

What do you do when you've been David Cassidy, though? You can't just vanish back into the chorus-line. After a brief brush with the charts again in 1985, he spent the rest of his life appearing on the nostalgia circuit and struggling with his own demons; a long-running battle with alcohol and then the onset of dementia was followed by liver and kidney failure at the age of 67. Rodney Bewes was a decade older than Cassidy, but he too remained linked to his youthful self in the public eye. His falling-out with James Bolam not long after they ceased to be Likely Lads was never resolved, but even the knowledge of their sad spat doesn't sour the pleasure of watching the two of them together on DVD in a series that grows richer in its poignancy as the decades drift by. And there's a kind of immortality in that, at least.

2
The Wild West

Once upon a time in America

21st CENTURY BOY
9 March 2016

Remember that night back in November 2008, when the eight-year reign of George II came to an end? That itself would have been something to prompt half of the world's population into doing spontaneous cartwheels, but look what he was replaced by – a black man! In the White House! America was cool again! It had a dude for President! Civil Rights veterans from the 60s took to the streets, some with tears in their eyes, hardly believing they'd ever live to see the day. Considering the lengthy history of racial turmoil the US has experienced, it remains quite an achievement, even now. The colour of Barack Obama's skin almost felt like that was enough as a selling point. The Nobel Prize panel were swept up in the euphoria as well, awarding Obama the Peace gong when he'd barely switched on the central heating in the Oval Office.

Seems a long time ago, though, doesn't it – the momentary usurping of American political dynasties in order for a politician virtually unknown outside of Chicago a couple of years previously to go where no African-American had gone before. It seems especially distant now, when the USA is reverting to type by backing a right-wing lunatic to take over the Washington tenancy of the man who is counting down the days before moving out. And as Obama enters his final months in the top job, it's extremely hard not to think of his Presidency with a gnawing sense of frustration as something that should have been so much better than it has.

In the television age, American Presidents have often left their mark with a specific powerful image – Kennedy's brains being blown-out in the Dallas motorcade, Nixon announcing his resignation, Reagan's historic love-in with Gorbachev, even Bush's expression as events on 9/11 are whispered into his ear while he sits before a group of oblivious schoolchildren. With Obama, the images that are evoked as his tenure as leader of the free world draws to a close seem annoyingly trivial: his endless appearances on US chat shows; acting as a straight man to comedians in skits; dancing with Michelle; singing at showbizzy White House bashes; posing for a selfie alongside David Cameron and the Danish PM at Nelson Mandela's funeral – all very twenty-first century in their abundance of style and absence of substance. Is that really how Obama wants to be remembered? Wasn't he supposed to be a great intellectual – or did he merely appear to be on account of the man he succeeded?

Though America was clearly ready for him – he received the highest number of votes for a Presidential candidate in history – Obama certainly didn't come to power while the nation was enjoying a period of satisfied contentment, winning the Presidential Election just months after the worst global financial crash since 1929, and at a time when his country was still involved in not one, but two unpopular foreign wars. He regarded the economy as his first priority, but also stated his desire to end the detainment of terrorist suspects at Guantanamo Bay. Although he eventually presided over the withdrawal of US forces from Iraq and gave the go-ahead for the mission that resulted in the death of Osama bin Laden, the rise of ISIS has served to hamper Obama's hopes of ending military involvement in the Middle East, and his reckless reliance on drones to do the dirty work hasn't endeared him to the Muslim world. At least he could point to the resumption of diplomatic relations with Cuba as a foreign policy success, if not quite matching the international significance of Nixon's olive branch to China.

On the home front, an initial economic improvement stalled, while Obama's proposals for healthcare reforms were not helped by the capture of the House of Representatives by the Republicans in 2010 and the widespread publicity afforded the grass-roots Tea Party movement. Obama's attempts at arresting increasing racial violence and finally doing something about antiquated gun laws in the face of continuing massacres also appeared to achieve very little, with the latter stymied by the Republicans gaining control of the Senate in 2014. One cannot but feel Obama has reached for greatness, yet has always found it ultimately elusive. Whether that is a failing of the man or the American political system is open to debate.

With Barack Obama still resident in the White House, it's far too early to judge how his Presidency will rank alongside those that are still talked about with awe. It wouldn't be much of a substantial legacy if the only aspect of eight years in office that will mark him out in history forever simply centres on the unique factor that made him seem such a breath of fresh air in 2008 – the colour of his skin.

AN AMERICAN ALLERGY
13 September 2016

The health concerns surrounding Hillary Clinton now that she and Donald Trump are embarking upon the final phase of their run for the US Presidency – the coughing fits, the fainting at this weekend's 9/11 anniversary ceremony, and the eventual diagnosis of pneumonia – are a reminder of the stamina required to hold the highest office in the land; and she hasn't even made it to the White House yet. Ronald Reagan was 69 when elected in 1980, and if Mrs Clinton is elected in November she will have reached the same age - an age at which the majority would be enjoying retirement rather than beginning one of the most demanding jobs on the planet. She has so far brushed off any rumours of serious illness, though if the race itself proves to be a strain, how would she cope once behind the desk of the Oval Office (as opposed being *under* it, which was the preferred position of her husband's female aides)? Aside from Kennedy, McKinley, Garfield and Lincoln – whose demises came as a consequence of assassin's bullets – four other US Presidents have died in office.

First up was William Henry Harrison in 1841. An American Whig and ex-Major General, Harrison holds several notable records: He was the last US President born a British subject (1773), the first serving President to have his photograph taken, the oldest man elected to the job until Reagan (aged 68), and the first to die in office; his tenure at the White House also remains the shortest on record, just 30 days, 12 hours and 30 minutes; he died from pneumonia after catching a cold three weeks on from his inauguration. Less than a decade later, President Zachary Taylor died of suspected cholera, believed to have been infected by the open sewers of Washington; another Whig and former Major General, Taylor was just seventeen months into office when he passed away.

Warren G Harding had served barely two-and-a-half years as President when he died of either a heart attack or a stroke in 1923 (the cause remains debatable). Not only did none of these three men serve a full term of office; their deaths were all surrounded by speculation and rumour, proving that the JFK conspiracy industry had precedents. Zachary Taylor's remains were even exhumed in 1991 to finally resolve the mystery of his death.

Perhaps the most famous non-assassinated President to die in office was Franklin D Roosevelt, who passed away on the eve of the Second World War's ending in April 1945. Stricken by polio at a relatively late age (39), the then-practicing lawyer was paralysed by the disease from the waist down and could no longer walk or stand without assistance. Determined not to be broken by the paralysis, Roosevelt worked hard at walking again, supported by a cane and wearing iron braces on his legs; he was frequently wheelchair-bound behind closed doors, though he was careful never to be seen so physically incapacitated in public. Roosevelt tried various alternative therapies to mask the extremities of his disability and found the warm springs in Georgia conducive to improving his condition.

Roosevelt already had a career in public office before his debilitating illness in 1921 and he re-entered politics by successfully running for the Governorship of New York in 1928; his physical difficulties were no secret, though the extent of them was. Whilst sometimes supported by crutches or one of his aides when speaking in public, he could stand alone on a podium by gripping a strong lectern; the need to keep hold of it led to his trademark animated head gestures when making a speech. After being elected US President for the first of four record-breaking occasions in 1932, Roosevelt was careful to minimise the damage that his frailty could have on public opinion, avoiding the media when arriving at events in order that his difficulties in getting in and out of vehicles wouldn't be publicised. Any photographers that attempted to capture the President at his most vulnerable allegedly had their photos censured by the Secret Service.

The heavy strain of the War years took a further toll on FDR's health; running for his historic fourth term in 1944, it was evident to those around him that he was not a well man, though it's possible he may have wanted to see WWII through to its conclusion. He was eventually elected, but the three months he served before his death were characterised by the need to broker peace in anticipation of victory; he attended the famous Yalta Conference with Churchill and Stalin in

February 1945, returning home a month later. It was then that his increasing ill-health could be hidden no longer, especially when he was forced to address Congress sitting down. A few weeks later he was dead at the age of 63 - five years younger than Hillary Clinton is now.

That Roosevelt became the most dominant American politician of his generation and was the White House resident for twelve years is testament to his tremendous determination to overcome a crippling illness that would have broken many men. It also shows how badly some crave high office in the face of potentially impossible obstacles. The manner in which the media, both professional and social, has become so flustered over Hillary Clinton's health makes one wonder how far FDR would have been able to hide his considerably more serious ailments from the prying eyes permanently peering into the modern goldfish bowl. Even John F Kennedy managed to keep his own chronic back pain from all but his closest friends, family and advisers, the severity of it (and the amount of drugs required to numb it) not becoming public knowledge until years after his death.

The pressures public figures – particularly politicians – are placed under in the 24-hour 365-days-a-year spotlight when compared to their distant predecessors are undoubtedly something 'private' figures are relieved to be spared. However, entering public life is largely down to individual choice, unless circumstances push the anonymous onto the front pages; and today the general public as well as the politicians choose to do so, whether running for office and having the miniature of one's entire life forensically scrutinised or posting a gallery of selfies and being exposed to the wrath of trolls. And nobody yet knows if Hillary Clinton's decision to try to get her hands on the Presidency will ultimately do her more damage than it will her country.

FOUL AND FOULER
26 September 2016

The Luvvies are out in force again, though this time it's the Hollywood left, that pious, humourless and self-righteous branch of the acting profession who turned this year's Oscars ceremony into a sanctimonious PC rally that was straight out of 'Team America: World Police'. Interpreting their participation in blockbuster movies that make millions as indicative that the audience stuffing itself with popcorn as they fly around in tights will also sit and listen to them preach as well is a measure of their colossal egos and sense of self-importance. They never learn. Lecturing the American electorate and commanding them to choose Clinton over Trump will probably be as counterproductive for Hillary's campaign as their British equivalents promoting Remain were for that particular cause. Trump Republicans may be content to fill the multiplexes when actors are doing their day-job, but the minute thespians start preaching politics, the effect is to push a sizeable chunk of their audience into the arms of the enemy.

When Hillary Clinton referred to Trump supporters as 'deplorable', it was a rather sweeping statement that I have no doubt contained a grain of truth in the case of the narrow-minded bigoted redneck faction; the problem is that by tarring all Trump supporters with the same unsavoury brush, Clinton is delivering an almighty insult to those Americans whose fortunes have plummeted under the Washington regime of both blue and red persuasion over the last twenty years. Many Americans hold Hillary's husband, Hillary herself *and* Obama responsible for the state they're in; they may have previously voted Democrat and placed their faith in the man who said 'Yes we can', but the ultimate impotence of the office for resolving the problems of what Nixon referred to as the Silent

Majority has hit them hard. In their eyes, Clinton's statement seemed to represent both her contempt and cluelessness when it comes to vast swathes of a vast country's population.

Many of that population have flocked to Trump simply because he's telling them what they want to hear – not in an airbrushed and (for want of a better word) 'politically correct' way, but in the brusque, blunt and unvarnished manner of a barroom braggadocio; some of the things Trump has said in public are indeed deplorable, yet one could probably hear the very same things in any drinking den in any corner of the US; to hear them on the political podium is a novelty that makes some voters believe he speaks their language.

A showy, egomaniacal maverick multi-millionaire whose luxurious lifestyle was inherited from his father is hardly the kind of candidate one would imagine capable of captivating those struggling to make ends meet, let alone taking on and defeating the sophisticated Republican establishment; yet the elements of Trump's personality that alienate his detractors are the same ones that have attracted his supporters.

Both Clinton and Trump have the kind of income and fortune that only a small percentage of their respective supporters will ever enjoy, so for either to declare themselves to be at one with The People is laughable; but the uncouth bluster of Trump has a kind of Homer Simpson appeal to many Americans, whereas Clinton's public image is closer to that of Mr Burns. Trump has sold himself as the outsider, and pitching himself as an antidote to the formula so many blame for their ills is a pitch that has precedents.

The antipathy and envy Richard Nixon exhibited towards the Kennedys – seeing their movie-star glamour, wealthy privilege and aristocratic aura as everything he craved but knew he would never have – was to him the embodiment of East Coast elitism, a world that had been barred to him all his life, as it is to most; but the grudge he bore was one he used to his eventual advantage. Post-Watergate, it's easy to forget that Nixon won a huge landslide in 1972; despite his many enemies, he connected with the same kind of voter that Trump is connecting with today.

Ironically, Clinton herself shares much with Nixon. Tricky Dicky's political career had a vintage of over twenty years before he was finally elected President. He'd played a prominent part in HUAC activities in the late 40s/early 50s, spent eight years as Eisenhower's Vice President, famously ran for President in 1960, and had a taste of future questions over his trustworthiness as early as 1952, when he utilised the relatively untested power of television by defending accusations of financial impropriety in the so-called 'Checkers' speech. After several years in the wilderness following his 1960 defeat to JFK, his capture of the Presidency in 1968 was undoubtedly one of the great political comebacks of all time. Clinton's political career stretches back even further than Nixon's did in 1968, and eight years after her first attempt to become the Democratic candidate she has returned for one last battle.

Like Nixon, Clinton has had her fair share of scandals that her opponents have pointed to as proof she cannot be trusted. There was the Whitewater controversy, which emerged even before her husband had been elected for the first time; there was her alleged compliance in buying off the victims of Bill's extramarital philandering; there were a couple of 'gate' affairs – Travelgate and Filegate; there was the email controversy; there was her dubious recall of events when she landed in Bosnia in 1996; there have even been criticisms of her not being entirely truthful as to the state of her health during the current campaign – enough scandals, in fact, to fill a book, which Christopher Hitchens partially did in his merciless 1999 dissection of Bill, 'No One Left to Lie To'. If only Hitch was still with us. What a mouth-watering commentator on 2016's no-holds-barred battle he would have been.

This Presidential race is unlike any other in that both candidates are so intensely loathed by great sections of the American electorate. Hatred of Hillary goes back a long way, but Trump has done his best to catch up over the past twelve months. Perhaps it's inevitable that someone as ghastly as Trump is the type that emerges when the masses feel disenfranchised and dispossessed, because it is only the Donald Trump's of this world that can boast the requisite ego, fearlessness and unshakable self-confidence in their own magnificence, the only ones that have the gall and gumption to push themselves forward for the job and genuinely believe they can do it. His complete inexperience in public office next to someone with more experience than anyone else is, on paper, a non-starter, yet his supporters bizarrely regard that factor in his favour, as much as it fills his opponents with dread.

The vacuous slickness of Obama and eight years of achieving very little beyond being the first black President can be perceived as a lack of guts, balls and the stomach for a fight; by comparison, Trump has convinced his supporters the opposite approach will achieve everything they desire. If recent events are anything to go by, America is indeed broken; but is Donald Trump capable of fixing it? And what does that say about the American political system that a man such as Trump is even in with a shout of fixing it in the first place?

The first TV debate between the two most polarising Presidential candidates in US history will air in the wee small hours of tomorrow morning. It could well be worth staying up for, if only as a dispiriting and masochistic wallow in how low we've sunk.

THE GREAT AMERICAN OBITUARY
10 October 2016

Perhaps if Washington, Jefferson, Franklin, Adams and the rest could have glimpsed 240 years into the future on the day they were poised to sign the Declaration of Independence, they might have come to the conclusion that taxation without representation wasn't really that bad a deal after all. Would they have committed the Thirteen Colonies to breaking from the Mother Country had they been able to see what their great democratic experiment would descend to by 2016? Mind you, I suppose that bit about all men being created equal was somewhat contradicted by the fact that most of the Founding Fathers were slave-owners – an issue it would seem the nation that became the United States of America has yet to fully come to terms with.

The seven years of war that followed events on 4 July 1776 may have eventually established American independence from Britain, but it was a fragile independence that the huge land mass absorbed into the Union appeared to exacerbate. 78 years on from the Treaty of Paris, the new nation (now comprising 34 states) was at war with itself. The sheer size of the country – on a par with most continents – has always presented its President with problems, ones so persistent that it seems almost impossible for the US to really be regarded as One Nation. After the end of the Civil War in 1865, there was a slow, gradual forming of a new genuinely post-colonial identity that shaped the country we know today, yet it was still one that the old Confederate States continued to resist for another hundred years.

As post-Civil War America expanded, the speedy industrial overtaking of Europe that was to shape the forthcoming 'American Century' may have made it the richest nation on Earth, but jarring inequalities on a par with those of the Old World have never been far from the surface. The US now stands on the cusp of making a decision that seems poised to extend the various racial, regional and economic disparities beyond what they even have been since World War II, yet this is just the latest in a long line of challenges to the aims of the Founding Fathers; that it is undoubtedly the most ugly example in living memory doesn't necessarily mean it's the worst, but it sure as hell feels that way right now. A historical perspective is often the only reminder of how young a country the US still is, and the contemporary state of the nation suggests it remains in the throes of teething troubles – which brings us nicely to Hillary Clinton and Donald Trump, again.

The airing of an old recording in which Trump exhibited his gentlemanly charm when it comes to the fairer sex has been received as though his previous public image had been on a par with Cary Grant. Numerous Republican bigwigs have excommunicated Trump as a consequence; but wasn't the truth staring them in the face the minute the billionaire celebrity first announced his intentions to run? How could anyone not know what Trump was like from the off? After all, he's been a household name in the States for over twenty years, and he's never been a shrinking violet when the camera points in his direction. It's a measure of the dearth of talent the Republican Party can call upon that Trump even got this far, so they've only themselves to blame. For so many to now express shock and horror is a bit rich.

Anticipating the Clinton team to use such 'revelations' against him in the second TV debate, Trump ensured his apology would contain a dig at his opponent and her husband for equally reprehensible attitudes towards women in the past. Hillary would have to be very clever to successfully use the Trump archive as a stick with which to beat her nemesis when Bill's own closet is crammed with enough skeletons to fill the grounds of a small provincial cemetery. With one more distasteful warm-up missive shot, the unedifying scene was set for the next head-to-head in the most vile and vulgar car-crash in American political history; and episode two made it to TV screens in the wee small hours of this morning UK time.

First time round, Trump's shaky opening reminded me a little of Jemini's memorably off-key live vocal at the 2003 Eurovision, though as soon as he was on the attack his bullish confidence surfaced and he was reborn as Dana International. This time, he didn't hang around, with his response to a question about 'that' old recording the cue to revive some of Bill's past misdemeanours whilst the ex-President sat just a few feet away. No knives were on hand to cut the atmosphere, but it was gruesomely electric. The nature of this debate was different to the first; there was a 'Question Time' vibe to proceedings, with selected members of the audience dictating the discussion. Both participants had stools to occupy when the other had the microphone, though as the programme progressed Trump prowled around the set when Hillary spoke, carrying the menacing air of a caged lion eyeing up the zookeeper when feeding time had been delayed.

During Trump's most personal assaults, Hillary's lengthy experience in public life was evident by the way in which she kept her cool and took the blows. Exhibiting the characteristics that have won him appeal amongst a sizeable chunk of the American electorate, Trump was more emotional; whenever he overran or wanted to respond to something Hillary had said about him, he questioned the fair share of time both had to make their respective points. He also sniffed a lot again, which will no doubt form part of his post-match criticism of how he was treated by the presenters. Hillary slickly skirted around some of the more probing questions of her own conduct, especially the 'email' issue, though whether her skilful avoidance of that perennial topic showed her expertise under pressure or preserved the popular image of her as a liar without compare remains to be seen.

What impact the second debate will have on the eventual result is too early to predict. Both contenders essentially lived up to preconceptions and nothing new was really learned about either of them. Its main purpose was as entertainment, a gladiatorial horror show that said more about the irresistible urge to watch two unpleasant individuals slugging it out to the death than it did about the optimistic ideals of the eighteenth century Enlightenment as a viable political blueprint that retains its relevance 240 years later. But who really expected it to?

THE LAST LAP
31 October 2016

Timing is everything in a race. The old cliché (usually applied to the football season) that it's a marathon rather than a sprint, has certainly been proved true on endless occasions, not only when it comes to the national sport, but also when it comes to politics. The 1970 General Election, in which serving PM Harold Wilson was expected to extend his Labour premiership to a full decade, was derailed by adverse balance of payments figures published during election week, though many believe world champions England losing to West Germany in the quarter finals of the World Cup just days before polls opened also played its part in the electorate delivering Wilson a bloody nose. It served as a warning to all hares speeding ahead of competing tortoises that the winners are declared as such only on the final day of the contest.

The timing of the FBI's decision to reopen the investigation into Hillary Clinton's 'email affair' less than a fortnight before election day in the USA has been downplayed as a political ploy, though the FBI certainly has history; under its first director J Edgar Hoover, the Federal Bureau of Investigation was far from impartial. Democrat President Truman had observed Hoover's stewardship of the FBI as the emergence of a private police force separate from presidential control. 'We want no Gestapo or secret police,' said Truman in the early 50s. 'The FBI is tending in that direction. They are dabbling in sex-life scandals and plain blackmail. J Edgar Hoover would give his right eye to take over, and all congressman and senators are afraid of him.'

Instigator of the 'dirty tricks' wing of the organisation, which became known as COINTELPRO, Hoover was in charge of the FBI from its 1935 inception until his death in 1972, and it is generally accepted that President Nixon refrained from removing Hoover from office over fears that Hoover would release the hounds; bearing in mind the skeletons that Nixon had nestling in his closet it was probably one of Tricky Dicky's most astute decisions. Since Hoover's death, the head of the FBI has been restricted to a 10-year tenure in order to avoid the perceived abuses of power Hoover oversaw; yet one cannot but feel the announcement to renew the entire Clinton email saga so close to polling day has been a concerted attempt to kindle fresh doubts in the minds of floating voters regarding Hillary's suitability as President.

Prior to the weekend's announcement by the FBI, Clinton had established a comfortable (albeit not exactly commanding) lead over Trump in the polls, though this has been slightly destabilised since. It goes without saying that Trump has revelled in the reopening of the investigation, claiming with customary melodrama that 'this is bigger than Watergate'. However, as much as it appears to be appeasing the Republican candidate's constant demands that Hillary be exposed as a crook, the FBI's decision to once again stir up a controversy that has already been dealt with and dismissed presents us with yet another unedifying chapter in a gory story that has dominated world headlines for the past few months.

Donald Trump's failure to present himself to the American public as something other than an egomaniacal sociopath telling the disgruntled and dispossessed what they want to hear (without any discernible solutions to the nation's problems) has sorely required ammunition to aim at his opponent; and the former First Lady has gifted him with a succession of dodgy rumours that has turned their TV debates into a theatrical equivalent of constantly arguing parents.

As to what impact the FBI's announcement will have on the outcome of the Presidential race, it's too early to say. Trump has uttered enough contentious statements during the campaign to have fatally damaged most candidates, though his blunt speaking candour has appealed to a sizeable majority of the American public that is thoroughly sick of Washington spin. Whether the official stamp of approval on his opinion of his opponent will affect the outcome of the election depends upon the don't knows out there who have yet to decide between the most experienced (albeit allegedly corrupt) practitioner of the Washington Dark Arts or a billionaire TV celebrity selling himself as an outsider in synch with public disillusionment over the way things have been run in the

American capital in the post-war era. And Jennifer Lopez flashing her gargantuan arse at a Clinton rally probably won't make much difference either way.

There's no doubt that Trump moving into the White House would utterly obliterate the vice-like grip the professional politicians running both Democrat and Republican parties have on American governance, belonging as he does to no real traditions of either party and being in possession of an ego determined to dismantle an ancient network of cronyism that has done few favours to anyone residing beyond the borders of the District of Columbia; and I suspect many mischievous critics of the system would welcome his tearing down of the status quo. But the stark choice the American electorate faces is that of the known knowns or the unknown knowns (as another Donald once said), and whether or not they are prepared to gamble the future of the western world on the outcome probably has little to do with anything the FBI has to say. Our life is in their hands; and if that doesn't fill you with dread, I don't know what will.

THE NIGHT BEFORE
8 November 2016

We think we've got it bad over here. I've got friends in Canada – can you imagine what it must be like for them? They're the next-door neighbours of the country upon which the world's attention is focused today, yet they've no more ability to participate and affect change than we have. It's akin to the Scots voting in an independence referendum in which the rest of the UK has no say and...oh, sorry, I forgot; we've already been there. Anyway, the disqualification of one half of North America in deciding the fate of the western world aside, the fact that the USA has to choose between a devious upholder of Washington's status quo and a misogynistic billionaire narcissist is surely something nobody would envy. Suddenly, having to weigh-up the respective merits of David Cameron and Ed Miliband just last year doesn't seem like such a terrible dilemma after all. The fact that both are now parliamentary toast shows how far we've travelled since the spring of 2015, whereas the US is now confronted with a similar scenario, albeit on a Hollywood blockbuster scale.

The first Presidential Election I was aware of took place forty years ago, when the incumbent occupier of the White House, Gerald Ford, took on the virtually unknown Georgian peanut-farmer Jimmy Carter. The former probably stands as the luckiest man in American history, becoming Vice President due to the resignation of Spiro Agnew in 1973 and becoming President due to the resignation of Richard Nixon the year after. I remember the Ford family being photographed during a visit to Disneyland in 1976, an image reproduced in the weekly I was subscribing to at the time, 'Mickey Mouse'; but Ford's luck ran out not long thereafter. He was defeated in November by Carter. Since Jimmy Carter ingratiated himself in the collective memory of my generation via his visit to the UK the year he was inaugurated, I have been a long-distance witness to nine further Presidential Elections, and this is the tenth. I can't remember another like this one, though.

We've become accustomed to our own excessive political circuses in the age of 24-hour news media – two General Elections and two Referendums in the last six years – but being bombarded by Trump and Clinton these past few months has been especially frustrating in that we can look but not touch. Many comparisons have been made between the northern industrial wastelands that voted Brexit here and those poised to vote Trump there, and it's hard to avoid such comparisons when the impact of globalisation has hit traditional providers of British and American economic prosperity with such devastating ruthlessness. Figures were bound to emerge to speak on behalf of those deprived of a voice, though it's a shame they had to be figures like Nigel Farage or Donald Trump.

Donald Trump I find fascinating, if only as a classic American sitcom character ala Archie Bunker or Homer Simpson; that he's actually on the cusp of being elected leader of the free world places this fascination in a state of disbelief. This can't be for real, can it? So it would seem. History has taught us that a vacuum can be exploited by any opportunist, and if that opportunist be a reality TV star, that seems perfectly in tune with twenty-first century sentiments. In many respects, it's a miracle Trump didn't select Kim Kardashian as his running mate.

Trump may have attached himself to the Republican Party, but he has no real affiliation with the issues that have dominated Republican politics over the last decade or so; he certainly hasn't played the God card, which has been the default position of every Republican candidate since Reagan, and one wonders if he's hitched a ride on the Republican express simply because starting his own party would have rendered him a minority independent with no chance of gaining the keys to the White House. That he managed to blow the true Republicans (and their fanatical obsession with what their fellow Americans do below the waist) out of the water says all you need to know about that party.

Yes, he has galvanised the majority of fervent blue-collar Republicans who couldn't get excited over John McCain or Mitt Romney, but he has also caught the attention of non-partisan voters in desperate search of someone to offer an alternative to the production-line politicians Washington produces with the same slick ease as Westminster.

Hillary Clinton's FBI reprieve last weekend places the decision of the organisation that named and shamed her the week before in a curious situation; did the FBI announce the reopening of the email investigation to simply cover their backs on the off-chance that, should Trump become President, they could point to that announcement as evidence they were prepared to pursue it and therefore weren't politically biased? The haste with which they subsequently declared there was no foul play on Clinton's part makes their initial announcement appear even stranger. Why bother intervening in the campaign if there was nothing to report anyway? If that was the FBI's strategy, it has ultimately backfired, as changing their minds just a couple of days before polling merely gives fresh ammunition to Trump's avowed belief that 'the establishment' is against him.

Oh, well. Time's up for speculation now. Come this time tomorrow, we'll know where we stand – more of the same or a leap into the unknown. And no one here will have any say either way.

THE MORNING AFTER
9 November 2016

Confronted by the sight of the decaying Statue of Liberty rotting away on a beach, Charlton Heston's astronaut character at the classic climax of the original 'Planet of the Apes' movie realises he hasn't landed on some alien planet where man's evolution occurred in reverse, but has been flung into the far future and is home – albeit a post-nuclear apocalypse home. Falling to his knees, he pounds away at the sand in despairing rage. 'You finally really did it!' he cries; 'You maniacs! God damn you all to Hell!' He didn't add 'You put Donald Trump in the White House!' Who would?

Who can even really believe this has happened? *Donald Trump? Donald f***ing Trump?* Yup.

Let me make it clear that I didn't think Hillary Clinton was perfect by any stretch of the imagination. If anything, her absence of perfection on so many levels enabled Donald Trump to inflict a humiliating defeat upon the most qualified candidate for the Presidency America has probably ever seen. Had she won, however, it would have been an achievement solely based on her gender. History would have been made, though we shouldn't forget that history was also made in 2008. Being America's first female President would have been a big deal, as being America's first black President was eight years ago. But had Hillary Clinton cruised along on that achievement alone – as Obama has often seemed to cruise along on his – the achievement would have paled very quickly.

When Obama came to office, the western world had just experienced its most severe economic collapse since 1929; though the climate has improved slightly since then, there remain vast areas of America that have yet to receive any signs of an upturn in their fortunes, and this was the climate prime for exploitation by Trump. Frustration with this state of affairs has manifested itself in many ugly ways in the US over the last twelve months, and having a black man in the White House doesn't appear to have made a bit of difference to racial tensions whatsoever; if anything, they're worse now than at any time since the Civil Rights movement half-a-century ago.

Barack Obama was swept into power on a tide of unrealisable optimism; hopes rested heavily on his shoulders after eight years of George II and the two unpopular wars he dragged the nation into, and Obama's colour – coming from a country with such troubled history in that department – was an undoubted selling point that suggested America could finally shake off the toxic legacy of slavery and segregation. There was faith in the future again. When Americans got there, however, the limited extent of the President's ability to enact the changes he and the country desired when confronted by a Republican-dominated Congress determined to thwart him at every opportunity seemed to highlight the impotence of the American political system. And that should serve as a timely warning to his successor and his myriad mad ideas. The Republicans may have retained control of Congress, but most of them don't even regard Trump as a genuine Republican; one could argue that has been his ace.

Bernie Sanders was the anti-Trump candidate far more than Hillary Clinton was; the bullish billionaire tapped into the same blue-collar discontent Sanders could have appealed to. Two outsiders versus each other instead of one outsider versus the advocate of the system so detested by great swathes of the electorate would have been a far superior contest, and one I have a feeling Sanders could have won. A proud socialist against a shameless capitalist, both latecomers to the parties they represented – that would have dealt a fatal blow to the professional party machine more than a thousand Brexit's.

Instead, we now have a President loathed by all but his fanatical supporters, a man whose very presence in the White House is the most telling example of an American political system that can be bought if you have enough bucks in the bank. The old cliché that every American child can grow up to be President in a way that every child can't grow up to be a king has belatedly been exposed as the myth it always was. If your father is an extremely wealthy man, you're certainly in with a shout. And JFK would have concurred with that truism.

Kennedy represented more than he ever delivered, and that probably would have been the case even if he had never travelled to Dallas in November 1963; he represented something so positive in the collective imagination, something youthful, regenerative, glamorous, new – a break with the grey old men who governed the nations of the western world, a man who appeared to be in tune with the spirit of the fresh decade he came to power in; and despite the unsavoury stories that have emerged in the fifty-plus years since his murder, that image continues to possess an irresistible allure. By contrast, it's hard to think of any President in US political history – and I include Nixon and Dubya – who radiates so much negativity as Donald Trump. And yet, conversely, he represents a similarly radical break. This is a rejection of the American party system as well as the final rejection of the Obama era. Yet for all the expected talk of 'uniting America', it's hard to see how somebody so divisive can unite after having alienated so many members of the electorate before even being declared the winner.

Trump's combative personality and arrogant, unapologetic coarseness is seen by many Americans as a sign of his unvarnished honesty; what you see is what you get. He's viewed as 'one of the guys', somebody you could share a few cans with as you watch the ball-game. He'd be the kind of guy you could go hunting with. Alien as that may seem to European sensibilities, in America it counts for a lot. But Trump's tasteless braggadocio could be regarded as the same spiel a prize-fighter spews forth during the weigh-in alongside his opponent; having won the fight, his acceptance speech after Clinton conceded was remarkably subdued.

If the election of Donald Trump is the end of the world as we know it, I doubt many would dispute the world as we know it is a pretty bloody awful place, anyway. But it's the world as we *don't* know it that we now face; and God only knows what that's going to be like.

ENTERTAINMENT USA
11 January 2017

Ever since Gettysburg, the Great American Speech has not only been the aim of every US politician seeking to define their time and enshrine their place in it; the moment talking pictures appeared, the movie industry realised few tactics served better as the denouement of a drama than the lead character pausing to passionately speak his mind to an assembled group of characters (and the audience) in a highly theatrical manner, as though he too was on a podium addressing the nation. This week has seen two examples of this enduring gesture – one coming from an outgoing President and the other coming from an ageing actress.

Like Barack Obama and his predecessors, Meryl Streep's field of expertise is speaking lines written for her by somebody else. Frank Sinatra and Elvis Presley *sang* lines written for them by somebody else; they were aware they didn't possess the talent to write their own, so they focused on what they did best and didn't lose any sleep over it. But professional actors are a different breed of entertainer and they often make the mistake of believing the adulation and awards that shower down on them for doing their job is somehow a reflection of them as individuals rather than the characters they've portrayed. When they sever the strings of the scriptwriter and, like Pinocchio, imagine they're flesh-and-blood instead of wood, the illusion is shattered and the audience winces.

It doesn't matter if it's Charlton Heston cheerleading for the NRA, Clint Eastwood interviewing an invisible Obama,

Michael Caine endorsing Cameron, Sean Penn intervening in the Falklands or the conveniently-distanced George Clooney lecturing Europe on its refugee crisis, the impact is the same. We belatedly (not to say disappointingly) realise they're not who we thought they were when we watched them on the big screen. Tell an actor he's wonderful and he'll do anything for you – something those who benefit from a celebrity endorsement know all too well.

With last year's PC Nuremberg Rally masquerading as the Oscars ceremony still sending a lingering shudder down the spine, 2017 hasn't even got as far as the Academy Awards before the same narcissistic urges have claimed centre-stage again. The Golden Globes is the Song for Europe to the Oscars' Eurovision, but the woman one US critic referred to as 'America's Judi Dench' decided to pre-empt the biggest bash in cinema's calendar by using the Golden Globes as her own personal platform, knowing full well she was playing to the adoring converted.

Actors will become increasingly dispensable in the next few years; the CGI 'reanimations' of Peter Cushing and Carrie Fisher in the latest 'Star Wars' movie are probably the shape of things to come, and as the technology advances more and more thespians will have to specify beforehand whether or not they consent to their image being resurrected in the event of their death. Therefore, Streep, as the reigning *grande dame* of Hollywood, grabbed the headlines with her own words in a way a CGI version of herself from twenty years hence would be incapable of; she never said the words 'President-Elect' or 'Donald Trump', but her target was implicit in the speech. She delivered it with the kind of faux-earnestness she's called upon in a hundred movies – the final scene in which a solitary piano accompaniment gradually builds up into a rousing, swooping crescendo of soupy strings cynically engineered to provoke tears and applause. She may have had a salient point hidden behind the hammy window-dressing, but it was buried beneath a landslide of emotional apple pie.

As a man who has yet to come to terms with at least the pretence of dignity that is supposed to compliment his office, Donald Trump responded to Streep's speech in the style of a petulant Twitter troll, oblivious to the fact he should be above all that by now. He's no longer merely a reality TV star anymore, lest we forget. But Trump is at war with anyone who mocks or criticises him; he's Richard Nixon taken to an online level, not simply dismissing his knockers with foul-mouthed vitriol behind closed doors, but engaging with them in unedifying internet fisticuffs in full view of the world.

He could have made Meryl Streep look even more foolishly self-indulgent had he just ignored her; but what he shares with Hollywood royalty is his inability to relent from imposing his opinions upon a populace he genuinely believes is enamoured with everything he says or does. In this respect, Trump and the red carpet A-listers should be natural allies, for their conceit and vanity is their dominant mutual personality trait.

As with the pyjama-clad slovenly shoppers captured on camera last weekend, who responded to being rightly shamed by crying racism, the majority of Trump's most vociferous critics fall back on wearisome buzzwords that ironically mirror the similarly simplistic and crude playground taunts of the man himself. By contrast, Hollywood's pampered starlets, labouring under the misapprehension that their public edicts carry the kind of weight ordinary Americans lack the intellectual capacity to articulate, clearly imagine that the audiences who pay good money to watch their overhyped brain-dead blockbusters will instinctively agree with their anti-Trump rhetoric just because they have achieved the wealth and privilege every US citizen is duped into believing they too can attain.

But perhaps there is one saving grace to emerge from this sad little war of words between America's ultimate showbiz elite and a President-Elect who himself is more showbiz than political: George Clooney has hinted Hollywood will go 'on strike' until the President-Elect is booted out of office. Just think about it – no mainstream Tinsel Town popcorn slopping around the multiplex aircraft hangers like a celluloid slick for four years! Go for it, George!

Everyone is acting out their preordained parts because none of the participants are smart or shrewd enough to see that they're doing so; their egos are too immense to discern anything beyond the shadows they cast to recognise the clichés. Like two competing B-movies at the local fleapit, the right-on left and the rabid right are back where they belong, engaged in a tired battle neither will concede and neither will win. They both deserve to drown in a perpetual golden shower.

TRUMPETTY-TRUMP
20 January 2017

Well, what can I say? Donald Trump is now officially President Trump; no great surprise, as his inauguration *was* advertised well in advance of the event. The talking point in the week leading up to it was the paucity of performers willing to participate, though I was relieved to be spared all that as a viewer. A Presidential inauguration ceremony isn't half-time at the Superbowl, and I don't recall entertainers being an intrinsic element of the ritual on the steps of the Capitol Building before the 'Rumours' Fleetwood Mac line-up reunited for Bill Clinton's first bash in 1993 – or perhaps the Glenn Miller Band played at one of FDR's numerous inaugurations and I was unaware of it.

The anticipated protests took place on the streets of Washington, but didn't get anywhere near the parade route; as far as I can tell, the activities of the masked men were limited to smashing a few windows and – Shock! Horror! – pushing a few bins over. That should send out one hell of a message to the Donald that he's up against a formidable enemy; ditto that chinless cinematic faux-anarchist Michael Moore, a man who pleaded on camera for Hillary Clinton not to become the Democratic nominee as he listed her failings and then pleaded on camera for the American electorate to vote for her when she *did* become the Democratic nominee, failings still intact.

The initial entertainment factor at Trump's inauguration, rather than coming from pop stars, largely emanated from spotting ancient ex-Presidents arriving, none more so than Jimmy Carter, 92 years young; the only living post-Carter President absent was George Bush Senior, currently in hospital. Seeing Clinton, Bush Jr and Obama sharing the same podium did have the look of a 'Doctor Who' story when the Timelord's previous incarnations get together; but it is strange when one considers Trump was sworn-in for the first time when he's already the same age as his distant predecessors Bush Jr and Clinton are today. After eight years of a President born during JFK's era, we're back to the Truman generation.

Watching Trump hold up his little hand and repeat those famous lines certainly had more than a touch of parallel universe unreality about it; everyone knew it was coming, but it needed to be seen to be believed, to finally confirm it had really happened. When rain began to fall as soon as Trump had taken the oath of office and prepared to make his speech, no doubt some would melodramatically claim the Washington skies were symbolically weeping, though watching on TV, all I could think of was wondering what shape his hair might take when exposed to the elements.

Trump's speech stuck to the core rhetoric at the heart of his campaign when going head-to-head with Hillary – the promise to revitalise the dead industries of America's rustbelt, to end inner-city gang warfare and to give the country back to the people; what Obama must have thought when the inaugural address of his successor implied his Presidency had achieved very little on the home front probably won't be known till the 44th President gets round to writing his memoirs; but I doubt Obama was reflecting on all the innocent lives his drones had extinguished during his two terms.

The headline-grabbing statements and choreographed controversies Trump specialised in during both his run for the Republican nomination and his clash with Hillary was akin to the chest-beating bravado that boxers exhibit at the weigh-in before their bout; come the moment he finally achieved the impossible by ascending to the White House, it was expected he no longer had any need to employ such contentious and divisive tactics, something that his unexpected conciliatory attitude towards his opponent re the fate he threatened her with during the Presidential Election seemed to point towards once he won the Presidency. However, Trump's ongoing Twitter spats suggest it's simply not in him to tone down his naturally combative nature, even when installed in the Oval Office.

How this nature will play out on the world stage, let alone domestic politics, remains to be seen; and I suppose it is the unpredictability of such an erratic character attaining the ultimate seat of power that is the main cause for concern when it comes to his detractors. At the same time, after years of persistent accusations that politicians are a bland breed straight off the android conveyor belt, having someone as the western world's unofficial leader who bucks that trend with such brash vulgarity is part of Trump's appeal, not dissimilar to the way in which many people find the eccentric persona Boris Johnson has cultivated a refreshing alternative to his fellow Parliamentarians.

The curious traditions of the US Presidency, whereby the new man at the top doesn't take charge till two months after winning the Election, present the incoming holder of the office with customary American theatrically on the day he can actually be addressed as Mr President. As someone who has become a household name as the star of a reality TV show, it seemed fitting for Donald Trump to begin his reign in such settings, though what comes next is something that even Trump has never experienced before – the genuine power to affect the lives of millions who've never even seen his crappy television programme. So, strap yourselves in; it's going to be a very interesting ride.

28 DAYS LATER
16 February 2017

On paper, it's already beginning to resemble a bizarre social experiment – replace the time-honoured tradition of a country being run by career politicians schooled in years of public office and hand over the reins of power to a man whose sole working experience has been within the field of big business and entertainment. Light the blue-touch paper, stand at a safe distance and watch the fireworks.

It won't be until next Monday that Donald Trump marks just one month as resident of the White House, yet so much has been crammed into the last four strange weeks that it feels much longer. Just this week has seen the first resignation from his administration – his National Security Adviser, Mike Flynn, over allegations of uncomfortably close associations with the Russian Ambassador to the US; the FBI are currently investigating Flynn and perceiving his relationship with Sergey Kislyak as part of the ongoing suspicions over the Kremlin's involvement in the Trump Presidency.

Trump has already set himself against the judiciary following the ramifications and legal challenges to his 90-day ban on visitors from seven selected Islamic countries, not to mention invoking the ire of those who were opposed to his Presidency from day one. Ordinarily, Americans will display inbred respect towards their President, whichever side of the political divide he stands on; all of this has been turned on its head by Trump; displaying that inbred respect in 2017 is the aberration, not the norm. Every policy so far announced has been a red rag to the liberal bull, yet every policy also appears to have reinforced the majority of his campaign promises – something most imagined would be quietly swept under the carpet once he took the oath of office. Even that bloody wall has been threatened. This isn't what usually happens when people are elected.

Then again, under normal circumstances, when people are elected they've usually become so skilled in the art of saying one thing when in opposition and then doing another when in government that the public are accustomed to being let down. Lest we forget, however, these are not normal circumstances. Donald Trump is not a normal politician. In fact, I'd question whether or not he'd even find that job description as applicable to him, despite the lofty position he now finds himself in.

Previously, outsider was a term political observers had used to describe the likes of Jimmy Carter or Margaret Thatcher. In the case of Carter, he was a State Governor barely known outside of that State, but a country decimated by the fallout of Watergate turned to him as a break with the established Washington elite that had let the nation down; in the case of Thatcher, she may have had prior government experience, but she too was seen as a break with the recent past of continuous industrial turmoil that had characterised the British 70s; and, of course, she was a woman. Both were outsiders, albeit outsiders on the inside. The same could be said of Barack Obama, who was at least a State Senator before running for President. Trump has never been on the inside and that was his genuine outsider's sales pitch; it worked.

Disillusionment with the old order has been gathering speed for the last decade, with the 2008 economic meltdown cited by many as the moment when the public realised things were not going to get better and the powers-that-be had no interest in making any country great again. The ground had been laid for a figure like Trump to come along a long time before he actually emerged as a candidate, yet a media machine in bed with those powers-that-be was not going to benefit from them being deposed; therefore, Trump's campaign was understandably mocked and ridiculed from day one – an eventuality he himself aided and abetted with his behaviour. Even some of us not belonging to that media machine couldn't really foresee Trump actually going all the way because it was such a dramatic severance of the world order as we had always known it that it seemed impossible to imagine that kind of surreal scenario. But it happened.

I often doubt the sanity of those who hanker after the highest office in the land, whether President or Prime Minister; we can all cite examples of past Presidents or PMs who were either chronically stupid or criminally devious – or both; the aphrodisiac of power has always eluded me, but there's no doubt it serves as an irresistible element for the men or women in public office who crave it like a drug. That in itself suggests to me symptoms of mental disorder and potential demagoguery, so amateur diagnoses of Trump's state of mind shouldn't be restricted to him alone; they should be applied across the board.

Former Labour Foreign Secretary and founding member of the SDP, Dr David Owen combined his medical knowledge with his political experience by covering the subject in a couple of books, 'The Hubris Syndrome: Bush, Blair and the Intoxication of Power' and 'In Sickness and In Power: Illness in Heads of Government during the last 100 Years'; and I reckon the connections are entirely relevant. You'd have to be mad to want to run a country, and I guess that's why so many world leaders are.

As for the Donald, what happens next is anyone's guess. 2020 seems a hell of a long way off at the moment and right now it's difficult to picture him reaching the end of four years, let alone contemplating a second term. But for all the wishful thinking by the left of impeachment, we shouldn't forget his Vice President Mike Pence. Trump may be an outsider, but he's chosen to surround himself with some Republican stalwarts whose narrow minds make Trump's stated vision of America seem radically liberal. Many may not be comfortable with the thought of Trump's finger hovering above the button, but the prospect of President Pence is considerably more concerning; Pence is an insider, the kind of establishment figure Trump was supposed to be a break with. So, be careful what you wish for, you Twitter Oswald's.

There was an abundance of memorable moments during the Watergate scandal, but none managed to condense as much drama into such a short space of time as the so-called 'Saturday Night Massacre', which occurred on October 20 1973. The reputation of Nixon's administration had suffered additional embarrassment ten days earlier with the resignation of Vice President Spiro Agnew whilst he faced charges of tax evasion unrelated to Watergate; but when the President ordered the Attorney General Eliot Richardson to fire Archibald Cox, the man Richardson had appointed as an independent special prosecutor to investigate the June 1972 break-in at the Democratic Party offices in Washington's Watergate building, the Attorney General refused to do so.

As part of his investigations, Cox had issued a subpoena to Nixon that ordered the surrender of taped conversations between the President and his aides recorded in the Oval Office; Nixon had refused in recognition of the threat Cox posed to his story of events. By ordering his Attorney General to dismiss Cox, the President assumed the problem would be solved; he hadn't anticipated Eliot Richardson would refuse the order and then resign in protest. Nixon's response was to demand Richardson's deputy William Ruckelshaus do the deed instead; Ruckelshaus also refused and resigned.

Desperate to save face, Nixon initially claimed Ruckelshaus had been sacked and turned to Solicitor General Robert Bork to fire Cox; Bork did so after being sworn-in as acting Attorney General, though the whole unedifying affair served to finally turn public opinion against Nixon. An NBC poll a week after the Saturday Night Massacre showed a plurality of Americans supported the impeachment of the President for the first time, even though it took another nine months before the House Judiciary Committee approved its first article of impeachment; and Nixon resigned before the process could even begin.

What an excitable US TV news presenter referred to as the biggest constitutional crisis in the history of the nation as the Saturday Night Massacre unfolded has had echoes in the past couple of eventful weeks in Washington. The main difference between 2017 and 1973 is that Nixon's credibility began to disintegrate when he had already served one full term in office and had retained power on the back of a landslide victory. As for the Donald, it's only four months since he took the oath of office for the first time and there seems to have been enough constitutional crises to make Richard Nixon's spell as President seem like an uneventful and rather dull period of American history.

The dismissal of FBI Director James Comey on May 9 certainly revived memories of the Saturday Night Massacre for those either old enough to remember it or those who have read about it since. Comey's termination came in the wake of the FBI investigation into the Hillary Clinton email affair as well as the organisation's conviction that Russia interfered in Trump's election campaign. Subsequent revelations that Trump had shared classified information with the Russian Ambassador and Russian Foreign Minister during a recent visit to the White House have done little to dispel the lingering belief of Russian involvement in the Donald's rise to power. Comey has claimed the President asked him to cease investigations into the short-lived National Security Adviser Michael T Flynn's Russian connections, something Trump has naturally refuted.

Lyndon Johnson's opinion of the FBI's fearsome first Director J Edgar Hoover, that it was 'better have him inside the tent pissing out than have him outside pissing in', suggests simply sacking James Comey might not be the end of the affair for Trump. Despite the President's intervention in Syria not exactly easing US relations with the Kremlin, the Russian issue won't go away. The appointment of a special counsel in the shape of former FBI Director Robert Mueller to continue the investigation hasn't necessarily met with Trump's approval, with the President referring to the ongoing efforts to establish a direct connection between him and Russia as a witch-hunt. Mind you, Trump's tiresome whinging about the media and how everyone is against him is only unprecedented on *his* side of the Atlantic; he's more than matched over here by the most frothing-at-the-mouth Corbynistas and their incurable persecution complex.

Trump has already taken his 'You're fired' catchphrase from 'The Apprentice' into his Presidency, sacking the likes of acting Attorney General Sally Yates for disputing his executive order to bar citizens of certain specified Muslim countries from entering the US; he also demoted and replaced acting Immigration and Customs Enforcement Director Daniel Ragsdale the same day he dismissed Yates. No explanation for this dismissal was given, though mere coincidence in what was labelled by some as the *'Monday* Night Massacre' seems unlikely. In this context, his firing of James Comey makes perfect sense. Trump still sees himself as the head of a company and everyone else as his employees. Anybody challenging his authority has to go.

Watergate was a slow burner of a scandal that unravelled at a sedate pace worthy of a weighty novel; it confirmed suspicions of Nixon that his most committed critics had harboured for a long time and cast a cynical shadow across

Washington that has never really gone away. What's happening now isn't quite the same. In contrast with Richard Nixon's unattainable ambition to be loved, Donald Trump couldn't care less; Nixon's downfall had all the elements of a Greek Tragedy, whereas Trump entered the political arena looking for a fight and now he's got one. As long as Russian rumours continue to circulate and talk of invoking the 25th Amendment if impeachment fails giving his opponents hope, the Donald's capacity to govern is entirely in his own hands. We shall see.

DIG FOR VICTORY
13 July 2017

Trump and Russia – it's the gift that keeps giving and one that continues to give hope to those who couldn't accept the Donald's victory last November. Fake news issues aside, the problem with the constant insinuations and rumours that have bedevilled the Trump presidency ever since before the inauguration is that they simply won't go away; even if there has yet to be any absolute and indisputable proof that Russia played its part in Trump's triumph, small scraps are being constantly thrown up as teasing trailers for the Big Reveal. How long do we have to wait for it, though? Shouldn't we have had it by now?

There are too many with a vested interest in Trump's removal from office to let the Russia connection slip off the radar, and their constant carping in media circles makes it hard to sometimes see the wood for the trees. How deep does Russian involvement in Trump's victory go, and was there any real involvement at all? Some of us just want the facts, but there are so many conflicting elements at the heart of this ongoing story that it's often difficult to decide what genuine crimes have been committed and what angles are being promoted merely to undermine the current administration at the White House.

President Trump's son Donald Jr meeting a Russian lawyer during the Presidential Election campaign and being promised 'dirt' on Hillary Clinton was something daddy's boy decided to confirm to the media this week as a pre-emptive strike against the New York Times. Even if Trump Jr claims the meeting was 'a wasted 20 minutes' and excavated no desired dirt, the release of emails confirming the heir to the Trump fortune did indeed meet with a certain Natalia Veselnitskaya during the campaign in the hope of gaining an advantage over his father's opponent can be viewed as further proof that the Kremlin had an influence on the outcome of the 2016 Presidential Election – or not. Ms Veselnitskaya apparently carries no weight whatsoever in Russian government circles.

Those of us who remember the 'hanging chads' debacle of 2000 will know by now that long-running sagas arising from contentious Presidential Elections are nothing new, and the allegations surrounding Russia and Trump are the latest in a series of awkward associations that perhaps stretch as far back as JFK's Mafia connections in 1960. Unless definite evidence emerges one way or the other, the rumours will linger as long as people are interested enough to pursue them, and Trump has so many enemies in America that the interests of those who are desperately seeking any advantage they can gain over the Donald will naturally receive excessive media coverage, whether rooted in genuine fact or not.

The President has unsurprisingly leapt to his son's defence this week via the medium that Trump Senior depends upon as a means of sidestepping what he perceives as a perennially hostile press – Twitter; he regards coverage of Trump Junior's confession as 'the great witch-hunt in political history'. At the same time, the Kremlin has denied the lawyer who had dealings with Trump's son had any damaging info on Clinton, while the lawyer herself also claims she wasn't in possession of the kind of goods that could have been useful to the Trump campaign, despite the fact that she met the President Elect's son at Trump Tower in June 2016.

It goes without saying that any kind of dirt on one's political opponent can be regarded as an advantage during a campaign, so if Trump's son thought he had the likelihood of receiving any last year he'd have been foolish to spurn the opportunity; but Hillary Clinton had such an impressive back catalogue of accessible dirt already available in the public arena that one cannot but wonder why Team Trump had to enter into any association with Russian representatives to add to that back catalogue. One can only assume naivety played its part, perhaps; after all, this was one of the most inexperienced teams in terms of public office ever to run for the White House. Then again, that's assuming there was any collusion between Trump and Russia in 2016, and the jury remains out on it.

2016's no-holds-barred campaign was characterised by dirt-digging; yes, dirt is an integral element of political campaigning, but both sides dug deeper for it in 2016 than had ever been seen before. The bizarre line-up of women pushed forward who claimed to have been sexually preyed upon by either Trump or *Mr* Clinton was just one ugly aspect of the campaign that marked it out as uniquely amoral. But a foreign government allegedly intervening in a US Presidential Election is a new development; lest we forget, it's a tactic usually reserved for the US itself, certainly where numerous South American countries have been concerned over the decades.

Trump claims he asked Putin if Russia had intervened when the pair met in person for the first time during last week's G20 summit; naturally, Vlad denied the allegations, and the President appears satisfied with that denial. He also claims he had no idea his son met the Russian lawyer until a few days ago, though added he wouldn't have objected had he known at the time. It must be endlessly frustrating for Trump's opponents that they just can't get hold of what they really want; maybe they never will because it simply isn't out there. But I've no doubt they'll keep digging.

BACK (STABBING) IN THE USA
28 July 2017

All too often, that celebrated US sitcom known as 'The Trump Presidency' hits heights worthy of a script penned by Larry David. With the disappointing departure of wacky White House Spokesman Sean Spicer, it seemed the loss of such a colourful cast-member risked the show never being the same again; lo and behold, however, the Donald hired his replacement on the same day, and Anthony Scaramucci has quickly settled into Spicer's shoes by proving to be instantly popular with viewers. Mr Scaramucci made an immediate impact in a classic episode that saw him interviewed by Emily Maitlis, and has also maintained the tradition of washing dirty linen in public by launching a personal attack on White House Chief of Staff Reince Priebus – with hilarious, as they say, consequences.

Beyond the fourth wall, the serious business of running the USA hasn't been quite so side-splitting. Over on Capitol Hill last night, it was drama rather than comedy that dominated proceedings as the Senate debated the President's repeal of 'Obamacare'. This was the third attempt to repeal the healthcare act of Trump's predecessor, and the third failure.

126

The bill became known as the 'Skinny' repeal, due to it being a scaled-down version of a total repeal that it was reckoned all Senate Republicans could agree to. Had the bill succeeded, it would still have left an estimated 16 million Americans losing their health insurance within a decade as well as a 20% increase in insurance premiums for those fortunate enough to keep it.

What made the defeat an especially bitter pill for the Trump administration to swallow is that three prominent Republican Senators – Susan Collins, Lisa Murkowski, and former Presidential candidate John McCain – voted against the bill and contributed significantly to its defeat in the process; the latter member of the trio was apparently badgered by Vice President Mike Pence for the best part of 20 minutes in a desperate attempt to get the veteran Republican to vote according to the President's wishes, before taking his place alongside a group of enthusiastic Democrats as the bill was voted down by the tantalisingly tight margin of 51 votes to 49. Trump's response was to claim all three Republican turncoats 'let America down'; but for McCain in particular it was an opportunity for revenge.

During his run for the Presidency in 2008, much was made of John McCain's Vietnam War record. After being shot down on a bombing raid over Hanoi in 1967, McCain was a Prisoner of War for six years and suffered appalling torture at the hands of his captors that has left him with lifelong physical disabilities, most famously the fact he cannot raise his hands fully above his head. McCain entered politics a decade after his return from Vietnam, but has long had something of a reputation as a 'maverick', not always prone to toeing the party line. His run for the Presidency in 2008 saw him lose to Barack Obama, though his cause probably wasn't helped by the selection of the execrable Sarah Palin as his running-mate. Nevertheless, he has remained one of the most recognisable and respected Washington veterans – not that this counted for much where Donald Trump was concerned.

During the embryonic stages of his efforts to gain the Republican nomination for 2016, Trump mocked McCain's record in Vietnam by saying he preferred 'heroes who weren't captured'. It should be noted that, though of an eligible age, Trump himself conveniently avoided the Vietnam draft like one of his White House predecessors, Dubya; he also didn't enlist as a volunteer or consider joining the Reserve Officer Training Corps; as a student, he obtained four deferments and was given a further medical deferment when threatened with the draft in 1968 on the grounds of 'heel spurs', which was nice.

A man such as McCain, with over thirty years in politics, will have developed an extremely thick skin by now, but a crass comment along the lines of the one Trump made was bound to rankle; last night, he had the chance to give the President the finger and he took it. Trump's avowed intention to get rid of Obamacare now seemingly stands in tatters, largely thanks to a man whose recent diagnosis with a serious brain tumour means he really doesn't have anything to lose. That he returned to active politics just a couple of weeks after brain surgery shows he's quite a tough cookie.

Ironically, McCain had spoken out against Obamacare and the need for it to be replaced during his re-election campaign in 2016, though by the time he came to cast a decisive vote yesterday evening, his opposition to the proposals on the table appeared to stem more from his disapproval of the clandestine manner in which the bill was prepared. McCain made a speech a couple of days before last night's vote calling for a 'return to regular order' when it comes to lawmaking, so it was perhaps no surprise that – coupled with the urge to get one over the President – McCain should side with Democrats at the eleventh hour.

The 'Skinny' repeal compromise was regarded as the only version Republicans might be able to get through Congress; its defeat means there are no other prospective bills on the cards to repeal Obamacare; despite this, Trump tweeted in the aftermath of the vote 'As I said from the beginning, let Obamacare implode, then deal.' At the same time, one of Trump's early rivals for last year's Republican nomination, Texas Senator Ted Cruz, declared 'Mark my words, this journey is not yet done.' It probably won't be in the long-term, but for now it is; and the Republicans have one of their own to thank for it.

SONG OF THE SOUTH
14 August 2017

When Belfast City Council voted to break with tradition in 2012 by reducing the flying of the Union Flag atop City Hall from 365 to 18 days a year, the more vociferous wing of the Unionist community greeted the announcement with violent protests. A couple of days ago, marking the anniversary of the Battle of the Boyne, bonfires were lit across Unionist strongholds of the province, many of which were decorated with photos of prominent Sinn Fein politicians. I only nod to our neighbours over the Irish Sea to make a roundabout point on how the issues that enflame passions on both sides of the sectarian divide in Northern Ireland barely register on the mainland; they're viewed by the rest of the UK (with the possible exception of Glasgow) as parochial concerns unique to Ulster and characteristic of a land with an extremely long memory.

Even with the high profile suddenly afforded the DUP in the wake of Theresa May's golden handshake, the 'street politics' of Northern Ireland rarely attract outsiders to the barricades, something that can't be said of another divided community from a region with a similarly turbulent history several thousand miles away – Virginia. The dramatic and ugly events that took place in Charlottesville, Virginia at the weekend didn't have their source material in religious divisions, but race – the most contentious of all American issues that just won't go away. Not even eight years of a black President could sort it.

Virginia was one of the four slave states from the 'Upper South' of the US that, along with Arkansas, Tennessee and North Carolina, joined the original seven Southern secessionist states in the Confederacy during the Civil War. Its history, now so bound-up with the Confederacy and its aftermath, predates that era considerably, with Virginia being the first English colony in the New World, established as far back as 1607. But it was also prominent among the 13 colonies that broke with British rule and has a claim as being the birthplace of the USA; it certainly was the birthplace of eight US Presidents, for one thing.

Like the rest of the states in the South, Virginia had a segregationist policy in place until the civil rights movement of the 1960s gradually led to a repeal of the remaining Jim Crow laws; but its past, like many of its neighbours' pasts, continues to attract the attention of those for whom integration remains a greater threat to making America great again than the hardware in Kim Jong-un's toy-box.

Recent attempts to reduce the high visibility of the Confederate Flag in the Southern states have gone hand-in-hand with a concerted programme to remove statues of, and monuments to, Confederate heroes from public places; and these efforts at erasing a history that sits uncomfortably on the shoulders of modern America have served to ignite the ire of white Southern natives proud of their inheritance, as well as white supremacists from different parts of the country who exploit the situation to promote their cause. When Washington belatedly addressed the iniquities and inequality of the South in the 60s by outlawing its segregationist traditions, the white population claimed the rest of the US didn't understand the South and there's probably a grain of truth in that. The South was seen as something of an embarrassment that contradicted America's international reputation as the Land of the Free; the South was a place where the past remained present.

The ongoing contemporary operation to change the perception of the South, not only for outsiders but also for those who live there, has been characterised by the official removal of 'negative' symbols relating to its past; though whereas the pulling down of statues during an uprising or revolution tends to come from the emancipated population itself, the policy of removing them that has been taking place across the South of late is a decision of federal government. Many have viewed this decision as symptomatic of rewriting American history, a rewrite that fails to acknowledge aspects of it that don't complement the image America likes to project of itself. There are also concerns that by erasing the visible legacy of the Confederacy, future generations are being presented with a lopsided story of their country, one without warts and all, and one depriving them of a history they could learn from.

Plans to remove a statue of Robert E Lee, Confederate Civil War general, in Charlottesville led to the town being invaded on Saturday by a 'Unite the Right' march, bringing in angry white men from all over America for a rally that was destined to be met with a counter-rally. Whatever valid points had a right to be made didn't stand a chance of being heard; both sides were infiltrated by those whose intentions were obvious from the start, many of whom had little or nothing to do with the part of the country they headed for.

The relatively liberal college town of Charlottesville was hijacked by opposing sides looking for a battlefield. The far-from spotless 'Black Lives Matter' crowd were accompanied by the masked men from 'Antifa' – an abbreviation of 'anti-fascist' – who have a reputation as violent left-wing anarchists; they were the group responsible for the trouble that occurred in Washington on the day of Donald Trump's inauguration. Those under the Alt-Right banner included neo-Nazis as well as that old mainstay always up for a fight, the Ku Klux Klan. The KKK are almost to the South what the Orangemen are to Ulster, though for all their shared pseudo-Masonic ritualism and shameful record of gerrymandering, the Orangemen are a long way from the Klan when it comes to provoking and stoking hatred in the most sinister manner.

What was already a predictable and unedifying clash on Saturday plumbed especially appalling depths when one lunatic ironically took a leaf out of the Jihadi manual and drove a car directly at protestors; his efforts were responsible for 19 injuries and one death. The white supremacists, who view President Trump as 'their man', were gratified that the Donald seemed reluctant to attribute blame for events to them, though the majority of the Alt Right (to whom Trump owes a great debt) probably regard the extremists who descended upon Charlottesville with the same abhorrence as the left views the 'Antifa'. It would certainly suit the narrative of the moment to lump together anyone who questions or challenges the anti-Trump consensus into one hate-fuelled, racist mob; but unfortunately, it's not quite so...erm...black and white.

AFTER THE FLOOD
18 September 2017

It's an old question – 'What would you take with you if your home was on fire and you had to make a dash for it?' For years, my answer to the question was the same: my cat and my memory stick. I sadly no longer have my cat, so it's just the memory stick now. Touching wood, I'll never be faced with that dilemma; but it's not just fire that can provoke a swift and sudden flight. Hurricane Irma's trail of death and destruction across the Caribbean and the southern coastal States of the US has forced people into giving their own answers to a similar question. Unfortunately – and, to me, inexplicably – many of them didn't regard their pets as being top of the list; some didn't even put their pets on the list at all. For such a God-fearing country as America, it's amazing how many Americans failed to take a leaf out of Noah's book.

Living in Blighty, we tend not to experience such extreme weather conditions. Yes, we've suffered some terrible floods in recent years and there have been the odd occasions in which Michael Fish has had to regret not taking a can of Mr Sheen to his meteorological crystal ball; but by and large most of us have no concept of having to make a rapid exit in the knowledge that the Big Bad Wolf will probably huff 'n' puff and blow our house down in our absence. Having said that, knowing it was coming would enable us to hastily gather our loved ones together and get the hell out of there quick. Nobody but a complete bastard would leave their children behind, so why would anyone abandon such significant family members as their pets?

Wind speeds of 135mph, a storm surge of 10 feet, three inches of rain every hour – that's what was predicted when Irma came to town, and the people responded accordingly, by packing away all essential possessions and running to the hills; a pity pets weren't regarded as essential possessions. The sad fact is that animals kept in the home are no more important to some people than disposable and replaceable items like furniture; there might be a hurricane coming that will more than likely condemn the poor beasts to a certain death, but hey, we can always get a new one once we rebuild our wrecked nest, just like we can a widescreen TV set. The mind boggles.

Over the past couple of weeks, I've seen several heartbreaking videos online of admirable animal rescuers travelling down residential streets transformed into the residential rivers of JG Ballard's 'The Drowned World' in search of pets left behind; and they found plenty. In Florida's Palm Beach County, the first 48 hours of Hurricane Irma saw Animal Care and Control officers come to the rescue of 38 dogs and two cats that their owners clearly didn't view as worthy of joining them on the journey out of town. With the saddest of ironies, such a socially gregarious animal as the dog appears to have received the worst of this careless cruelty from its best friend.

Despite the fact that there were many evacuation centres accommodating pets along with their owners, some still chose to not only abandon their animals, but in the case of several dogs, to leave them chained up to poles or in kennels; the dogs couldn't even make their own escape as a consequence. In Polk County, four dogs were mercifully saved from a watery grave by members of the public; the rising water level in the kennel they found them in was apparently as high as the dog's chests and the grimy pool was also swimming with horrific-sounding fire ants. It's worth remembering too that the Animal Care and Control officers have to deal with dogs whose bewilderment with, and fear of, their predicament in such a situation can be manifested as aggression, making their lifesaving work all the more heroic under the circumstances.

Flying debris can be as big a danger as flooding in the conditions that descended upon Florida; experts said as little as a single grain of sand in winds of 100mph can cause a serious injury. The image of confused dogs tethered to immovable objects when Mother Nature is inflicting such a violent onslaught in the vicinity is one that should haunt the guilty parties forevermore; but if they had a conscience, they wouldn't have left their pets to face it alone in the first place. Some simply dumped animals at shelters before fleeing and probably believe they're somehow more responsible and humane than those who didn't think even think their pets deserved that much; but they still left them.

In Palm Beach County, chaining dogs outside a property if the owner is absent is actually a felony offence, so doing so in a hurricane means some stiff penalties are imminent. Returning home, these 'victims' of Irma for whom it's difficult to have much in the way of sympathy can look forward to fines and even prison sentences for their callous actions. The maximum sentence, incidentally, is a mouth-watering five years. The State Prosecutor for Palm Beach said, 'This is a prime example of animal cruelty. We will find you and we will prosecute you.' The Animal Care and Control Captain of the same county added, 'The animals should be a valued part of your family and they should be part of your plan.'

Those who may well receive time behind bars will also not get those pets back and will be banned from owning any pets ever again; meanwhile, those who dropped their pets off at animal shelters before hot-footing it out of town will be placed on a 'Do Not Adopt' list; they too will not be reunited with the animals they rid themselves of. Sure, none of us on this side of the pond can picture the nightmarish scenario that people in the path of Hurricane Irma found themselves in; but that's still no excuse for the cruelty some of them exhibited towards animals in their care. I hope their new homeless status lasts until at least the next storm. Serves them right.

YEAH, WHATEVER...
21 April 2019

I suspect people had more blind faith where their leaders were concerned before 1973. If Watergate or a comparable scandal (in terms of cultural impact) was to happen now, how would we respond to the revelation that the biggest elected representative in the land was a bit of a crook? Shock! Horror! Yes, certainly in the media's delivery of the news to the masses; but what of the masses themselves? A shrug of the shoulders and a resigned 'Well, they're *all* bent bastards', perhaps; indeed, one wonders if Richard Nixon would simply serve out his second term of office today and face down the challenge of impeachment as Bill Clinton did. The general consensus now we are sufficiently distanced from the activities of Tricky Dicky's inept White House mobsters appears to be that what Nixon got up to behind closed doors was no worse than what many of his predecessors got up to, not to mention his successors.

It would now appear that, as a collective, the Kennedys got away with far more than Nixon ever managed; this could have been because they always looked good; and in politics, particularly *American* politics, that helps. Regardless of all the unappetising worms that have slithered out of the Kennedy can over the past half-century, the JFK model remains a potent political sales technique, seen just last week as desperate Democrats continue to submit a succession of bland shirt-sleeves-rolled-up congressmen, senators, governors and mayors from those States where hair is nearly always thick, black and slicked-back. Perhaps it's a sign of the cynical times that whenever I catch sight of these showroom dummies on TV, my first thought is to wonder how long it'll be before their campaign is derailed by the inevitable story of an affair with a call-girl or, worse, an allegation of a college rape. In the twenty-first century, it's become second nature that we eventually expect our leaders to be revealed as bent bastards; in the twentieth, it wasn't necessarily so.

Yes, opinion of politicians in general languishes so low today in comparison to forty or fifty years ago that it's hard to think of a profession that outranks politics in terms of eliciting public revulsion. The only one that springs to mind – tabloid journalism – is probably as responsible for this state of affairs as any other, salivating over every scandal it has helped to break with as much energy as the politician has sought to cover-up the one he helped to make. The negative view of politicians has been largely generated by their own wicked deeds, though repeated exposure to them via the media has helped fan the flames. It's been a partnership that has had disastrous consequences for both parties; and the more polarising politics is, the more determined each side becomes to destroy the other at the expense of everything else that needs dealing with.

Therefore, though I've only skimmed through the findings of the Mueller Report (or those sections highlighted online and on television) since its publication last week, skimming was as much as I could be bothered doing. I mean – is anyone going to be remotely surprised by anything it has to say, even its most damaging indictments of a presidency few outside of the most devoted rate much higher than the nearest sewer, anyway?

The reaction to the Mueller Report from both sides of the ideological barricades is a perfect portrait of a wider political divide and how the media has played its part. The anti-Trump brigade, religiously dedicated to every website and rolling news channel that reinforces their viewpoint of the Donald as the Devil incarnate, furiously rifled through the report in search of anything that confirmed what they already believed – and that was all they were looking for; similarly, the pro-Trump crowd did likewise, bringing all their gun-totin' baggage and unswerving love of the Man from Del Monte to the table, solely seeking to finally prove he ain't no buddy of Putin. Consequently, Mr President can confidently declare the findings exonerate him and extinguish the Russian rumours once and for all, whilst his more vocal political opponents can also locate plenty in the report that supports their opinion of Trump and can perhaps act as the launch-pad for a renewed attempt to oust him from office. Who in 2019, I wonder, could possibly approach such a report with a totally unbiased perspective?

Numerous senior Democrats have played the part of TV talking heads in the wake of the Mueller Report, furtively speculating on what fresh opportunities for attack its revelations have presented them with. But Democrats really need to get over Trump. I think western liberals in general need to get over Trump, but US opposition politicians and their supporters *especially* need to get over him. Their fanatical, foaming-at-the-mouth obsession is proving an obstruction to the one legitimate and indisputable means of evicting him from the White House – the ballot-box. If they don't get their act together soon and push forward a candidate the entire Democratic Party (and then the majority of the country) can rally round before 2020, their nightmare is simply going to be prolonged for another four years and make their meltdown a permanent one.

The Democrat fixation on dislodging Trump by any means, fair or foul, is almost comparable to the similar tunnel vision some backbench Tories have on Brexit, with the potential to destroy their party if they don't put the brakes on. The man's not going anywhere for at least another eighteen months, so cease and desist from wasting time trying to evict him other than by persuading the electorate to do so when the time comes. Otherwise, Democrats risk being defined solely by their disproportionate hatred of Trump as much as the ERG is defined by its disproportionate hatred of the EU.

Yes, we've all enjoyed Alec Baldwin's impersonation of the President, but let's not pretend poking fun will change anything. One could evoke Peter Cook's sarcastic summary of the spectacular success German satirists had in preventing the Nazis' rise to power or perhaps remember how the Alternative Comedy generation had a thing about Thatcher without their fury making the slightest bit of difference to the Iron Lady's staying power; in the end it was her own insane sense of invincibility that did for her, without any assistance from Ben Elton. Indeed, as a stand-up, Elton was as indebted to Margaret Thatcher as Mike Yarwood was to Harold Wilson. Lest we forget, one prominent member of the 80s comedy club is now a Dame of the British Empire; she burned a pin-prick in the ozone layer last week by jetting over to Central London during its reinvention as Glastonbury to link arms with trustafarians and tell us how we're killing the planet. Some of us already knew that, just like we know the best way to get rid of Donald Trump is to find a better man – or woman.

THE PISS-POOR RELATION
4 June 2019

Having known a succession of non-bedroom flats as home during the past 15-20 years, I've been deprived of one conundrum that those with a 'spare' are occasionally faced with – the visitor who stops overnight and then extends his stay to several days. I'm sure the majority of these are welcome guests who are sincerely invited to treat the place like their own; and I'm equally sure this majority are courteous visitors who volunteer to do the washing-up. Surely not all take the piss – emptying the fridge of its contents and leaving the bathroom a bombsite of wet towels and poo balls, for example.

Uncle Donald's long-trumpeted state visit is, I suppose, the dreaded scenario of the embarrassing overseas relative whose brief return to the mother country has been made easier (for him) by the emotional blackmail he employed to secure the spare room for three days. Families, eh? He'll probably want to be introduced to your circle, even though you'll spend the whole excruciating meeting hoping he doesn't say something racist or grope your girlfriend; and after just one night of being bombarded by his braggadocio bluster, your pounding head will be pleading with you to concoct an excuse that will force him into finding a hotel ASAP. 'I know, it's dreadful; but the bloody landlord says he needs to hire out the premises for an Icelandic jazz festival tomorrow. There's nothing I can do about it.'

No, I'm not keen on Donald Trump; I never have been. I think he's a boorish, charmless, combative, coarse vulgarian. But I will say the fact he pisses off a lot of people who piss me off tickles my funny bone – far more than the puerile playground response of some to his presence on these shores. Hell, I'm no

140

stranger to the puerile playground, as the video accompanying this post once again demonstrates; but when Dubya flew-in and raised similar hackles a few years back, the protests against his visit – at a time when war in Iraq was ongoing – were grounded in something substantial and seemed to have a genuinely valid politicised edge to them. I mean, a baby blimp? Come on – is this the best we can manage now? I suppose a giant cock only visible from the air could be said to be in the vein of traditional English humour; but it still feels like the nation is dropping its trousers and desperately mooning Air Force One because it can't articulate its objections better than a five-year-old.

Despite Sadiq Khan's attempts to promote the capital as though it's one long Pride parade, the appalling roll-call of murders on the streets of London during his mayoral tenure – let alone in the six months of 2019 so far – really should focus his attention away from Twitter spats with a man who does this for a living. The public petulance of the London Mayor – not to mention the Leader of HM Opposition – is also counterproductive; Mr President draws most of his political strength and support from playing the outsider up against the establishment, and were leading Labour figures not so preoccupied with signalling their collective virtue, they'd realise their attitude is playing right into the Donald's tiny hands.

Worse still, building up Trump to be the towering monster he likes to see himself portrayed as serves to make his predecessor in the White House look better than he actually was, conveniently airbrushing his less attractive legacies from the record books. The former drone-happy President was also guilty of sticking his nose into Brexit business last time he was here, but all has been forgotten during the wistful longing for the nauseating hero-worship that followed Obama around the UK like a gaggle of weak-kneed teenyboppers. I'm pretty sure Theresa May would love her final moment as PM to be flipping burgers in the back garden at No.10 with the 'cool President', but it ain't gonna happen. She'd probably burn them to an inedible frazzle, anyway.

Mrs May can leave the wining and dining this time round to Her Majesty, and Brenda certainly has the experience, playing hostess to some exceedingly dodgy characters over the decades – everyone from Idi Amin and Robert Mugabe to the Shah of Iran and Nicolae Ceauşescu; and let's not forget Brian's buddies in the Saudi royal family. Compared to that notable rogue's gallery, Trump is Nelson Mandela. We really should put him into perspective, but the febrile climate in Blighty at the moment isn't very conducive to perspective, alas – witness the casual dispensing of meaningful historical terms like 'Nazi' and 'Fascist' so they are reduced to meaningless insults on a par with 'knob-head' or 'wanker'.

Trump's behaviour so far – including his retort to Sadiq Khan before he even set foot on British soil – is entirely in keeping with the man, so nobody should feign surprise or outrage. Boris Johnson's uncharacteristically low profile at the moment – a deliberate tactic to avoid the fate that always befalls the early favourite in a Tory leadership contest, one suspects – could probably do without the endorsement of the President, mind. Nigel Farage has less to lose, though being seen in the same light as Piers Morgan when it comes to one's choice of friends isn't the best boost either man's aspirations could wish for at such a crucial juncture.

One of Trump's duties before he departs is to be present at a commemorative ceremony in Portsmouth, marking the 75th anniversary of the D-Day Landings. The last time D-Day was marked on such a grand scale ten years ago, Gordon Brown as

PM practically had to invite himself to Normandy when Nicolas Sarkozy's ego and eagerness to be photographed alongside Obama implied the British RSVP had got lost in the post. The former Co-Prince of Andorra might have neglected to remember, but the opening shot of liberating Nazi-occupied Europe was pretty much an Anglo-American operation at the western end; it's therefore only right and proper that whoever happens to be the incumbent US President should be present on such a significant occasion, and the event being marked should override any personal gripes with the man occupying the office. If anything is capable of really putting 2019 into perspective, remembering 1944 should be – shouldn't it?

3
Listen to the Banned

Censorship, culture wars and the politics of identity

'Bangkok Chick-Boys' was the documentary Alan Partridge alleged he wanted to switch off his hotel cable TV in favour of 'Driving Miss Daisy', though mysteriously found himself unable to work out a way of doing so. Grilling his Geordie sidekick about his experience of Ladyboys during his military outings to the Far East, Partridge's fascination with these exotic self-made hybrids isn't uncommon, as the queues of western male tourists eager to sample their talents will testify. Elsewhere in Asia, Indian culture has the Hijras, castrated men dressed as women who are supposedly blessed with gypsy-like mystical powers to bestow bad luck upon those who seek to banish them from society; despite this, most simply end up living a grubby existence as low-level prostitutes (I won't describe them as 'sex-workers', as that implies a degree of career choice to their miserable little lot).

As a collective group, the Ladyboys and the Hijras largely refrain from seeking recognition as Real Women. True, their appearance may dupe the odd unsuspecting foreign punter, but they are clearly posing as the opposite sex by exaggerating stereotypical feminine traits. The same could be said of the old Warhol transvestite superstars such as Candy Darling and Holly Woodlawn, who knowingly resided in a harmless fantasy world that reinvented them as the most glamorous divas Tinsel Town never had. The latter two's roles in Paul Morrissey's trashy early 70s underground movies contained both humour and an undeniable degree of risqué excitement that inspired both Bowie and Divine; as far as the heavyweight drag queen was concerned, his cinematic collaborations with John Waters took the humour to a glorious plateau of bad taste that has never been bettered.

Quentin Crisp, a remarkably brave man who took his life in his hands every time he stepped out into 1930s London with his painted face and nails and dyed red hair, was once criticised by the New York gay 'community' in an early example of libertine censorship for daring to air reservations over the OTT excesses by which being out and proud had to be advertised in the manner of a New Orleans Carnival. Crisp did so with his customary caustic wit, though this didn't square with the witless, fanatical demands to be 'accepted' by a straight society that Crisp had never sought to win the acceptance of.

Ah, yes – wit, the vital element missing from the rulebook of the transgender police who pretend the glorified middle-aged Ladyboy, Bruce 'Caitlyn' Jenner, is a woman. With their endless additions to the Uxbridge English Dictionary and on-the-spot fines for those who dare to use terms that are no longer allowed in polite society, these humourless enforcers would actually find their Orwellian credo very much at home in Iran. There, any man prepared to publicly proclaim his homosexuality is encouraged to undergo a sex change, which the state will pay for. Subsidised gender reassignment has become commonplace in Iran, and those who emerge from the operating table are thereafter officially recognised as Real Women. Who'd have thought it? The transgender capital of the world is the land of the Ayatollah.

At one time, donning the apparel and mannerisms of the opposite sex was a deliberate act of subversion, a conscious affront aimed at the straight society that associated any hint of gender bending with deviancy – or in other words, homosexuality. The thought that a heterosexual man could adorn himself with cosmetics was such a challenge to the stringent specifications of what maketh a man that it contained genuine rebellious connotations, even in a country like Britain, with a rich history of theatrical female impersonation stretching through the music hall and all the way back to the time when pre-pubescent boys had to play Shakespeare's female parts on account of actresses being banned from the stage. Whether Mick Jagger in a dress or Marc Bolan sprinkling stardust on his cheeks, there was always a playful, mischievous aspect to the practice that reflected the traditional British sense of the absurd; in the wider canvas of America, which has a far more prevalent macho lineage, such behaviour was restricted to isolated pockets of resistance like LA and New York. The chic freaks rejected the straights and their society and didn't want to be embraced by it.

How times have changed. A man paints his lips or eyes today and he's immediately claimed by fanatical lobbyists demanding he be recognised as a woman in order that he can be neatly categorised, labelled and accepted. How would the transgender police have reacted upon entering the cornucopia of sexually ambiguous individuals dancing the night away at Steve Strange's Blitz club in the early 80s? Standing out from the crowd was crucial to any adoption of female accoutrements back then; nowadays the crowd mentality, whereby everyone has to be part of some 'community', has become so entrenched that the natural assumption is that a man in makeup is not expressing his individuality but seeking to be co-opted by an officially-sanctioned group. Stripped of its fearless sartorial radicalism, what was once the ultimate outsider's challenge to the masculine straitjacket has been stolen by those who have no comprehension of the thrill embodied in blurring gender lines as a means of spurning safety in numbers; they ask why would anybody *not* want to belong, whereas I ask why would anybody *want* to?

So many are so incensed by the increased policing of the English language that they often rally round those who delight in calling a spade a spade for all the wrong reasons. Whether Donald Trump, Jeremy Clarkson or Tyson Fury, it's a measure of how oversensitive the arbiters of what can and can't be said in public have become that some react to the latest linguistic directive by cheering on a professional gobshite whose relish in causing offence has no point beyond the causing of offence. One would struggle to find the poetic vitriol in a column by, say, Kelvin McKenzie that was once the trademark of Ian Nairn, the late great architectural critic who offended all the right people with eloquence and wit because his anger came from the heart and was motivated by a deep desire to make the world a better place rather than craving a self-promoting platform to point a gesticulating finger.

It was announced the other day that Salford Council plan to introduce on-the-spot fines for anyone caught using 'foul and abusive language' in the area of Salford Quays, a slick and soulless neighbourhood that contains luxury apartment blocks as well as the BBC's very own 'Northern Powerhouse', Mediocre City UK. Liberty have written to Salford Council to clarify what they would constitute as foul and abusive, including inquiring if a foul and abusive word being uttered would count as a criminal offence if there was nobody else present to hear it. Should someone bang their shin on an inanimate object whilst passing through the Quays, unleashing a simple expletive to verbally articulate pain when reciting a Shakespeare soliloquy just won't do, have they then broken the law?

Salford Council claims this monitoring of 'speech crime' is a response to complaints from residents of the Quays regarding antisocial behaviour. Correct me if I'm wrong, but Salford Quays does not consist of sheltered housing for the elderly, the demographic within society that traditionally have a problem with fruity vocabularies. Besides, Salford Council's own account of these complaints mentions uprooting wheelie bins from their prominent and aesthetically appealing positions on the pavement; did whoever threw the bins into the Manchester Ship Canal issue a series of rude words as they did so? F*** knows. A Public Space Protection Order has been utilised in order to enforce this unenforceable law, and calling Salford Quays a public space is something of a misnomer if the public are to be policed in such a manner. At least be honest and refer to it as a private space – or perhaps a 'safe space', those newfangled wombs specially designed for the most easily offended group of the moment, university students, to flee to when their delicate little sensibilities are thrown into turmoil as someone says something contradictory to their manual of what is and isn't acceptable.

The most vocal monitors of the English language have made it clear they won't tolerate half of the words in the dictionary over the last few months, censoring and hectoring veteran advocates of free speech such as Germaine Greer and Peter Tatchell and issuing evermore ludicrous decrees that we disobey at our peril. Swearing doesn't seem to have come under the radar of the Stepford Students yet, though I suspect those words that are perceived as insulting to the anatomy of the shrinking violet probably have – cunt, fanny, twat etc. I would imagine bollocks, knackers, dickhead, knobhead, wanker et al are probably still acceptable in that they refer to the naughty bits of men, and these naughty bits can of course constitute a dangerous arsenal if not belittled by insults.

It goes without saying that someone whose every other word is fuck or fucking can quickly become tedious, not so much by using those particular words but just by the endless repetition of any words; I find those who pepper their sentences with 'like' or 'y'know' as irritating as anyone who substitutes these words with profanities. However, there are certain social situations in which constant recourse to swearing suggests a lack of general etiquette. I wouldn't, for example, reply to an old lady making an innocent inquiry in a supermarket queue by showering her in a stream of four-letter words, nor would I adopt the tactics of the infuriatingly oblivious self-centred tosser conducting a loud sweary conversation on his mobile in the same environment, treating his local branch of Sainsbury's as though it were a taproom. And there's nothing worse than a parent effing and blinding at their small children as he or she waits impatiently to buy their scratch-card. I don't swear in front of my mother or my nine-year-old niece because I'm conscious they're not the right audience; but with friends, it's different. Perhaps because I'm not in love with the sound of my own voice, I doubt I'd offend any residents of Salford Quays, anyway, on account of speaking at a level intended solely for the ears of the person I'm speaking to.

This week, Donald Trump marked his Super Tuesday success by making penis jokes during a live televised debate with one of his Republican rivals; yes, it was just like Kennedy and Nixon all over again. One feels the only way the brakes could be applied to the Trump juggernaut would be if he were caught saying 'nigger' within range of a TV microphone. Even then, however, there would still be a large section of the huntin', shootin' and fishin' American public applauding his perceived rejection of PC politeness by not being afraid to speak his mind.

And that in a way is the danger of policing language to such an extreme that nobody seems to know what is or isn't acceptable to say in public; more and more become weary of these endless rewritings of verbal intercourse and many instinctively flock to those who deliberately flout the new rules, finding them a breath of fresh air. Unfortunately, these tend not to be fiercely intelligent individuals such as the much-missed Christopher Hitchens, who would support their spurning of speech crime enforcers with a superlative counter-argument that utterly trashes the agents of serial censorship, but those who have nothing else in their armoury other than a playground insult. And my dick's bigger than yours.

WE ARE NOT AMUSED
8 March 2016

Have you heard the one about the anti-fascist protest where protestors were there to prevent libertarians from exercising their right to free speech, hid their identities behind masks, poured a bottle of piss over someone who had the guts to stand up to them, and generally behaved with all the restraint of fanatical Jihadists setting fire to the stars & stripes? Unfortunately, there isn't a funny punch-line. This happened in Canada – yes, the laidback, easygoing next-door neighbour of the USA; but it could just as easily have happened here in Blighty. The recipient of the unwanted golden shower didn't go running and crying to a 'safe space' to suck her thumb and dial 911 (or whatever number Canadians dial for law enforcement), followed by a crash-course in therapy to reiterate that she remains 'special'; she walked away with as much dignity as she could muster because *she* wasn't the fascist present; the spoilt brat who doused her in wee-wee was. And those who couldn't make it to the latest Nuremberg Rally aired their opinions of the punishment dished out to the

153

she-devil with a series of sympathetic commiserations on twitter.

It's no wonder the regressive left is an apologist for Islamic Fundamentalism and every other crazed faction that is hailed as a heroic bulwark against the white, straight, women-suppressing, ethnic minority-suppressing, gay-suppressing, homophobic, transphobic, misogynistic and racist world elite that controls the planet. They share the same narrow worldview, only differing in the route that brought them to it. That their Vancouver branch expressed the intolerance of their secular Puritanism by aiming their ire and bodily waste at Canadian broadcaster and vocal critic of their manifesto Lauren Southern is not merely the action of overgrown children to whom 'no' was never said; it also lays bare their belief that a man who still has his tackle intact but chooses to play the part of the opposite sex is more of a woman than the real thing, should she happen to disagree with them.

The British branch of the international prohibitionists have mainly focused their attention on inanimate human facsimiles rather than living, flesh-and-blood people who can provide a counter argument, with the honourable exception of those renowned fascists, Tatchell and Greer; the targets of their illogical and ill-educated fury are old statues of prominent figures usually emanating from a past that Blairite educational reforms deliberately provided them with no history of, other than labelling everyone who wasn't a slave or repressed colonial as a rabid racist. The empire-builders and military leaders are easy targets, as they tend to be the ones who had statues sculpted in their honour; but to dismiss Britain's imperial past in one ignorant swoop is also a slur on the thousands of Brits who spent their entire working lives out in the colonies, ones whose unvisited resting places crumbling in overgrown graveyards on the Indian Subcontinent (amongst other locations) are testament to their forgotten contribution in establishing the best of British principles – not to mention the English language – on foreign soil. Anyway, unlike most of our European colonial competitors, Britain rarely *invaded* another country; the majority of Britain's overseas possessions grew organically over decades from their humble beginnings as trading posts, the classic mark of a maritime nation.

Queen Victoria herself is the latest focus of the Ministry of Truth's brown-shirt brigade, though it will be difficult to remove all of her stone likenesses from the landscape, considering every city in the country erected a statue to her when she died. Even during her long lifetime, Victoria was immortalised as the embodiment of Britannia, a symbolic mother figure to the Empire, thus singling her out as another representative of our shameful history. How many of these foaming-at-the-mouth revisionists know anything about the woman – one possessing natural breasts and vagina – who reigned for over sixty years and gave her name to an entire era, the only time a woman has ever done so other than Elizabeth I?

Are they, for example, aware that in her later years, Victoria became enamoured with Indian culture and had a Muslim secretary called Abdul Karim, who was her close confidant for the last decade of her life, much to the disapproval of her less enlightened staff and family? She was ahead of her time in the case of Karim, whereas her disapproval of women's suffrage was more typical of her time. Contrary to her popular image, Victoria was a passionate woman who revelled in the sexual relationship she enjoyed with her husband Prince Albert, something that the brood she brought into the world underlines, despite the fact that continuous pregnancy got in the way of these erotic interludes. In this, she was very much in tune with her female subjects at a time of primitive and ineffective contraception.

For at least the second half of her reign, Queen Victoria was the most famous woman on the planet, and despite the lack of electoral representation for women in the mother country, great strides were taken by many women during that reign, strides that ended the absolute power of husbands in marriage, strides that challenged the exploitation of low-paid women workers, strides that curtailed the legal abuse of prostitutes, strides that broke down the barriers of higher education, and strides that contradict the retrospective image of Victorian women as shrinking violets forever fainting and swooning.

On International Women's Day, how ironic that these great strides taken over a century ago have been conveniently buried in a past that we are now supposed to be ashamed of, leaving us with a generation of women reverting to playing the victim, either of unequal opportunities in the workplace or the wicked libido of the male sex. Carping on about how hard done-by they are seems to be the default button of some women to elicit sympathy and to be in denial of just how much has changed, particularly in the western world, over the past 100 years. One would almost think being the underdog is some form of feminine comfort zone. But then, there's more to women today than a pair of breasts and a vagina – like a penis.

OUT OF THE FRY PAN...
12 April 2016

Though I've never subscribed to the opinion myself, there have long been some for whom Stephen Fry is viewed as a slightly smug PC luvvie and leading light in the so-called 'gay mafia' media establishment, beloved by certain sections of the left for his anti-Tory sentiments and endorsement of atheism, beloved by certain sections of the right for his embrace of old-school aristocratic tweeds, gentleman's clubs and Shakespeare. For me, what Stephen Fry has always represented is a continuation of the subversive posh bloke within comedy, something that was pioneered by the likes of Peter Cook and Graham Chapman.

'A Bit of Fry and Laurie' was far more radical than 'The Young Ones' because it could sneak anything under the light entertainment radar on account of the surface safeness of two Oxbridge boys with the diction of cricket commentators. Stephen Fry and Hugh Laurie weren't middle-class drop-outs slumming it with the common people by being overtly crude and self-consciously plebeian; it would have been far easier to have taken the Ben Elton route, but they instinctively tapped into what had made the Ministry of Silly Walks so funny – taking the most humourless, strait-laced elements of quintessentially English upper-class respectability and turning them on their heads.

Fry won further points with me for his TV series of a decade ago, 'The Secret Life of the Manic Depressive', especially when this seemingly confident household name allowed himself to be captured on camera languishing in a depressive episode of wretched self-loathing. For anyone without Fry's celebrity status who had been there, it was curiously encouraging to witness it happening to someone who had achieved so much within his chosen field, highlighting the fact that depression doesn't recognise wealth and success any more than it recognises penury and failure. After a groundbreaking series addressing a major taboo and the ongoing marathon of 'QI', Fry's position as that most overused of labels, a National Treasure, seemed secure. And then he had the temerity to say what so few beyond the blog and the Twittersphere dare.

During the period when Paul Gambaccini was on permanent police bail while the Met desperately dug up every little bit of dirt they could to justify their persecution of a prominent media voice, Stephen Fry criticised the police tactics on TV. A cynic might say what happened to Gambo had been happening to both the once-famous and the un-famous for a long time without anyone speaking out against it, and alternative opinions were only being belatedly aired due to a respected broadcaster being the latest target of a witch-hunt that was already two or three years into its reign of terror. But that the likes of Stephen Fry should question the wisdom of the inquisition was a sign that it had reached such ludicrous proportions that it now warranted an overdue critique from a personality with considerable clout. Broadsheet columnists quickly followed suit and finally enabled the subject to be debated in a wider public arena without those asking salient points being branded witches as they did so.

Stephen Fry has now voiced the concerns many have been discussing online for months regarding regressive left censorship, particularly on British campuses. The generation of narcissistic little Hitler's who are currently reversing the time-honoured traditions of universities as cradles of free speech and debate as they seek to impose their increasingly illogical and obsessive declarations of offence upon any perceived symbol of repression need to be stood up to. As their bullying, fascistic tactics are causing spineless university governors to crumble in the face of relentless intimidation that is labelling anything that veers from their cotton wool-wrapped infantile vision as 'offensive', more respected voices that carry some weight in media circles have to speak out against this insane tide of fanatical secular Puritanism.

Germaine Greer and Peter Tatchell have already fallen foul of an Orwellian army who recently proclaimed white gay men as another social demographic to be branded an enemy, and as one of the country's most notable white gay men, Stephen Fry was probably in their no-platform sights even before he had the nerve to condemn their Stasi-like policing of what can and can't be said.

Fry has rightly honed in on the immature spoilt-brat nature of this wave of censorious foot-stamping and its social media Rottweilers haven't wasted any time in attacking his (add the appropriate prefix to 'phobic') assault on their totalitarian plans for a new world order. As with the Paedogeddon witch-hunt before it, this latest curb on the freedom to express a personal opinion contrary to the consensus has now got seriously out of control and requires people to stand up and be counted without fear of online reprisals. That Stephen Fry has done so is to his credit and gives hope to those of us who are observing events from the outside without his platform...or no.

GOODBYE SAM, HELLO SAMANTHA
18 May 2016

I've spoken before of pushy parents projecting their failed ambitions upon the vanity projects they call children, of vicariously living thwarted dreams through offspring, regardless of how unfair a burden it is for that offspring to carry. I'm not speaking of it again, though certain aspects of a new odious development remind me of it. This is parents picking up on a particular personality trait in their mini-me's and coming up with a psychological diagnosis that ticks the PC boxes and enables them to advertise their right-on credentials by using their children as a sandwich board. I'm talking about parents who come to the decision that any characteristics of the opposite sex displayed by the kids evidently means the kids are gender-dysphorian, non-binary, tiny tot trannies.

I used to go to school with children, so I can recall what they were like. There were always boys who were routinely called 'cissies', the ones who appeared to have no male friends in the playground and always hung out with the girls, doing as the girls did; moreover, there were always girls who rejected girlishness and preferred the rough 'n' tumble of male company. The Nancy Boy and the Tom Boy are enshrined as archetypes in British pop culture, from Dennis the Menace's effeminate nemesis, Walter the Softy to 'George', Enid Blyton's butch little ball-breaker in 'The Famous Five'. Both were defiant aberrations, going against the stereotypical grain; both may have grown up to be gay. But being in closer contact with their respective feminine and masculine sides than the majority of their contemporaries didn't necessarily mean either wanted to eventually assume the full gender reassignment process. They were unselfconsciously taking a stance against what society defined as masculine or feminine.

I'm not ashamed or embarrassed that I've always been 'in touch with my feminine side', nor should I be. I've always believed a man who aggressively fights it is half-a-man, in denial of what is a biological truth. When that femininity is manifested as visual flourishes of a kind that an overtly masculine male culture reacts to with hostility, it's not the easiest brand of honesty to embrace; but to volunteer for a two-dimensional testosterone straitjacket is not in my nature, and I'd be less of a man if it was. Any past problems I may have had with being a man were, I can now see, a direct consequence of being presented with such a limited portrait of the sex. The hair is short, the clothes are colourless, the drink is beer, the passion is sport, the libido is triggered by the Page

3 Girl; and any deviation from the rulebook is precisely that – deviation. But as I instinctively reject imposed rulebooks in other aspects of life, why should gender be any different?

Ironically, the haste with which some misguided parents are now prepared to redefine their sons as daughters (and vice-versa) at the slightest hint of a preference for aping the opposite sex plays straight into the hands of the narrow male/female stereotypes they smugly imagine they're challenging. Little Sam prefers to play with the girls and their dolls, therefore that must mean he's a girl trapped in a boy's body; we must start calling him Samantha and send him to school in a skirt next term while letting his hair grow long; that, after all, is the extent of what a girl is, isn't it? If we swap one set of gender clichés for another, then everyone will then know he's a girl. No shades of grey there, just black-and-white boys and girls where there is no room for the Nancy Boy or the Tom Boy, those genuine rebels.

Girls and boys pass through numerous phases as they grow-up; that's what growing-up is about. I changed the comics I read on a virtually monthly basis; one week I was in love with Joanna Lumley in 'The New Avengers'; the next, I was in love with Jaclyn Smith from 'Charlie's Angels'. My female cousin's bedroom wall had a different pin-up staring down at me every time I visited. 'I thought you liked David Cassidy?' 'No, I like David Essex.' The first song I apparently proclaimed to be my No.1 'Desert Island Disc' was 'Yellow River' by Christie; 46 years later, I can honestly say I've never cared for it since it was a chart-topper in the summer of 1970. Anyone with anything about them experiences life as a permanent state of metamorphosis, changing opinions on subjects every ten years or so; a great deal of what I thought at 18 I now consider bollocks – and it's only right I should. The concept of development being frozen at any age is a particularly horrific one for me, let alone life choices being set in stone by parents when still a child and some distance from even puberty, let alone adulthood.

Gender identity is an especially delicate area of a child's life for parents to play with, far more serious than them mapping out their child's career or drilling a religious belief, a forced dedication to a musical instrument or a specific sport into them. More than anything, it is something the child needs to formulate when it has experienced a little bit of what life has to offer beyond the nursery or the playground, when it actually ceases to be a child and can be classified as an adult. There's nothing wrong with a boy finding more affinity with girls or a girl finding more affinity with boys; by surmising this implies a desire to actually become that which the child has an affinity with is to expose a parent's own limited awareness of the rich variety of what being a boy or a girl actually has the potential to encompass.

ALL YOU NEED IS HATE
15 August 2016

Perhaps it was only when time-travelling 21st Century DI Sam Tyler was confronted by racism in 1973 and expressed his opinion that he suspected a 'Hate Crime' that the ludicrousness of the term seemed more blatant than ever. 'As opposed to an I-really-love-you crime?' asked his guv'nor in response. Okay, so DCI Gene Hunt in the celebrated BBC drama 'Life on Mars' may not have been the most sympathetic or sensitive of characters, but the notion of a separate category for a criminal act based solely on 'hate' is a contentious one that deserves to be questioned. At the time 'Life on Mars' was set, there were certainly plenty of retrospective Hate Crimes being committed on British streets; the daily murders by both sides of the sectarian divide in

Northern Ireland could be considered so – using today's definition, anyway.

The impression sometimes given is that Hate Crime was hatched as a catch-all umbrella label to Hoover-up lots of little offences and assemble them all in a neat package that could also encompass other 'offences' not already catered for by the law. Many of the actions by individuals that fall under the Hate Crime banner would once have been dismissed as little more than playground-level name-calling; it's a definition open to abuse like few others. It's as though officers arriving at the scene of a crime who may be bemused by the evident absence of a motive pull the Hate Crime card out of a hat because it not only makes their job so much easier; it also pleases those who demand recognition as Victims.

There are numerous subdivisions that are encompassed by the Hate Crime tag. These include racially motivated violence, transphobic violence, violence against LGBT people, violence against men, violence against women, violence against people with disabilities and so forth – all of which are horrible, but all of which are virtually identical and unpleasant crimes committed by one human being against another. Should they not simply be considered age-old acts of violence full stop? Why do they require their own little label that immediately puts them in a 'special category'?

The need to categorise everything and everyone so that every item of information on a database can be referenced and cross-referenced to see which box it belongs in has been extended from data to people; and people are utterly complicit in this. The desire to be a 'joiner' and belong to an officially recognised Community seems to have superseded religious definitions in many cases as a means of self-identification, and would appear to fulfil a deep need to be a member of a crowd in a world that has been shorn of its older certainties. The advent of Hate Crime could be considered a symptom of this need.

Actively promoted by pressure groups and self-proclaimed minorities seeking a pigeonhole to comfortably slot into, Hate Crime is not only redefining genuine crimes and grouping them with incidents that should barely register as such, but it appears to be a term that is being applied to any manner of minor insults, an extension of the PC Police in monitoring free speech. The whole 'you can't say that' argument has been given one hell of a boost with the inception of Hate Crime.

Nowhere is this more obvious than online, where the anonymity a fake identity provides apparently gives the troll carte-blanche to say whatever he or she likes and receive no comeback. Hate Mail existed long before email, let alone Twitter, so it's nothing new. Technology has merely facilitated a faster means of sending abuse than it used to take when posting a letter, just as it has enabled messages of a more benign nature to reach the recipient in an instant. For those who live online and can barely survive a minute without gazing at their Smartphone, any abusive text or message is bound to have a greater impact, as this is impinging upon the central hub of their existence.

The Metropolitan Police Force is clearly taking the concerns of online obsessives into account by setting up a new unit to tackle the problem for the princely sum of £1.7m. A spokesman for the pilot project claimed there was 'no place for hate in London' and also used that awful term 'zero tolerance', which always sounds too uncomfortably reminiscent of old phrases such as 'short, sharp shock' or even the inappropriate application of the word 'Tsar' to anyone heading such a taskforce.

It is the vagueness of Hate Crime as a description and how easily it can be attached to an opinion that contradicts the current consensus that makes it such a problematic term. Any police involvement in a dispute between one individual and a Community (especially an online one) always seems an unnecessary intervention, something that grown adults should be able to deal with on their own and not go crying to the Boys in Blue about. After all, they have enough issues of their own making to deal with, such as murdering former Premier League footballers by applying 50,000 volts to them simply because they resisted being restrained. That might not be a Hate Crime, but it's pretty bloody hateful. RIP Dalian Atkinson.

DEFENSIVE PLAY
14 September 2016

Whenever I sign out of my inbox, Yahoo automatically takes me to what passes for their 'headlines', which usually consist of the kind of showbiz fluff I cross oceans to avoid. One I saw today was referring to some actress in some movie where she apparently drags up (i.e. wears a fake beard); I only know because there was a photo of her. I didn't bother reading it because I couldn't care less, though the headline itself caught my eye because it claimed said actress 'defends her trans-role.' Curious choice of word – 'defends'. Sorry, it was my understanding that the only people who have to defend their actions are those on trial for murder and other such serious crimes. Am I missing something? What is there to defend about playing a part, which is indeed the definition of being an actor?

'Plumber defends his decision to unblock drain!' 'Mechanic defends changing tyre!' 'Postman defends delivering of letter!' Any sillier than 'Actress defends pretending to be a

165

fictional character in a completely made-up story'? Not really, though public figures over the years have often had to answer to the archetypal 'Disgusted of Tunbridge Wells' figure incensed by something they've seen on the TV, at the cinema or in the paper – or haven't seen at all but have surmised they would find offensive. This seems to have expanded in recent years, perhaps a consequence of the democratisation of fame, so that those who grab their fifteen minutes also have to be scrutinised by Mr and Ms Disgusted, now firmly on the left where once they were on the right. It gives the impression that society as a whole has been transformed into one giant court of law, one in which we are all permanently on the defensive, having to justify every move in anticipation of criticism from the unofficial PC police who guard against offence.

This is a court bereft of statute books so that nobody is entirely sure what can and can't be said and what can and can't be done, hence the increase in habitual criminality. How helpful then, that we have our self-appointed online lawmakers who are on hand to recite the dos and don'ts, as well as intervening if we unknowingly break their laws. The novelist Lionel Shriver gave a lecture in Australia a few days ago, one that received publicity across all mediums; generally, the sense she spoke was well-received, though there was the predictable backlash from those that enjoy the lashing of backs. Shriver appeared on 'Newsnight' to...yes, you guessed it...defend what she had said.

Essentially, Lionel Shriver accused the scourge of so-called Identity Politics and accompanying disgust with Cultural Appropriation of stifling the creative and the imaginative – which those who propagate such Orwellian control are not. This is the attempted policing of creativity that says writers of fiction can only write from the point of view of their own gender, sexuality and race; and if 'ethnic' characters are introduced into their stories, they have to be non-caricatures and inoffensive, officially approved representatives of their individual ethnicity. What a remarkably philistine set of rules and regulations.

Any good novelist researches the background and environment of any character that isn't based directly upon them or somebody they've known – or they simply use their imagination, which is one factor that distinguishes the writer of fiction from the writer of fact. Beatrix Potter couldn't converse with ducks or mice, so she had to imagine what it would be like to be a duck or a mouse.

I've written stories myself that have been set in, say, Georgian London. I was born 200 years too late to have lived in Georgian London and to have known anyone who did. So I research. I get the historical facts right in terms of surroundings, social manners, dress, diet, language *et al* – in short, making sure my characters and the world they inhabit are as accurate as somebody living in the twenty-first century can possibly portray them. Graft contemporary mores onto the past and you end up with an invented ideal that says more about now than then. Hollywood does it all the time because America doesn't want to accept that many of its revered Founding Fathers were slave-owners.

The ludicrous 'outrage' a couple of weeks ago over a funny line in 'Coronation Street' provoked a silly storm in an even sillier teacup, whereby a reference to a character from 'Roots' was deemed to be racist. Considering the amount of black and gay characters in Weatherfield, there's a surprising absence of racism or homophobia from those who fall into neither camp. I would hazard a guess that the majority of those who were sufficiently outraged were white and probably of middle-class descent.

It's that familiar condescending middle-class white guilt which prompts such people to speak 'on behalf' of the perceived persecuted minority, which ironically makes them sound more colonial in their attitudes than those who don't take offence if a campus 'Mexican' night deigns that wearing a sombrero is crucial to the event. They feel compelled to appoint themselves as spokesmen and women, as though the minority in question are incapable of articulating any outrage themselves. A verbal pat on the head which says 'Don't worry, poor ignorant little coloured person; we can be your mouthpiece, what with you being denied our privileged education'. It's laughable.

I've cheered myself up of late by watching episodes of 'The Goodies'. Aside from the nostalgia factor and the surreal madcap humour which still makes me laugh, one element that really struck me was the freedom the trio had to poke fun at anyone and anything. A series that was unfairly regarded at the time as 'Python-Lite' today seems incredibly subversive. Indeed, it's hard to watch it now and not mentally note all the jokes that could no longer be made on television, let alone the piss-taking of celebrities we're not allowed to mention anymore, such as Rolf Harris, Clement Freud or Jimmy Savile. There's no what used to be called 'bad language' on any episode of 'The Goodies' whatsoever, yet whilst one can now swear to one's heart's content on TV comedy today, the field has narrowed beyond belief as to targets of jokes.

As regular readers will know, my sideline online identity as a purveyor of satirical and silly videos enables me to get away with things that television would no longer permit. Comments often say 'You should have your own TV show; you're funnier than anything currently on telly', which is immensely flattering, but also misses the point. I'm not on the telly because nobody would dare commission anything of a humorous nature that refuses to acknowledge the boundaries established that define what can and can't be laughed at. Well, sorry. I'm not prepared to defend myself or my work to people I neither respect nor recognise as creative peers. You either find it funny or you don't; and if you don't, I'm not especially bothered; go and watch 'Mrs Brown's Boys'.

Any unwritten rules when it comes to any artistic medium stinks of puritanical censorship and the policing of creativity by the non-creative. Sorry if I offend, but you can go f**k yourself. I'm not living under Stalin, the Stasi or the Spanish Inquisition, so your opinion carries no weight and has no authority.

NO COUNTRY FOR SQUARE PEGS
8 October 2016

When people speak of the Great British Eccentric being a dying breed, most of the examples given of the species do tend to be over a certain age – 50, at least. Granted, there are a few defiant exceptions (certainly in terms of dress, someone like Paloma Faith, perhaps), though the famous names that spring to mind are usually past their half-century. I think the claims of the species bordering on extinction aren't too far-fetched in that it's hard to foresee another generation spawning any. It isn't just the large-scale homogenisation of genuine individual thought and/or appearance within society that could be held responsible, nor the fact that every suspected 'Paedo' exposed by the press is painted as 'a bit weird' because he doesn't adhere to an imposed dress-code (thus marking out sartorial originality as totally toxic); but when any potential eccentricities surface in children today parents, teachers and doctors alike are a tad too quick to diagnose a 'syndrome'.

You may or may not have heard of Oppositional Defiance Disorder, but that is the tag that has now been attached to children who misbehave – yes, fancy that! Children misbehaving and refusing to do as they're told! What an uncharacteristic behavioural trait! Children doing what children have always done can no longer be just that; there has to be a medical condition to cover all eventualities that can be tamed with both medication and counselling.

The feminisation of our leading institutions, along with the box-ticking bureaucracy that negates common sense, seems determined to prevent little boys in particular from being little boys. There is also the plethora of self-help 'how to be a perfect parent' publications, an entire literary industry that has had a pernicious influence on the attitude towards children and remains in perpetual denial of the fact that some of them are strange little bastards.

Ever since the recognition of dyslexia as something to be distinguished from basic stupidity, there has been a conscious rush to judgement on classic childhood symptoms that veer from the desired ordinariness that is a by-product of perfection. All the numerous minor strands of autism are examples of this, and Attention Deficit Hyperactivity Disorder is another that has now become utterly accepted as a bona-fide syndrome, a condition that is hastily diagnosed and in many cases treated with a course of medication. In recent years, the transgender issue has also reared its head, especially amongst right-on parents who seize upon any indication of effeminacy in their little boy as a sign his 'true' sexuality must be determined by them before he's even hit puberty.

The dangerous fad for labelling every aspect of a child's natural behaviour a syndrome is a panicky response when so many are afraid of standing out from the crowd and expressing any notion of individuality that contradicts the consensus. The ghastly competitiveness of parents that rests on one-upmanship faces a severe threat if their little angel is exhibiting any signs of being 'different', so a convenient pigeonhole that is accepted as a syndrome by the teaching and medical profession is an easy solution to a problem that doesn't actually exist.

Like most of us, I grew up around many children who displayed personal eccentricities that would now probably have a ready-made diagnosis on hand. One girl I was at primary school with used to bite her toenails. I wonder what that would be categorised as today? Keratin Carnivore Disorder? And I suspect we all knew one or two who would eat their own bogies. Mucus Consumption Disorder? Keeping children on a tight leash and denying them the freedom to express themselves through the kind of behaviour adults aren't able to get away with is a modern trend that only has a few caveats, such as when it comes to 'artistic' expression – which basically amounts to those bloody awful pictures proud parents stick on their fridges as a sign of what creative geniuses they've spawned.

But genuine creativity often goes hand-in-hand with unconventional outlooks and attitudes that are commonplace amongst children and rare amongst adults; the adults that retain them are ones that resisted having them drilled out by the educational system. It must be harder than ever to uphold such resistance and be a little Winston Smith today, however.

Not only does one have to risk being diagnosed with a syndrome and being forcibly drugged to wash the nasty thoughts away, but there is also the league table-obsessed educational system itself, which like all institutions – whether the NHS, DWP, police force or legal profession – has become a training camp for the appliance of politically-correct robotic responses in which impromptu personal judgment not listed in the script has no place. The fear of litigation or ostracism enables such Orwellian Ministry systems to flourish unimpeded by common sense and ideas that risk being labelled that most dreaded of contemporary ailments, eccentric.

That each new crop of recruits to these institutions now instinctively follow the rulebook to the letter of the law (and probably had early resistance suppressed by a syndrome diagnosis and accompanying medication) means the likelihood of the Circumlocution Offices the institutions have gradually evolved into ever reverting to what they were before virtually zilch. Anyone at the frontline of having to deal with said institutions will know what an uphill struggle it is to make representatives of them understand that everything they've had programmed into them is counterproductive to an actual result. Add the inherent conservatism of social media as a further tool for falling into line and it would seem any future eccentrics that are lucky enough to slip through the net will be few and far between. And our society will be all the poorer for their absence.

CARRY ON UP THE AMAZON
24 October 2016

Anyone who watched 'The Day Today', 'Brass Eye' or even the more obscure 'Jam' several years ago may have wondered of late where Chris Morris is. After his involvement in the prophetic 'Nathan Barley' and suicide bomber comedy 'Four Lions', he seems to have been inactive; not true, of course. I suspect he's currently the criminal mastermind behind the world we live in, creator of comic characters as wide-ranging as Ed Miliband and Boris Johnson, and perhaps his greatest work of fiction, Donald Trump. He also scripted the long-running saga of Samsung's exploding mobiles and the recent clown craze, and was even making his mark at the United Nations last week by pulling off a magnificently mischievous conceptual art stunt in persuading that august institution to make a comic-book superhero an ambassador.

Okay, so there's no evidence Mr Morris was involved, but surely he had to be, right? Wonder Woman belongs to the same DC universe as Superman, Batman, The Flash and The Green Lantern – in other words, she exists only when an artist draws her. *She's not real.* She was played on the small screen by Lynda Carter in the 70s and will shortly be portrayed by another actress on the big screen as the Wonder Woman character is added to the never-ending superhero cinema franchise. Yet, the key point is that neither Lynda Carter nor the weirdly-named Gal Gadot has been nominated as a UN Ambassador, whereas the character they've played has. Imagine Sherlock Holmes being given a peerage. Granted, probably more deserving than most recipients, but that's the ball-park of unreality we're in.

For all the Nobel Prize Committee's whinging about Bob Dylan's silence on winning the literature gong, Bob's failure to fly down to Stockholm and collect his award was probably to be expected, knowing the kind of erratic and unpredictable individual he is; but the UN will be waiting forever if it expects Wonder Woman to take up her ambassadorial role for the simple reason that she doesn't actually exist.

The official title that the creation of William Moulton Marston and his wife Elizabeth has had bestowed upon her by the UN is that of 'honorary ambassador for the empowerment of women and girls'; giving that role to a fictitious character suggests either the UN doesn't regard it as an important task or that an organisation formed to be the ultimate arbitration service between warring nations has been reduced to a subservient marketing tool for the forthcoming Wonder Woman movie.

Wonder Woman will be used to promote women's rights and gender equality, apparently; this is one of the UN's 'sustainable development goals'. The UN's Under-Secretary General for Communications and Public Information (yes, unlike Female Superhero, that really *is* a job title), Cristina Gallach, was quoted as saying 'Gender equality is a fundamental human right and a foundation for a peaceful, prosperous and sustainable world.' And the way to achieve it is to hire a cartoon woman with the vital statistics of a young Pamela Anderson, who walks around in nothing more than a bodice, skin-tight knickers and knee-high boots. The UN couldn't have scored a greater own-goal if it had borrowed a couple of bunny-girls from the Playboy Mansion.

The initial early 40s creation of Wonder Woman by a prominent psychologist and his missus, both of whom were involved in a polyamorous relationship with the same woman, was supposed to introduce an emancipated feminist heroine into the men-only club of superheroes; in that respect, their creation was genuinely groundbreaking, especially when the best a female character in a comic-book could hope for at that time was to be the Lois Lane girlfriend figure. But the character has developed such ridiculously perfect physical proportions over the decades (mirroring the similar transformation of her male counterparts) that for her to make the transition to the movies an actress probably has to submit herself to the kind of intense daily work-out regime beyond the budget and available leisure time of most girls who will see the film. She is as unattainable a physical ideal as Barbie, and this is one of the more prominent objections to her adoption by the UN - once the fact she doesn't exist is put to one side, that is.

An in-house petition by UN staff protesting against the decision cites this aspect, claiming 'It is alarming that the United Nations would consider using a character with an overtly sexualised image at a time when the headline news in the United States and the world is the objectification of women and girls.' Some of those behind the petition turned their backs on the ceremony (attended by Lynda Carter) announcing Wonder Woman's appointment, and there was a predictable storm on social media decrying the decision, coming as it did in the aftermath of the latest 'Trump tape' revelations.

If the aim is to move away from the common media and advertising image of a woman's sole role outside of motherhood as being a desirable sex symbol, a character whose visual appearance embodies the latter certainly seems a strange choice. But for me it is the simple fact that the UN opted for a fictional character rather than a living breathing human being that remains the oddest element of this whole PR disaster. Then again, at least they recruited Wonder Woman rather than that other fictional character and parody of feminine assets, one who doesn't even possess any super-powers, Kim Kardashian.

EVERY BELITTLE HELPS
5 January 2017

Long-term followers of my 'oeuvre' may recall a weekly YouTube series of mine that spanned a year from the spring of 2014 to 2015; called '25 Hour News', it parodied rolling news channels by presenting a satirical spin on the headlines of the preceding seven days. Although most episodes have

175

since been deleted on account of their irrelevance to the here and now (not to mention a few 'copyright' issues), there are still a small handful of specials available, including my takes on both the Scottish Independence Referendum and the 2015 General Election as well as a compilation review of 2014. Revelling in freedom from the permanently anxious censorship committees that police the potential for offence re most television comedies these days, I viewed everyone as fair game for having the urine extracted from them.

At the time when ISIS decided American journalists would function better by having their heads removed, I recall concocting a spoof on a certain 70s game show called 'Muhammad Forsyth and the Decapitation Game'; I only put together the opening titles and a description of what the programme consisted and that was that – job done. The audience was in the thousands rather than the millions, so I didn't have to respond to the kind of ludicrous Twitter outrage that this week greeted a rare comedy parody of our friends in the Middle East.

The blurb in the Radio Times accompanying the new BBC2 series 'Revolting' painted it as a hidden prank show, to which my reaction was 'just what the world needs – a hipster Beadle's About'; it wasn't until the online serial offence-takers kicked up a fuss yesterday over a sketch from the show spoofing those horrific reality TV 'rich wives' programmes that I realised the series apparently amounted to more than a 'Candid Camera' for the Instagram generation.

The skit in question was called 'Real Housewives of ISIS' and was, I thought, a pretty funny piss-take of both a nauseating television genre and the equally nauseating principles of those stupid enough to seek salvation by selling themselves into Jihadi slavery. Lest we forget, British Muslim women who have made the journey from the UK to Syria haven't been kidnapped; they volunteered. And if they're dumb enough to fall for the ISIS PR, they're worthy of ridicule, as is the organisation nobody forced them to join. Considering the absence of sensitivity to non-believers and infidels that the ISIS philosophy promotes, why should anyone spare them the deserved scythe of satire? According to the ISIS apologists on the left, however (those for whom Israel is the only Middle Eastern nation that has blood on its hands), this sketch was beyond the pale.

'Real Housewives of ISIS? Wow, the BBC got some explaining to do'; 'The Real Housewives of ISIS is so distasteful. Lowest of the low from BBC2'; 'Sick, you are truly sick in the head and morally bankrupt' – just a small selection of the Twitter comments that followed the programme's broadcast. I suppose the 'morally bankrupt' accusation is the one that stands out; morally bankrupt by taking the piss as opposed to the unimpeachable morality of the suicide bomber? One can't help but think that the same voices would probably have reacted in similar fashion to 'The Great Dictator' had Twitter existed in 1940. 'Chaplin, you are morally bankrupt 4 attacking Nazis and Hitler'!

To be fair, Chaplin himself later admitted that had he known of the Final Solution when he made 'The Great Dictator', he wouldn't have poked fun at Adolf in quite the same way, but by making a movie satirising Hitler in the US at a time when America had yet to enter the Second World War, he was putting himself out on something of a limb. The great exodus of European Jews from the continental film industry to Hollywood bore fruit for American cinema in the years to come, but the stories they told upon arrival were ones Chaplin absorbed when formulating the concept of 'The Great Dictator'; he'd also viewed Leni Riefenstahl's grandiose Nazi propaganda movie, 'Triumph of the Will', and had apparently found it unintentionally hilarious. The end result of these influences was one of the first comedic takes on Hitler and the Nazis, but not the last; as the conflict escalated, Chaplin was hardly alone in mocking the Führer.

Cartoons and comics aimed at children were crammed with humorous interpretations of Hitler and Mussolini throughout the war years; wartime strips in The Dandy and The Beano included 'Addie and Hermy, the Nasty Nazis' (Hitler and Goering reborn as archetypal DC Thompson dimwits) and 'Musso the Wop (He's A Big-A-Da-Flop)'. It's an age-old truism that one way an enemy can be belittled by those not in a position to take them on with force is to laugh at them; just look at James Gillray's caricatures of Napoleon in the early nineteenth century, whereby the physically inaccurate portrayal of Bonaparte as a short-arse *literally* belittled him and established the myth of the French Emperor's size that still lingers. I wouldn't go so far as to say this image contributed towards Napoleon's eventual overthrow, but it definitely served to make him less of a bogeyman in the popular imagination and defused the fear of him that he undoubtedly drew strength from.

It's a measure of how effective the PC intelligentsia have been in dictating to TV companies what we can and can't laugh at that something such as the 'Real Housewives of ISIS' sketch is seen as outrageous. A fashionably dismissed comedy from the 70s like 'The Goodies' had a dig at Apartheid in an episode simply called 'South Africa', one scene of which features a spoof travel ad for the country wherein the Black & White Minstrels act as salesmen for the system that had its fair share of appeasers in Europe at the time. It all sounds very radical and daring by today's standards, but this was a pre-watershed mainstream series that was even regarded as lightweight back then.

There are so many aspects of contemporary life that often seem more like parody than the real thing, and I sometimes think the architect of the present day's culture is not some great political thinker, but Chris Morris. And, as the old adage goes, if you don't laugh, you'll cry. Laughter is an essential salvation at times like these, and the BBC should actually be applauded for allowing 'Real Housewives of ISIS' to air; they've nothing to defend or apologise for.

SHE WHO MUST BE OBEYED
6 March 2017

First it was Germaine Greer, now it's Jenni Murray. Their crime? Daring to voice an opinion that contradicts the doctrine of the new order consensus, specifically the clause that declares we must never question the authenticity of men who have undergone gender reassignment surgery and must automatically place them in the same category as women who were born with full female anatomy. And this despite the fact many Trans-Women invite such distinctions. No doubt the po-faced funereal spectre of Professional Northern Trans-Woman Paris Lees will be prompted into one of her regular 'Channel 4 News' or 'Newsnight' comedy turns in response, hurling the 'old bigot' slingshot at the latest target.

The veteran 'Woman's Hour' presenter who has provided the serial offence-takers with a new hate figure is 66 years-old; Germaine Greer is 78. Unlike their hysterical detractors, both women were born into a world that had clearly defined boundaries based on class, race, sexuality and gender; and Greer in particular played a hugely significant part in changing the perceptions of those boundaries where gender was concerned, far greater than her twenty-something critics could ever imagine. She and Murray have been witness to arguably the most revolutionary breaking down of those boundaries that the western world has ever experienced; and it has happened in the space of barely half-a-century.

More than one generation has had to overturn all its inherited beliefs and opinions on society's so-called 'minorities'; and this takes the kind of time that those born into a world where the contemporary consensus holds sway have no comprehension of. To use just one personal example, I recall my mother expressing her embarrassment when my deaf granddad (her father) used the word 'nigger' loudly in a supermarket, yet she herself still uses the word 'paki', which makes me wince every time she says it. That she could find 'nigger' unacceptable whilst simultaneously not thinking the same of 'paki' highlights how her own inherited beliefs and opinions have changed, albeit not quite reaching the acceptable standard demanded by the speech police.

Expecting the grandparent generation to mirror the approach to what can and can't be said in either public or private discourse as practiced by their grandchildren is not that different from expecting them to have unnaturally coloured hair, piercings and tattoos. The under-40s blame game from the losing side in the EU Referendum, reserving Remoaner vitriol for pensioners who had the audacity to hold a different point of view, largely based on life experience and a wider knowledge of the lengthy European project rather than 'racism', was a telling demonstration of that generation's narcissistic refusal to accept there are contrary opinions to their own; and this extends into other facets of life in which their inability to respond to these contrary opinions with nothing more than lazy labelling is revealing a worrying absence of emotional maturity.

If a trans-woman wants to be recognised and accepted as a 'real' woman, why is there the need for the 'trans' prefix? One is either a trans-woman or a woman; one cannot be both, surely? It's almost as though some want the benefits each can bring – acceptance as belonging to the sisterhood yet also requiring 'special treatment' that a natural-born woman is exempt from. Here's your cake, and you can eat it too! I've met a couple of women in my life who were born male, and I wouldn't have known if I hadn't been told. To me, both resembled middle-aged Avon Ladies and they seemed happy in their skins, which is great; they weren't declaring to all and sundry that they were spokeswomen for the LGBTRSVPABCXYZ community and demanding to be treated as a Third Sex.

The majority of men who have endured male-to-female surgery do so because they genuinely believe themselves to be women trapped in men's bodies; therefore, once they re-emerge from hospital, their bodies are finally in-synch with what their heads have always held to be true and they are, to all extents and purposes, now bona-fide women. Yes, they have no menstrual cycle and cannot get pregnant, but other than that, there's little to distinguish them from women whose bodies were compatible from day one.

I don't believe the constant carping from militant Trans-Women or those professing to speak on their behalf really has anything to do with gender identity, more another example of the contemporary craving to sign-up to an officially designated minority, to uphold the trend for comfortable pigeonholing and membership of a 'victimised' collective that can gather together and share placards.

The original 70s Gay Liberation movement in the US often saw conflicts between those who preferred the traditional masculine male role model and those who revelled in their feminine side; the latter was seen as 'letting the team down' by camping it up and aping the flamboyant vanity and cartoon frivolity of girlie girls, thus reinforcing the archaic effeminate stereotype. But there was still room for both in the battle for acceptance. Today, any prominent gay media man, whether Stephen Fry or Peter Tatchell, faces the threat of the no-platform treatment if they dare to say anything that shatters the facade of everyone being in it together. Ridiculously, they can be labelled 'homophobic' just as Germaine Greer can be labelled 'misogynistic'.

Virtually all of the men or women who have been targeted by the speech police in the last couple of years have been over-45 at least, and most were on the frontline of the actual battles that obliterated the old boundaries, something their wet-behind-the-ears opponents have benefitted from. More was achieved by 'The Female Eunuch' than mixed-gender lavatories, so it's time the kiddies cut their predecessors some slack and stopped trying to impose their own rigid framework on generations that were far more fluid and broad-minded when it came to sexuality and whether or not their own predecessors agreed with them.

AFFIRMATIVE ACTION HEROES
6 April 2017

1966 was a landmark year in the history of the American comic book; it saw the introduction of the first regular black superhero to the roll-call of hip Pop Art icons. It's worth bearing in mind that The Black Panther debuted in the pages of Marvel's 'The Fantastic Four' several months before the formation of the actual Black Panther militant civil rights group, so there can be no accusations of cashing-in on the part of the character's creators, legendary double act Stan Lee and

Jack Kirby. Further additions to the 'ethnic minority' league of superheroes came in the early 1970s, with the likes of The Falcon and Luke Cage, Power Man; the latter was a blatant attempt to capitalise on Hollywood's 'Blaxploitation' era, though as a 70s child randomly picking up imported US Marvel comics, the skin colour of said superheroes wasn't an issue; all that mattered to me then was whether or not the stories and (especially) the artwork were worth shelling out 6p for.

A lot has changed in forty years. Ever since the Marvel Corporation was purchased by the Disney Corporation, Marvel is not so much seen by the general public as a comic book business than as the source material for an ongoing motion picture franchise. The need to appeal to the movie industry's imposed diversity agenda has seen Marvel's line-up undergo the kind of severe PC surgery in recent months that smacks of pure tokenism rather than a natural reflection of the changing American idea of what constitutes a 'hero'.

Not so long ago, Spider-Man's secret identity was redesigned as that of a mixed-race adolescent; Ms Marvel – one of Marvel's second division characters – was remodelled as a Pakistani immigrant for no reason other than a presumed need to tick a few politically-correct boxes; Norse God Thor received a sex-change during the same period, as did Iron Man, when millionaire playboy-cum-scientist Tony Stark made way for (in the words of Bonnie Greer) an *African-American* woman. The comic branch of Marvel seems to have bowed to external pressures and thrust the 'ethnic' members of its universe into the limelight whilst its movies continue to boast a largely white cast appealing to a largely white audience. No wonder its sales have plummeted.

In 2014, 9 out of 10 of the best-selling comic book titles were produced by Marvel; last year, following the aforementioned revamps, it could only claim 3 out of 10. Between 2015 and the beginning of this year, Marvel launched a ridiculous 104 new titles, with a quarter of them being resounding flops. It would appear the department upon which the entire Marvel industry was built is currently being run by right-on headless chickens responding to a perceived need for a narrow definition of diversity, without any real clue as to what it is that makes the superhero genre work. Even a Senior Marvel Executive, David Gabriel, has admitted as much, though was predictably forced to retract his honest observation when it received the usual howling accusations of racism.

From its 1930s beginnings, the superhero as a character was a square-jawed strongman clad in the skin-tight costume then more commonly associated with circus entertainers. He was a one-dimensional figure without any trace of an internal life because he had one simple function that didn't require much in the way of existential analysis – to fight crime. All the superheroes that sprang from what comic book historians refer to as 'The Golden Age' – Superman, Batman, Captain America, Captain Marvel *et al* – adhered to this successful formula. Wonder Woman was a novel deviation from the norm, but what essentially made her different was her sex; other than that, she was cut from the same cloth as her male counterparts.

It was only when Marvel rebranded itself as a major challenger to the dominance of DC via the launch of 'The Fantastic Four' in 1961 that the superhero acquired a level of realism he had never previously possessed. Stan Lee and Jack Kirby put together their crime-fighting team with unique human failings at a point when the superhero medium was emerging from a lull in which it had been superseded by romance, crime and horror genres. The latter had sparked a moral panic on both sides of the Atlantic akin to the 'Video Nasty' scare of the early 80s; the violence in comics was also linked to juvenile delinquency, leading to the introduction of the censorious Comics Code Authority. Superheroes suddenly seemed a safe option again.

Marvel's revolutionary redrawing of the boundaries of the genre included giving the bespectacled target of high-school bullies the ability to climb walls and spin webs. Poor Peter Parker always lost the girls to the jocks – probably like the majority of the Marvel readers – and this relatable factor was crucial; who could relate to Bruce Wayne, after all? But Parker's new identity as Spider-Man came at a price; initially a TV star showing off his superpowers, he declines to intervene in a robbery, only for the criminal in question to then kill his uncle. This twist, which saddles Parker with intense guilt, provokes him into fighting crime thereafter. There had never been that kind of mature storytelling in superhero comics before.

Marvel's phenomenal success in the 60s – and its extensive college-age readership – gave DC a kick up the arse, leading them to exploit the latent dark side of Bat Man and making him a far more interesting character in the process. The introduction of The Black Panther was a natural progression; Marvel were already reflecting the culture of the times, so a black superhero was an inevitable development rather than the knee-jerk response to a demand for diversity. By comparison, the recent rush to cobble together a line-up of PC-friendly superheroes feels like the decision of a focus group, characters created by committee; and the readership know this, which is why they've rejected them. Once again, the few are dictating their agenda to the many, and the end result is a disaster.

OVER THE RAINBOW
7 August 2017

Amidst the celebratory coverage of the 1967 Sexual Offences Act's fiftieth anniversary, it is certainly worth being reminded precisely how limiting the freedoms contained within the 'consenting adults in private' law actually were, and how these limitations made it easily open to abuse by the powers-that-be. After the Act was passed, it's surprising to realise that more gay men were prosecuted than before it. Perhaps the understandable precautions that had been crucial prior to 1967 were perceived to be unnecessary once decriminalisation came into force; the illusion of legality blinded many to the numerous areas in which homosexuality remained criminal; it also forced the police and politicians to focus on those areas with renewed crusading vigour in the years thereafter.

A timely reminder of this uncomfortable truth came via Peter Tatchell's excellent and eye (or ear)-opening Radio 4 documentary, 'The Myth of Homosexual Decriminalisation', broadcast on Saturday evening; it documented how 1967 was not so much an end as a beginning, the start of the long road to abolishing discrimination, altering attitudes and achieving an equal age of consent with heterosexuals – none of which were dealt with in the imperfect Act that came into being half-a-century ago.

Scotland, Northern Ireland, the armed forces and the merchant navy – all exempt from decriminalisation in 1967; much anti-homosexual legislation remained on the statue book for decades after 1967 and queer-bashing was a legitimate police pastime well into the 1980s. For out and proud young men today, barely old enough to even remember the last century, all of this must seem insane. The prejudices openly unleashed upon gay men and largely unchallenged by the majority of society combined with the AIDS hysteria (AKA 'The Gay Plague') and Clause 28 to create a climate of moral panic that would unthinkable to anyone under, say, 30 in 2017. Perhaps the inability to comprehend how we used to live has played its part in a lack of perspective where those too young to remember are concerned.

The sins of their forefathers for allowing this state of affairs to linger for so long without challenge has undoubtedly fuelled a militant bullishness amongst the young; this reaction demands the law and society in general adopt the consensus they've developed to serve as a severe redress to the past. It comes partly from retrospective guilt and is not unlike America's similar response to historical racism via the slave trade and segregation. At its most extreme, the new consensus is imposed with the same level of illogical fanaticism once employed by those who upheld and endorsed the previous prejudices this consensus reacts against, portraying anyone who is white as inherently racist and anyone who is heterosexual as inherently homophobic.

But the ironic outcome can often seem like less of a striving for genuine equality between the different sexual demographics – which is surely what should be aimed for – and more of a determined campaign to ensure the poacher is elevated to gamekeeper and vice-versa. The new consensus cannot alter the past, but the slightest sign of any attitude bearing a passing resemblance to the past – however mild in comparison – dumps the wrongs of the past on the doorstep of the present. The 'gay cake' saga in Northern Ireland a couple of years ago seemed indicative of this mindset; a refusal to countenance that there are many out there for whom homosexuality remains a difficult concept has created a climate of intolerance that excludes debate. If you don't embrace this consensus, you are a homophobic bigot – end of.

'Inclusivity' does not include those who deviate from the script.

The clamour to be seen as endorsing the consensus by political parties and other establishment organisations that maybe weren't viewed as so gay-friendly in the past resulted in the virtue signalling of the National Trust edict stating volunteers dealing with the public at Norfolk's Felbrigg Hall (whose last resident, Robert Wyndham Ketton-Cremer was recently posthumously 'outed') must wear rainbow gay pride badges. Those who weren't comfortable with wearing them were to be relegated to the backrooms of the property. The case was taken up by certain Fleet Street tabloids and predictably labelled a right-wing *cause célèbre* by the likes of the Grauniad; but the sudden reversal of the edict so that wearing the badges is now optional rather than compulsory seems a more sensible compromise that recognises inclusivity should mean what it says.

Many of the archive recordings of attitudes towards homosexuality excavated for Peter Tatchell's Radio 4 retrospective were as gobsmacking to hear as similar excerpts of unashamedly racist language from the same era; but whilst these attitudes survive on a smaller scale in private, the cheerleaders for our liberated society still turn a blind eye to one publically vocal section of it. Some of the vilest and most bigoted opinions on homosexuality expressed today emanate from Islam, yet the ultra-liberal left gives Islam the kind of leeway it won't tolerate in any other faith, let alone secular discourse. Why? Perhaps it's due to the fact that Muslims have been designated the left's persecuted pets; they are above and beyond the kind of criticism others are fair game for.

Of course, not every Muslim is virulently anti-gay any more than every Christian or every person without any religion whatsoever; I think most people aren't really that bothered, to be honest. It's just a shame the person who retains a problem with the notion of homosexuality – usually down to simple ignorance and lack of education – is lumped in with the genuinely homophobic in a rainbow that has no shades of grey.

FAMILY ENTERTAINMENT
12 August 2017

As with the two Peters, Hitchens and Oborne, Paul Joseph Watson is not a media figure whose every pronouncement provokes a nod of the head, yet as with those aforementioned grumpy grandees of Fleet Street, he often nails the ludicrousness of the world we live in simply by daring to challenge it. An unapologetic ambassador of the so-called 'Alt Right', Watson is the face of the UK branch of 'Info Wars', the US conspiracy theorist site fronted by the ranting human foghorn Alex Jones. Watson doesn't adopt the breathless bluster of his American sponsor; adopting that approach for a British audience would reduce him to the level of Jeremy Clarkson. Instead, he sometimes comes across as Owen Jones through the looking-glass, the flipside mirror image of the pocket Northern Socialist.

Watson has posted a series of regular videos on YouTube over the past couple of years, both highlighting and ridiculing the increasingly fatuous fanaticism of the extreme left's PC storm-troopers, especially on the other side of the Atlantic; as a result, he's made as many enemies as fans, and while one may not always concur with his conclusions, there's no doubt he's highlighted a lot of things that needed highlighting. Until now, that is.

Watson has temporarily drawn the blinds on his YouTube window due to the fact that he can no longer make a living from it thanks to a new Star Chamber of YouTube judges, installed by parent company Google to police the medium and crack down on any questioning of the consensus. Many may be unaware that 'monetising' one's uploads to YT can bring in a little revenue depending on the number of views the videos receive; Watson's videos received astronomical views and no doubt brought in a nice little profit on a monthly basis. However, the crackdown on anyone saying anything that could be perceived as 'offensive' means all of Watson's videos have now been deemed 'not advertiser-friendly', thus meaning he can't make a penny from them anymore.

I've written on more than one occasion in the past of the transformation of YouTube in recent years. What was initially an invaluable platform for, amongst others, lovers of archive footage unavailable on DVD and rarely screened on TV – often uploaded from decrepit off-air VHS recordings or sourced from actual television vaults by insiders – has slowly seen passionate promoters of the rare and obscure edged to one side by The Man and his corporate bullyboys. Copyright laws have been tightened to the point whereby every piece of film not actually shot on one's own camera is subjected to a 'third party infringement' order, regardless of how minimal its use may be. I once had a video stamped with copyright claims simply because I used the BBC4 ident for a handful of seconds as the intro to it.

This OTT enforcement of copyright has made navigating such rules something of an art-form for veteran uploaders, but perhaps responding to criticisms of alleged lax attitudes to 'hate' videos, YouTube has now embarked upon a censorious crusade in which any video that doesn't promote the Coca-Cola ideal of a harmonious multicultural/LGBT/Islam-with-asmiley-face society is penalised; anyone who takes the piss out of or merely questions this bland make-believe Utopia is denied an income as a consequence. People regularly air their grievances with the BBC as pandering to a left-leaning notion of 'Right-On' politics – often justified, viz. the hardly unbiased four-person panel of prominent Muslims discussing the latest Pakistani grooming network on 'Newsnight' this week; but YouTube has suddenly usurped Auntie Beeb as an intolerant home for one view and one view only.

Infuriatingly vacuous American airheads who call themselves 'vloggers' – usually squeaky-voiced teenage Disney Princess types who exude the air of hyperactive six-year-olds albeit bereft of infantile charm – make millions from their vapid videos that appeal to a generation whose heads have already been ground to slurry by being force-fed media sedatives; and these are the future of YouTube, not anybody with anything to say. My own personal speciality area tends to be satire, but satire is now as welcome on YouTube as a copy of Charlie Hebdo would be in a Parisian mosque.

A couple of days ago, the new YouTube constabulary provided me with a long list of my videos their panel has decided I can no longer make any money from. To be honest, I don't make much, anyway – around £120 a year; I have a loyal following who will view my output whatever I upload and I also pick up casual viewers en route, but I'm a cult presence and probably always will be. I accept that some of my output is coarse in the Derek & Clive tradition, but YT already had an age-restriction system in place where rude words were concerned, so anybody stumbling upon them knew what to expect beforehand.

None of the previous rules in place to protect a 'family audience' were apparently sufficient, however, for the strict new boundaries have narrowed the range of opinions on offer even further. Many of my own videos parody the politically-incorrect 1970s and therefore need to be viewed with that in mind, yet the humourless martinets Google has recruited to clean-up YouTube's lingering vestiges of its original freewheeling spirit can't even tolerate that. One particular video of mine was a spoof 70s BBC trailer previewing a night of programmes marking 'National Smoking Day'; it's so obviously a piss-take, yet it's been labelled 'not advertiser friendly'. Despite infringing no copyright, I can't earn anything from it anymore. But it's 2017. Sign up to the consensus or be cast out into the online free-speech wilderness.

DR. DIVERSITY'S CASEBOOK
15 October 2017

Although I haven't broadcasted it on here before, around two months ago I belatedly bowed to financial pressures and switched from smoking to vaping. My opinions on the rights of, and discrimination against, smokers haven't altered; the decision wasn't anything to do with me meekly surrendering to the fanatical anti-tobacco lobby, an admission that they were right and I was wrong all along; the simple fact is I couldn't afford it anymore. The rising cost of a packet of fags - £10.50 for 20, last time I looked – hasn't been in line with the price of everything else for a long time. The fact that, depending in which supermarket you shop, you can buy three bottles of wine for the same price as 20 cigarettes will cost you speaks volumes; and the drain on my finances was too much to sustain, so I stubbed out my final fag in August.

It helped that I instantly liked vaping and, as if to emphasise this, I still have a packet of Superkings containing four remaining fags that hasn't been touched since the day I received my first e-cigarette; after almost 30 years of smoking between 30-40 cigs a day, I suppose that's not bad going, and I can honestly say I don't miss it at all. If the buzz from the drag is the key hook of the smoking process, I can get just the same nicotine hit from vaping and replicate the former gesture at a fraction of the cost. The vapours don't linger in the room, they don't discolour the fixtures and fittings, they don't coat my clothes in a permanent odour, and they don't dissuade non-smoking visitors anymore.

Immunity to the smell of cigarettes was a consequence of smoking them; only since I stopped have I become aware of it. It's still entombed in my wardrobe because there are a lot of items on the coat-hangers there that haven't been washed or worn since I ceased; but it's amazing how strong the smell is on others now. When out and about, I can detect a cig from quite a distance, long before I see someone smoking it; and it's remarkable how everyone I see with a fag hanging out of their mouth seems to be the most slovenly, scruffy slob imaginable; the archaic images of Marlene Dietrich or Lauren Bacall using cigarettes as a crucial element of their effortlessly cool personas aren't being matched by the smokers I'm seeing. By contrast, the e-cigarette is a rather sexy, stylish object and, frankly, superior in all respects.

Not that the proven health (and financial) benefits of vaping deter the tobacco prohibitionists, who see it not as an escape route from smoking but as a gateway to the practice, the fools; the same limitations on ordinary cigarettes have been unfairly superimposed onto the e-cigarette, and I'm wondering when I'll encounter opposition to it from the medical profession. I say this because the first time I remember being singled out by a GP for smoking was in the early 90s. I can't remember the reason for being at the surgery, but I recall the doctor asking me if I smoked; when he received a reply in the affirmative, he placed a little sticker on the front of my file, which he presumably did for all smokers. Perhaps afterwards my file was slotted in a drawer along with the rest of his smoking patients, segregated from the non-smokers and downgraded in the case of an emergency when a choice might have to be made between the two groups.

Back then, it felt like a bit of an intrusion into my privacy, though smoking as heavily as I did was obviously a health risk, and I can understand to an extent that it would probably be in a GP's remit to hint at what I already knew – i.e. smoking wasn't good for me. What if it went further than that, though, into private areas that (unless the visit to the surgery was related to one's 'rude bits') have no relation to one's health in the same way? New NHS guidelines apparently imminent mean that health professionals will now be obliged to ask patients over-16 what their sexual orientation happens to be. It's both a further extension of the nanny state's nosy neighbour tendencies and the latest chapter in the ongoing 'diversity' agenda that has swept through every public body of late to seemingly appease a very small section of society with a very loud voice.

Doctors and nurses will now be recommended to inquire as to a patient's sexual orientation at 'every face-to-face contact with the patient, where no record of this data already exists'; what is horribly referred to as 'sexual monitoring' will be mandatory in England and Wales by 2019. Patients will be asked 'Which of the following options best describes how you think of yourself – straight/gay or lesbian/bisexual/other sexual orientation'; presumably, the 'other' is paedophile or zoophile? Might I suggest an additional response on the part of the patient – 'Mind your own f**king business'.

Thankfully, Dr Peter Swinyard, Chairman of the Family Doctor Association, was not impressed; in his opinion, the new guidelines were 'potentially intrusive and offensive', adding 'Given the precious short amount of time a GP has with a patient, sexuality is not relevant', rightly pointing out that sexual choice affected 'relatively few medical conditions'. On the other hand, Paul Martin, chief executive of Manchester's LGBT Foundation, says he is 'so proud' of the intrusion into patient's private lives. His organisation has pushed for 'sexual monitoring', as it views the change as some kind of step forward to address perceived medical inequalities for those happy to be defined by the LGBT pigeonhole. Those patients who don't want to disclose their sexual preferences – and why indeed should they? – will be placed in the 'not stated' category.

This compliance with the Equality Act 2010 by the medical profession is allegedly intended to ensure no patient is discriminated against; but if someone's sexuality *isn't* advertised on their file, no rush to judgement based upon it by a doctor who might hold prejudicial views can then be made – and doesn't *that* make all patients equal? A doctor's role is to treat whatever is wrong with the patient; a doctor doesn't need further unnecessary data that bears no relation to the patient's presence in their surgery - unless the patient smokes or vapes, of course; and then they deserve all the stickers their files can handle.

ALAS, POOR LAVINIA
19 October 2017

It's easy to forget now, but there was a time in the middle of the 1980s when all the artistic gains made in the name of 60s and 70s libertinism seemed in peril; we were on the cusp of a potential rewind back to the censorious era of the Lord

Chamberlain's Office and the Hays Code. Channel 4, which has made its early 80s name as a fearless purveyor of 'anything goes in the name of Art', was a frontrunner in this sudden and abrupt reversal of attitudes when it introduced its red triangle season of films circa 1986. These were movies that nowadays wouldn't (or shouldn't) provoke outrage, but at the time appeared shocking even by the easygoing standards of a TV station that had promoted the brief usage of an expletive such as 'frigging' in a primetime soap opera ('Brookside'). The fact that characters on soaps are generally the only people in Britain who never swear was something 'Brookside' momentarily challenged until it became as blandly unrealistic as the rest of them.

Channel 4's red triangle season featured TV premieres for the likes of Derek Jarman's Romanesque gay fantasy, 'Sebastiane', as well as Dennis Hopper's 'Out of the Blue'; for those who weren't around, the red triangle in question would be a permanent fixture in the top left of the TV screen whilst the movie aired, which allegedly served as an early warning system for the unsuspecting viewer who might switch over from something less contentious on ITV or BBC1. Most of the films screened as part of the short-lived season weren't that different in content from what had already been shown on Channel 4 – it had premiered the infamous Sex Pistols movie, 'The Great Rock 'n' Roll Swindle', in 1985, for example; but the bizarre season can be seen in retrospect as a concession to the great moral backlash of the late Thatcher era, which also included Clause 28.

Back then, most of us watching thought that such unnecessary caution would be redundant by the time we reached the twenty-first century; we didn't bank on our contemporaries raising children with so many layers of cotton wool wrapped around them that coming into contact with the classics by the time they reached university age would necessitate a revival of the same red triangle approach that Channel 4 had pioneered in the middle of the 80s. Lo and behold, however, the loathsome 'trigger warnings' have now even crept upon the works of one of England's most revered wordsmiths like the kneejerk reorganization of the BBFC rules and regulations in the wake of the 'Video Nasty' moral panic of 35 years ago.

Apparently, students at Cambridge have been warned that certain masterpieces penned by an obscure playwright, name of William Shakespeare, might upset them; yes, the English lecture timetables have been marked with trigger warnings that take the shape of Ye Olde red triangle with accompanying exclamation marks. One play in particular has been singled out as specifically gory – and to be honest, it does read like the plot of an archetypal 80s Video Nasty in that a major female character is raped and then has her arms amputated by her rapists as well as having her tongue cut out.

Admittedly, 'Titus Andronicus' *is* a bit of a gore-fest, though is also one of the Bard's most invigorating works, one in which the sibling perpetrators of the crime in question receive their just desserts by being baked in a pie that is then eaten by their mother. Elizabethan audiences were seemingly less squeamish than their equivalents 400 years later, perhaps because they didn't question the eye-for-an-eye morality that was just as evident in the nursery rhymes they'd been raised on.

In defence, Cambridge University has claimed that such warnings are 'at the lecturer's own discretion' and 'not a faculty-wide policy', though at the same time the esteemed academic establishment has admitted that 'Any session containing material that could be deemed upsetting (and is not obvious from the title) is now marked with a symbol'. A representative from Derby University, Professor Dennis Hayes, commented 'Once you get a few trigger warnings, lecturers will stop presenting anything that is controversial...gradually, there is no critical discussion.' Critical discussion, for centuries a hallmark of university life, is now something to be avoided for fear of contaminating safe spaces. The impression given that universities today are akin to nurseries for mollycoddled adolescents who shirk from anything that contradicts the world as presented to them in infancy is hard to shake off when confronted by such ludicrous censorship; and if Shakespeare is fair game for the no-platform treatment, we really are f**ked.

The kind of guidelines familiar on the sleeves of DVDs now apparently apply to plays as well; if a sensitive seventeen-year-old objects to the content of something written by Shakespeare – and even the fastidious middle-aged Festival of Light brigade let the Bard off in the licentious 70s – chances are others will feel the need to be protected from centuries-old content that is hardly comparable to the kind of 'adult' material they've probably routinely scanned online. That 'To Kill A Mockingbird' has been removed from some US school syllabuses on account of it being 'uncomfortable' is a classic example of illiterate idiots taking over the asylum; as some wag on Twitter pointed out in relation to the 'uncomfortable' factor in Harper Lee's modern classic, 'that's the point'; but if even Shakespeare is targeted in this revisionist facelift, anybody seeking to say something about the here and now has no chance.

What that says about the world we live in, a world wherein British policemen are sent out wearing nail varnish to virtue-signal their stance against modern slavery when they're in a better position to stamp out the practice than the rest of us, is profoundly depressing. But this be 2017 in the septic isle.

Forty years ago, the most damaging verbal assault one could make upon the establishment was to say 'God save the Queen/she ain't no human being'; today, simply express reservations over Islam as a 'religion of peace' and give the thumbs-up to Brexit. To do so will earn you the same vitriolic condemnation from the establishment and expose you to an identical level of censorship. The main difference now is that the establishment is young and the dissenting voices are old. This upside-down reversal of battle lines has been a long, protracted process, building up over a generation spoon-fed a saccharine soundtrack by the Cowell industry and further sedated by social media. A consensus unquestioned and unchallenged, whether through fear of online ostracism or being lumped in with genuine extremist groups, has stifled debate amongst the young and left those with nothing to lose or prove as the only ones prepared to go against the grain. That these tend to be veterans whose key cultural contributions were made decades ago speaks volumes as to where we are now.

A couple of years back, Chrissie Hynde - feted as an embodiment of 'Rock Chick Cool' by a generation judging everything on a pose - spurned her unwanted canonisation by those young enough to be her daughters. She provoked Feminazi outrage with the publication of her autobiography by simply suggesting a little common sense be applied where young women on the town are concerned; and now her near-contemporary Morrissey has fired another contentious missive from his self-imposed exile across the pond, the latest in a long line of them that have served to keep his profile high as his music continues to languish in the same cul-de-sac it's occupied since the early 90s.

Stephen has always revelled in his contrariness, memorably proclaiming 'The Wild Boys' by Duran Duran Single of the Week in 'Smash Hits' back in 1984 when he would have been expected to favour some jangly Indie ditty; and whilst he was critical of Thatcherism during its heyday, his loathing never seemed to be a convenient hitch on a fashionable bandwagon in the way it was for many members of his generation, most of whom were later happy to cheerlead for New Labour as they collected their MBEs and Knighthoods. Ben Elton never said he enjoyed the sight of Norman Tebbit being pulled from the wreckage of the Brighton Bombing, for example.

When he was lumbered with the 'National Treasure' albatross a decade or so ago, lionised by the likes of JK Rowling, one had the constant suspicion that such plaudits were sitting uncomfortably on his shoulders; his one-time musical soul-mate Johnny Marr publicly expressed he didn't want David Cameron declaring 'The Queen is Dead' to be his favourite album, whereas Morrissey went even further in the eyes of those suddenly singing his praises by taking a big juicy chunk out of the hand that was feeding him. Should anyone have really been surprised, though? This is a man who had called Reggae 'vile' and 'racist' in the 80s and who was castigated for flaunting the Union Jack at a gig in 1992 by the same music scribes who eulogised Oasis (and Noel Gallagher's Union Jack guitar) a couple of years later.

Unlike Paul Weller, Morrissey never embraced a particular political party, let alone a specific left or right ideology. He appeared to be above all that and, like Orwell before him, refrained from nailing his colours to the mast. Whichever stance was flavour of the month, he seemed to instinctively adopt the opposite position, and I feel his much-publicised sound-bite support for UKIP was born of the same mischievous motivation rather than a wholesale conversion to Nigel's Barmy Army. It was just another antagonistic jacket for him to don as a means of getting up the noses of those who were patting him on the head for still being alive.

Yes, it's true that certain wordsmiths sharing a lineage with Morrissey, such as Philip Larkin or Iris Murdoch, lurched further to the right as they aged; and one could look upon Morrissey's opinions as belonging to the same process. On the other hand, one could view his refusal to kowtow to the consensus as another example of how his lifelong bloody-mindedness is still intact, even in the face of overwhelming pressure to conform. The furore unleashed by Morrissey's most recent statements has provoked the kind of demands for his head on a plate that used to accompany similarly provocative comments by those half his age – in short, the kind of reaction rock stars traditionally inspired in the old. What makes today so strange is that it is the old now outraging the young instead of the other way round.

One could equally argue that without his occasional rent-a-gob quotes, Morrissey would still largely be confined to a relatively brief moment in the 80s when he represented an alternative *zeitgeist* to the prevailing big hair and even bigger shoulder pads that lazy revisionists evoke to sum up the whole era for those who weren't there. At the same time, however, he no longer has to worry about the kind of career suicide such quotes would threaten twenty-something musicians with; he knows his hardcore devotees will continue to buy his output as they always have, regardless of whether or not their hero is fashionable again. If the mainstream decides it wants him, fair enough; if it doesn't, he couldn't care less.

With 35 years of recording behind him, Morrissey has the luxury of being able to afford nonchalance, but those thirty or forty years his junior don't; they have to conform or they risk losing everything. At a moment when Twitter, Facebook and YouTube are cracking down on any alternatives to the accepted design for life, dissenting voices are being silenced by a ruling class that don't want democratic debate; they want us all to think and speak the same language. It doesn't matter what one's actual political ideology is; we should all be allowed to express it, even if it isn't one that everybody wants to hear. Otherwise, we're back to burning books. And it says everything you need to know about 2017 that the only person getting the arbiters of taste frothing at the mouth is someone who arguably hasn't been relevant for three bloody decades

4

Overseas Development

And now for the rest of the world...

Five years have now passed since a 26-year-old Tunisian named Mohamed Bouazizi set himself on fire, a horrific act of protest that not only led to his death a month later but also inspired a nationwide revolt against the rule of Tunisia's President that rapidly brought his 23 years in power to an end. What happened in Tunisia sparked something remarkable in the Middle East that spread with breathtaking speed in the opening weeks of 2011; the people of Algeria, Oman, Yemen, Morocco, Egypt, Libya and Syria all took their cue from events in Tunisia as hereditary regimes that had generally been established following military coups decades previously suddenly seemed less invincible than they ever had before. The western world, still smarting from its interventions in Iraq and Afghanistan, held its breath and cautiously pledged moral support to what was christened the Arab Spring, even though many of the unelected leaders threatened by the people had received the backing of the west for years, regarded as a necessary evil in the battle with al-Qaeda.

Although history has shown that most revolutions tend to rise from the people, there is often a figurehead around whom the people rally and effectively nominate as ruler-in-waiting once the regime against which they're rebelling has been removed. However, what distinguished the Arab Spring from many previous revolutions on a similar scale was that there was no people's hero waiting in the wings to replace the toppled dictator; there was no Libyan Castro to succeed Gaddafi's Batista, just the euphoria of freedom from tyranny and no plan in place as to what came next. Following the collapse of the Soviet Union, it was only really the Balkans that underwent the turmoil that can come when a populace accustomed to being told what to do are suddenly left to their own devices;

most of the nations on the eastern side of the Iron Curtain adapted to change relatively quickly because there was a Yeltsin or a Vaclav Havel ready to step into the vacuum.

In scenes reminiscent of what had happened in Romania twenty-five years earlier, the astonishing daily gatherings in Cairo's Tahrir Square forced the resignation of Egyptian President Mubarak in February 2011 – though simultaneous demands for the end of long-running dictatorships in Syria and Libya didn't lead to surrender. Libya's uprising against Gaddafi was met with fierce resistance that quickly spilled over into civil war; by August of 2011, however, Tripoli fell to rebel forces backed by NATO and within a couple of months Gaddafi himself was cornered in his hometown of Sirte, where the same kind of bloody street justice once meted out to Mussolini by Libya's former colonial overlords awaited the man who had controlled his country as an effective Absolute Monarch since 1969.

While Libya was coming to terms with the death of Gaddafi, Egypt was adapting to democracy, voting in a June 2012 election that eventually saw Muslim Brotherhood candidate Mohammed Morsi declared President; in Syria, however, President Assad clung onto power with the military support of Putin's Russia by unleashing unprecedented savagery on his people as revolution morphed into civil war. The Syrian Army massacred 225 in the village of Tremseh in July and topped this the following year with a chemical attack on Ghouta, slaughtering over a thousand civilians. A month before, Egypt's strides towards democracy were delivered a setback when their democratically-elected President of a year was deposed in a coup d'état and the military were back in charge. The Arab Winter had set in.

Due to the ferocity of the ongoing civil war, the connections to insurgency in Iraq and the ramifications of fleeing refugees, Syria has claimed the majority of middle eastern headlines over the past three or four years, whereas Libya has been rather overlooked since Cameron and Sarkozy played the part of triumphant victors for democracy in Benghazi. Gaddafi had successfully suppressed any form of Islamic militancy throughout his reign, but in his absence violent lawlessness arose when regional militias that had formed during the civil war showed a reluctance to relinquish control of their corners of the country after liberation, often joining forces with hard-line Islamic militants from neighbouring Arab nations and engaging in battles with rival militias.

Former Gaddafi loyalists and members of his Army also grouped together, and ancient sectarian animosities re-emerged to present the newly-elected government in Tripoli with further security headaches. Following a second civil war, Libya was effectively left with two competing governments, a situation that continues to prevent any NATO intervention, despite the wishes of those attempting to prevent ISIS forces from spreading outwards from Sirte, which they captured exactly one year ago. At this moment in time, Libya is giving Syria a run for its money as the most f***ed-up nation on the planet, though there's no shortage of competition in the Arab world.

Yemen was initially regarded as a success story of the Arab Spring before the fragile democracy collapsed into civil war and eventual military intervention by Saudi Arabia. The high number of civilian deaths as a result of airstrikes conducted by the Saudis from March 2015 onwards have been blamed by the UN for an imminent humanitarian crisis in the country along with the Saudi-led naval blockade of Yemeni ports, yet the campaign continues to receive the support of the US and

UK, the former providing intelligence and the latter providing weaponry.

From supporting the autocratic rulers of the Middle East to supporting the revolutions to remove them to supporting the military coups to remove those who removed the autocratic rulers in the first place has been the pattern of the western position on the Arab Spring and its bloody fallout; giving power to the people may be admirable in theory but doesn't always lead to a satisfactory outcome in practice. As things currently stand, the conflicts that can be traced back to events five years ago seem to share only one guaranteed outcome right now – the prospect of more lives being lost.

HOMELAND
20 April 2016

Well, at least all the right boxes have been ticked now. The election of Malia Bouattia as the new President of the National Union of Students is the perfect appointment. Female – tick; black – tick; Muslim – tick; Pro-Palestine – tick; Anti-Semitic – tick. Whoops, slight error there; I meant to say Anti-*Zionist,* which has nothing remotely to do with Anti-Semitism, of course. It's cool to be Anti-Zionist, just as it apparently is in some circles to be pro-ISIS; not that I'm suggesting Ms Bouattia is, naturally. It's just that publicly rejecting a motion put forward by her fellow students two years ago to condemn ISIS activities does suggest she's not entirely opposed to the methods some adopt to cope with the 'Zionist' problem.

Funnily enough, I once had an 'uncle' (one of those non-blood relatives families used to attach that title to) who had been an officer in the Palestine Police when the country was under its guise as the British Mandate of Palestine, something

208

it became following the collapse of the Ottoman Empire in the aftermath of the First World War. The exit of the British from a state in which Jews and Arabs had co-existed in relative harmony for centuries to make way for the foundation of Israel in 1948 was not one of this nation's proudest colonial retreats, but it seemed as though keeping the peace was more trouble than it was worth, as proved to be the case in Cyprus, another sectarian powder-keg, a decade later.

There was an organised Arab revolt in 1936-39 and this was followed by wartime and post-war increases in Jewish – or Zionist – terrorism. Both camps knew the modern state of Israel would be an eventuality, proposed as far back as 1917, and a tussle for control began long before Israel came into being.

The understandable post-war displacement of those European Jews who had survived the Holocaust presented the British authorities in Palestine with a refugee crisis, the symptoms of which are all-too familiar today. American President Harry S Truman intensified the pressure on Palestine to admit 100,000 Jews, yet the British were acutely aware of the potential dangers of flooding a small landmass with so many people representing one of the two dominant religions in the region and upheld an immigration ban despite world opinion. Violent Jewish reprisals followed, and the years 1944-48 were the height of Zionist terrorist incidents in Palestine, something the British forces present were unsurprisingly at the receiving end of, including my Uncle Joe.

The bombing of Jerusalem's King David Hotel, which served as the British HQ in Palestine, in 1946 resulted in a death toll of 92. Perhaps first-hand experience of such an incident was to shape my Uncle Joe's undeniable Anti-Semitic opinions, the most extreme example of which was one he aired during my childhood, that those Jews who had died in the Holocaust deserved it. Not that such an opinion can be in any way justified, but it's easy to see why he might harbour a grudge, fishing the corpses of his comrades from the rubble of the King David Hotel.

Somewhere, I still have his badge from the Palestine Police, given to me when I was far too young to realise what it represented; I'm still not quite sure what it *does* represent.

The Anglo-American Committee of Inquiry was set up after the war to look into the problem of Palestine and came to the conclusion that the country should not be either an exclusively Arab or exclusively Jewish state. President Truman wouldn't acknowledge the committee's recommendations and pressed on with calling for the immediate admission of 100,000 Jewish refugees, something the British knew would lead to another Arab revolt. When the British requested US troops to prevent this from happening, the Americans baulked and the Brits decided to wash their hands of the problem by announcing the hasty termination of Mandatory Palestine and leaving it up to the United Nations to come up with a solution. The UN conclusion was to establish separate Arab and Jewish states, effectively partitioning the country.

Palestinian Arabs rejected the proposals, scheduled to take place the moment the British departed, with the Arab League threatening military opposition to the plan; and though the British reluctantly accepted it, they refused to enforce it as they regarded it as unfavourable to the Arab population. Zionist terrorist atrocities had turned British opinion against the Jewish cause, and the Brits declined to oversee the transitional period alongside the UN Palestine Commission, preferring to cut and run. Remarkably, the proposed partition was also opposed by future Israeli Prime Minister Menachem

Begin, though his was a lone voice amidst majority Jewish rejoicing.

On the eve of Israel's birth, a civil war erupted in Palestine that the British again felt the full force of. This conflict accelerated the exit of the British and made the end of Mandatory Palestine something that couldn't come soon enough for many in this country. As British rule rapidly broke down, Jewish leader David Ben-Gurion declared the State of Israel had been born, even though this declaration was unrecognised by surrounding Arab nations. The Palestine Mandate officially ended on 15 May 1948, bringing the curtain down on a thirty-year period in which the British had tried and failed to do what the Ottomans had succeeded in doing for far longer. And it's fair to say the situation has never been resolved since.

The Palestinian 'cause' over the last seventy years has become a *cause célèbre* for every generation of would-be revolutionaries and right-on rebels; it shouldn't instinctively lead to Anti-Semitic sentiments, though it has a habit of doing so, especially where those whose knowledge of its history is derived less from actual experience of its realities and more from propaganda garnered from the insulated cocoon of the demo and the debating society. That the new NUS President regards Middle East peace talks as 'strengthening the colonial project' highlights the fact that this dead-end is set to continue.

THE PRIZE: TURKEY
17 July 2016

Back when the world was a bigger place than it is today, the annual 'Blue Peter' summer expedition served as an eye-opening introduction to far-off foreign destinations and

211

indigenous cultures for a UK audience of children, many of whom (like me) had never ventured beyond the British Isles at the time. One particularly memorable moment came in 1975 when John Noakes stood in the middle of the Bosphorus Bridge and pointed to one end, declaring over there was Europe, before pointing to the other and declaring over there was Asia. Funny how these things have a habit of returning to the forefront of one's thoughts at the most unexpected moments. When news broke of an attempted military coup in Turkey a couple of days ago, the very same bridge was back in the headlines, closed to traffic due to the emergency.

The 'Blue Peter' trip to Turkey – just a year after the country had invaded Cyprus – was sandwiched between two other military coups, taking place in 1971 and 1980, though there had already been another (back in 1960) long before John, Pete and Lesley flew to Istanbul. That 2016 should witness a fourth is not really a great surprise. The Turkish Army takes its role seriously as an upholder of the Turkish Republic's secular constitution, as established by Mustafa Kemal Ataturk in 1922; and a country that acts as the gateway from one continent to another has always had powder-keg potential whenever relations between Europe and Asia are fraught, especially where interpretations of faith are concerned. Threats to Turkey's avowed intention to not be governed by religious doctrine, along with the increasing censorship of the polarising Islamist President Erdogan, appear to have sparked this latest military uprising which, unlike those of 1960, 1971 and 1980, has failed.

Erdogan has been a divisive and dictatorial figure ever since his election as President in 2014, following eleven years as the country's Prime Minister. His Islamist political stance was evident early on, even resulting in a prison sentence for inciting religious intolerance in 1998. His two years in office as Turkey's President have been marked by a clampdown on freedom of speech and regular accusations of human rights violations, both of which have continued to stall Turkey's ongoing attempts to join the European Union and both of which are too close to hard-line Islamic states for comfort. His conservative Islamist leanings have also been seen by some as placing Turkey's proud tradition of secularism in peril.

It was notable that the rebel forces within the Turkish military that spearheaded this aborted coup saw capturing television stations as a top priority, for Erdogan's attempts to control state broadcasting appear to have been based on the Putin model. Unlike the Soviet Union, the Ottoman Empire is no longer within living memory, and the independent republic that rose from the ashes of the old Ottoman possessions carved up by the allied European powers at the end of the First World War was a deliberate break with the old Islamic imperial past. However, just as the pop culture of the defunct GDR has something of a nostalgic cult following in East Germany, the legends of Ottoman conquest exercise a sentimental grip on many of those who subscribe to Islamic Fundamentalism; and President Erdogan often seems possessed by the spirits of the deceased sultans.

Anyone ascending to the pinnacle of political power in Turkey is conscious that the military's loyalty is not so much to the nation's leader, but to the founding spirit of the nation; and Erdogan has used canny means to neutralise any potential challenge from the military to his authority, rounding up hundreds of army officers in two separate high-profile court cases based on spurious rumours of coup-plotting. The removal of those whose loyalty to him wasn't guaranteed enabled him to promote those whose was. Along with military personnel sentenced to lengthy prison sentences were numerous journalists and opposition politicians hostile to

Erdogan's rule. Even before he became President in 2014, Erdogan's lengthy spell as Prime Minister served as a warm-up to his tyrannical presidency, with public protests ruthlessly crushed and controversial judicial reforms laying the ground for the virtual Absolute Monarchy he appears to be creating for himself. 'Insulting the President' has now become an offence of a nature that would be more familiar in Iran, bracketed as an effective terrorist act.

The manner in which Erdogan has imposed his law upon Turkey and the way he is viewed by his opponents as threatening the country's cherished secular foundations was bound to provoke military response sooner rather than later, yet the failed *coup d'état* of last week, which has so far claimed over 250 lives, has been suspected by some as a stunt instigated by the President himself. In many respects, it gives him the remit to suppress all dissent that he has been waiting for. His immediate response to the coup – arresting almost 3,000 soldiers and over 200 politicians as well as firing over 2,000 judges – has been swift; some foreign observers have made the point that the President's hand is now stronger than ever; he has carte-blanche to enforce his authority in what the New York Times has labelled a counter-coup.

'He is a weak ruler who needs religion to uphold his government; it is as if he would catch his people in a trap.' So spoke modern Turkey's venerated founder, Mustafa Kemal Ataturk. The country's unique geographical position has always placed it on the frontline of any East-West tensions, yet as a secularist state it has managed to act as a successful bridge between two regularly clashing cultures. How much longer it can continue to do so with a man like Recep Tayyip Erdogan at the helm remains to be seen; but the signs aren't great.

TURNING JAPANESE...OR CHINESE
9 August 2016

Brits say Falklands; Argentines say Malvinas; Japan says Senkaku; China says Diaoyu. Territorial claims are funny old things, often inciting the most fervent of passions over the least obviously appealing lumps of rock. Most such claims stretch back centuries and only acquire sudden value when ownership is threatened by a rival claim, usually provoked by the discovery of something with a far greater value lurking in the neighbourhood. In the case of the Senkaku/Diaoyu Islands in the East China Sea, these uninhabited locations resembling the landscapes upon which Godzilla battled his fellow mutant beasts are currently at the centre of a dispute between Japan and China, a dispute placing one of the most fragile fault-lines of the Far East in peril.

The waters encircled by Taiwan, China, South Korea and Japan boast a proliferation of tiny islands that even outnumber the similarly scattered little landmasses dotted around the tip of Scotland; for Japan, the most prominent served as a convenient barrier between it and the US Army during the Second World War, though the Senkaku Islands are more distanced from the Japanese mainland, closer to Taiwan. There were no real territorial claims made upon them in the eras of the ancient Chinese and Japanese Empires; British ships referred to them as the Pinnacle Islands and their value was solely as navigational markers.

The success of Japan in the First Sino-Japanese War (1894/5) saw the dominance of the East Asian region shift from China to the victor, marking Japan's beginnings as a major military power that would ultimately carry it all the way to Hiroshima. Although Korea was regarded as the main prize of the conflict, it was the Senkaku Islands that were first claimed as imperial possessions in the aftermath of the War, and China didn't seem particularly concerned. A Japanese fish processing plant was established on one of the islands, Uotsuri-shima, which remained active until WWII; the very presence of the plant on the island appeared to certify the claims that it and the neighbouring islands had been incorporated into Japan's sovereign territory.

Even when the Senkaku Islands fell under American control following Japan's surrender in 1945, China wasn't especially vocal about ownership claims. China only really began to make a fuss at the end of the 1960s when the United Nations Economic Commission for Asia and the Far East discovered oil and gas resources situated around the islands. Despite this potentially profitable future for the vicinity, the US returned ownership to Japan in 1971, something that prompted Chinese territorial claims to become official Peking policy. Taiwan had also been ceded to Japan in 1895, and it was the return of Taiwan into Chinese hands after the Second World War that China now retrospectively says should have gone hand-in-hand with the acquisition of the Senkaku Islands. History is certainly a flexible friend when it comes to territorial claims.

Bizarrely, some of the islands are privately-owned and are rented by the Japanese Government, though each outright purchase by Japan is regarded as a provocative gesture by China. One of the islands is used as a practice range by the US military, maintaining the presence America has had in the region ever since it funded the post-war financial reconstruction of Japan. That part of the demilitarisation of Japan involved the US taking on the role of the country's defender in the event of any attack places America in a difficult position during the current dispute. Add the unstable spectre of North Korea to the equation and it's plain to see how delicate the situation in the Pacific really is.

Strategically, the Senkaku Islands are situated in significant shipping lanes as well as fruitful fishing grounds, not to mention the oil and gas reserves, of course; but they also serve as a microcosm of the battle for control of the region between China and America. Over the last four years, China has deliberately flouted Japan's ownership of the islands by sailing its ships into Japanese territorial waters and has also created the 'East China Sea Air Defence Identification Zone' in an area covering Senkaku, one that the penetration of by non-Chinese aircraft apparently requires adherence to rules laid down in Beijing. Neither Japan nor the US has adhered to these rules.

Old enmities between China and Japan have been revived by this dispute, ones that rouse nationalist passions on both sides and ones that politicians of the respective nations seek to appease in the eternal quest for popularity. But while the world's attention appears perennially focused on the Middle East, it is perhaps the *Far* East we should be keeping a closer eye on, especially when one considers that a couple of months ago three Russian warships – accompanied by a Chinese Navy frigate – sailed past the Senkaku Islands in what could well be perceived as an act of choreographed provocation. Any Russian intervention in disputes between nations rarely bodes well for a peaceful resolution.

FIFTY YEARS OF HURT
29 August 2016

Anyone remember the World Cup in Colombia in 1986? If you do, you must have been ingesting a sizeable amount of hallucinogenics at the time, for it never happened. It was certainly scheduled as such following Spain in 1982, but the established pattern of never awarding the event to a country that had previously staged it was finally broken when FIFA opted for Mexico (hosts in 1970) at the eleventh hour. Up to that point, the World Cup tended to alternate between the soil of South America and Europe, the traditional powerhouse continents of world football; the first such tournament had been held in Uruguay, after all.

Having had Uruguay, Brazil, Chile, Mexico and Argentina all host the World Cup, Colombia was the next South American name out of the hat – winning the bid as far back as 1974; but by the time the 1982 tournament had ended, it became apparent that Colombia was in no fit state to take on the challenge four years later. Economic reasons were cited, but there was a hell of a lot more to it than that. The brutal murder of Colombian international Andres Escobar upon his return home from scoring an own-goal at the 1994 World Cup sadly proved FIFA all too right.

Today's announcement of a ceasefire between the largest rebel forces of the left (FARC) and the Colombian Government could potentially end a conflict that has spanned a staggering 52 years. FARC (an acronym derived from the Spanish spelling of the Revolutionary Armed Forces of Colombia) formed in 1964 as the paramilitary wing of the Colombian Communist Party and has largely based itself in the plentiful rural areas of the country for the past half-century, springing as it did from an impoverished agricultural community confronted by immense inequalities and suppression of all subversion within Colombian society. However, any hopes that FARC could replicate recent revolutionary events in Cuba at the time of its formation were dashed by the pact between the Colombian Government and wealthy landowners, who had already guaranteed US support against any guerrilla rebellion. Instead, the whole unedifying bloodbath has dragged on and on for five devastating decades.

The history of South and Central America is, with a few exceptions, largely a lesson of post-colonial mismanagement of the most disastrous manner over the last century and-a-half. Back in the fifteenth and sixteenth centuries, when the various British trading outposts dotted around the globe had yet to morph into overseas territories, the Spanish Empire was at its height, ruling over great swathes of land in the Americas; but by the turn of the nineteenth century, Spain was in terminal decline as a world power, overtaken by Britain and (especially) Napoleonic France. The Peninsular War of 1807-14 was a decisive conflict contributing towards the eventual defeat of Bonaparte, but only Britain emerged from it stronger than it had been before; the strain of the Napoleonic Wars on Spain and Portugal was a precursor of the strain of the Second World War on the UK, resulting in the loss of colonies neither country could afford to govern when in turmoil at home.

The independence of South American countries previously under Spanish and Portuguese rule in the early-to-mid-nineteenth century has parallels with the loss of British colonies in Africa during the mid-to-late twentieth century, and what happened next also has a ring of familiarity to it. The country that became Colombia had, under Spanish rule, been known as the Viceroy of New Granada, a huge colonial possession that also comprised modern-day Ecuador, Panama and Venezuela as well as parts of Brazil, Peru and Guyana. Left to its own devices following Spanish withdrawal in 1819, the future Colombia went through a series of name changes that must have given rise to several headaches for cartographers of the era – the Republic of New Granada, the Granadine Confederation, the United States of Colombia and finally, in 1886, the Republic of Colombia. There was a split with Panama, following the Thousand Days' War of 1899-1902, when the borders of modern-day Colombia were established, but the constant changing of names reflected a deeper degree of uncertainty in the country as to its identity.

The USA had played a part in the split with Panama, tied-in with the construction of the Panama Canal, and despite a subsequent war with Peru, the new nation of Colombia was largely peaceful until the period of the late 40s and early 50s known as 'The Violence', when the country's two major political parties engaged in a civil war and claimed the lives of over 180,000 people. The cessation of hostilities in the 1960s gave rise to somewhat superficial peace, though various guerrilla groups of both left and right below the surface were forming to take violence onto a new and bloodier level altogether.

The current conflict – though after half-a-century of it, the term 'historic' could also be applied – is reputed to boast a death-toll of more than 260,000, so any indications of genuine peace on the horizon are bound to be imbued with a great deal of good-will and optimistic hope on the part of the long-suffering Colombian people. As a continent, South America is oozing untapped potential and possesses the ingredients to eventually emerge from the lengthy shadows cast by drug barons, civil wars, pseudo-Marxist dictators and unhealthy US interference in the same way that Eastern Europe began to emerge from the collapse of the Soviet Bloc at the end of the twentieth century. But so much damage has been done since it wrestled itself free from Spanish and Portuguese rule that it could take at least another couple of generations before anything remotely resembling success can be discerned.

In the case of Colombia, a country with a richness of biodiversity that encompasses the Andes, Amazonian rainforests and coastlines on both the Caribbean and the Pacific as well as a healthy ethnic and linguistic mix, one can only hope some kind of stability can be achieved that will help it rise anew from decades of unnecessary bloodshed. Who knows, perhaps it can one day get round to staging the World Cup it was forced to surrender back in 1986. The world is crossing its fingers for a long overdue happy ending.

WASHINGTON – WE HAVE A PROBLEM
September 6 2016

These are strange days for America where its relations with friends and neighbours are concerned. We've had the unexpected ceasefire in the long-running feud with Cuba, Obama making veiled threats about the UK being at the back of the queue for US trade deals in the event of Brexit, Donald Trump's awkward encounter with the Mexican President following months of negative Mexican stereotyping by the tiny-handed gobshite, and now the incumbent resident of the White House being called a 'Son of a Whore' by the Filipino President Rodrigo Duterte.

The outspoken leader of the Philippines has previous – applying the same insult to the Pope a few months back and adding 'gay' to his favourite catchphrase when aiming it at US Ambassador to the Philippines Philip Goldberg. But it was aiming it (minus the 'gay' part) at President Obama that has caused the cancellation of a planned meeting in Laos this week between the two, in which Obama stated he would raise the tricky topic of the 2,000-plus lives lost in the Philippines' state-sponsored 'war on drugs', provoking Duterte's outburst. One wonders if Donald Trump has been basing his own charm offensive on the main man in Manila.

After 300 years as a province of the Spanish Empire, the Philippines wrestled itself free of Spanish rule in 1899 and proclaimed a Republic. However, the Pacific island was then caught-up in US interest in the region, following the Spanish-American War of 1898 – one of the endless conflicts the USA has been involved in for the majority of its existence. Capitalising on the vulnerable and diminishing remnants of Spain's ancient colonial possessions, the US supported Cuban rebellions against Spanish sovereignty in the late nineteenth century and went to war with the fading European power for ten weeks, a demonstration of America's imperialist expansionism that resulted in Spanish surrender and the Treaty of Paris. With Spain suing for peace, the ball was in the USA's court and the Treaty of Paris handed over the likes of Cuba, Puerto Rico, Guam and the Philippines to the Americans.

The short-lived independent republic that the Philippines proclaimed after overthrowing the Spanish was brutally crushed by the US in the Philippine-American War of 1899-1902, and the imperial plaything that the Treaty of Paris had ceded to America became the colony of a foreign power again. After hypocritically lecturing Britain for years on the need to grant independence to its own colonies, the US officially surrendered the Philippines in 1946, a year before the British exited India, though this was largely a consequence of the Japanese occupation of the nation from 1942-45. The US promised the Filipino people independence once the Japanese were evicted, and the US kept its word – after between 500,000 and 1,000,000 had died under Japanese rule, not to mention the thousands of Filipino girls and women the Japanese had used as 'Comfort Women', a euphemism for sex slaves.

There was an inevitable catch when independence came. The terms of this independence were heavily balanced in America's favour, with dozens of US military bases remaining as well as legislation granting American corporations access to exploit the Philippines' natural resources, turning an American colony into an American satellite state. As with the Soviet Union, once the US got its claws into a country, it stayed put. The American Empire of which Gore Vidal wrote – in the writer's eyes, a betrayal of the original intentions of the post-British US Republic – was never more evident than in the way America controlled the fortunes of the Philippines, with the possible exception of pre-revolutionary Cuba.

That a ruthless tin-pot dictator such as Ferdinand Marcos could be allowed to oversee a regime marked by human rights violations, state censorship and suppression of political rivals yet still be backed by the US speaks volumes. As long as he wasn't a Commie, he could clearly do whatever the hell he liked – the example of Batista in Cuba had already shown that an inhumane regime would be tolerated while ever it danced to America's tune.

Even The Beatles were on the receiving end of Marcos's rule when they were essentially thrown out of the Philippines after turning down an invitation to dine with the President and his shoe-fetish wife Imelda during their strained 1966 tour of the Far East. A decade of Martial Law and the 1983 assassination of Marcos's nemesis Benigno Aquino Jr upon his arrival back in the Philippines after a period of exile eventually sealed Marcos's fate – though it's telling that, rather than stand trial for his crimes, he was allowed to settle in Hawaii upon his abdication in 1986.

In recent years, the Philippines has built bridges with its wartime occupier Japan, has retained relatively good relations with is former colonial overlord Spain, and has also overcome its one-time hostilities towards China – though something has changed where America is concerned. Ironically, the man who was elected Filipino President just a couple of months ago has the kind of pedigree the US would once have vigorously endorsed: linked to a vigilante group called the Davao Death Squad, cited as responsible for the extrajudicial murders of alleged drug dealers, the very issue Obama sought to raise in the aborted Laos meeting with Duterte. Yet, despite past support for America during the Cold War and the War on Terror, the servant would appear to be finally standing up to its long-time master.

With the newly installed and unpredictable President Duterte at the helm, American-Filipino relations seem poised to enter a new and unprecedented phase. 'I am no American puppet,' he declared before making his unsavoury insinuations as to Obama's maternal parentage. How long this rather reckless antagonism will last remains to be seen; but as Duterte has threatened to withdraw his country from the UN and form an alliance with China and various unnamed African nations, we may perhaps be seeing the beginnings of a drift away from American influence after more than a century, and genuine independence at last – albeit with another nutter calling the shots.

FULL OF EASTERN PROMISE
12 September 2016

It has to be said - old-school crackpot dictators are a little thinner on the ground than they used to be. Yes, there's Assad, but as far as psychopaths go he's rather a weedy-looking runt of a man, short on insane charisma and therefore hardly worthy of comparison to Idi Amin, Ferdinand Marcos or Jean-Bedel Bokassa. Ever since Gaddafi received rough justice at the hands of the Libyan people, nutters in theatrical military dress or ones staging extravagant coronation ceremonies that bankrupted their country appear to be on the wane. And, mad though he may be, Donald Trump is aiming for democratic election as his nation's leader as opposed to seizing power in a coup. Ah, but there's still North Korea; and there's still Kim Jong-un.

Kim Jong-un ticks a fair few of the crackpot dictator boxes, for sure. He's never seen in anything other than his regulation Mao-style uniform; he has that strangely severe crop with little at the sides or back but plenty on top that was once *de rigueur* for members of bands clogging up the 80s indie charts; he has an unsettlingly smooth, plastic countenance that Hollywood has-beens would die for; he inherited the physical leadership of North Korea from his late father, who nevertheless remains celestial leader of the country for all eternity; he holds more official titles than he can probably even list; he has presided over numerous purges and executions on a whim, including members of his own family; he is head of an archaic Stalinist regime that controls every aspect of its oppressed subjects' lives, as though (as Christopher Hitchens once memorably observed) using 'Nineteen Eighty-Four' as an instruction manual; he is provocatively antagonistic towards the USA and the West; and he also now has his finger on the nuclear button. Yes, I think he's worthy of a spot in the pantheon under discussion.

North Korea's much-publicised nuclear programme has hit the headlines again over the past few days, but it now has an official history that stretches back a decade – according to the not-necessarily reliable PR machine of the 'Democratic Republic', at least. A 2006 underground explosion was detected by outside sources, and the North Koreans claimed it was their first nuclear test. Reports that the country was indeed a nuclear power followed over the coming months and years as the alleged underground hydrogen bomb explosions continued to register on monitoring mechanisms way beyond the borders of the secret state that is Kim Jong-un's private kingdom.

During the Cold War, North Korea allegedly requested assistance in developing nuclear power from both the Soviet Union and China, though only the former gave any kind of help, acting in an advisory capacity to build research reactors from the mid-60s to the late 70s. At the time, North Korea was a pretty minor member of the Communist club, with most of Eastern Europe answerable to Moscow, and China the dominant power behind the so-called Bamboo Curtain when it and the USSR were at odds with each other.

However, in the twenty-first century, the changing landscape of political ideology has pushed North Korea to the forefront of global tensions, with this last obstinate bastion of increasingly isolated designs for life being one of the few remaining countries still basing itself on an outdated model long since discarded by former Soviet satellite states and even China, following its phenomenally successful move into the free market. There is a novelty factor in place today, both in terms of the country itself and its worryingly Loony Tunes leader. North Korea is a curious anachronism in the Global Village, with only the testimony of the few to have escaped its clutches serving as reportage from the forbidden zone.

One unsung area of the North Korean economy has been its export of ballistic missiles, though speaking as an Englishman whose own nation's booming arms industry is currently profiting from Saudi strikes on Yemen I have no grounds to display superior smugness. Egypt, Libya, Pakistan, Iran and Syria have all benefitted from North Korea's militaristic hardware, yet the United Nations has still imposed sanctions against the country without any discernible impact upon Kim Jong-un's oblivious and immune regime. Too-close-for-comfort neighbour South Korea has become understandably jumpy with such an unstable enemy on its doorstep and has been forced to issue details of its plans to obliterate the North Korean capital of Pyongyang if its half-brother extends its nuclear experiments to the point where it can be perceived as a serious threat to its genuinely democratic sibling, claiming Pyongyang will be 'reduced to ashes and removed from the map.'

Earlier this year, North Korea declared it had sent a satellite into space, provoking condemnation from the US as well as near-neighbour Japan, and even China – traditionally the country's staunchest ally in the region. China's support remains crucial to North Korea's continuing existence as a bonkers rogue nation, and in theory China could bring North Korea to its knees without a single shot being fired. But Beijing is playing a very clever slow game where its Communist kindergarten colleague is concerned and the jury is out on how far it will allow the country to go when China itself is so preoccupied with building bridges in the West and expanding its business interests in Africa.

How much longer China's attempts at projecting a professional and reformed image whilst supporting an embarrassing throwback like North Korea will last remains to be seen; but if North Korea keeps on generating so much bad publicity, it's only a matter of time. As for the rest of the world, we can only observe events from afar and hope that the Supreme Leader meets his maker before his evident insanity curtails our own future ambitions.

PARADISE LOST
16 November 2016

There has been an abundance of media discussion on the 'Special Relationship' between the UK and the US in the wake of Donald Trump's victory in the US Presidential Election, and the haste of Nigel Farage to play the Blair poodle to Trump's Bush has been fairly excruciating to witness over the last few days. Obama's 'back of the queue' response to Brexit set the British cat amongst the American pigeons a few months ago, yet the extent of the UK handover to US interests in the wake of the Empire's dissolution half-a-century ago remains relatively under-reported.

Take the British Indian Ocean Territory, for example. Not familiar with it? Halfway between Tanzania and Indonesia, this area encompasses around a thousand islands within 23 square miles, the largest landmass of which is Diego Garcia, covering 17 square miles. Today, its inhabitants are US and UK military personnel and numerous contractors numbering up to 2,5000, though until the late 60s and early 70s the island had a native population of 2,000 descended largely from eighteenth century slaves originally emanating from Mozambique and Madagascar. Even after the abolition of slavery within the British Empire in 1834, the Chagos Archipelago remained a colonial outpost where the natives were very much second-class citizens; with the nearest imperial HQ in Mauritius, a considerable distance away, the post-slavery 'freemen' on Diego Garcia were poorly-paid contract workers employed by an absentee landlord, whose working and living conditions were rarely studied or improved.

During the Second World War, British and Indian troops were garrisoned on the island, with its strategic position attracting

228

the peacetime attention of both the UK and US Governments, who entered into discussions to establish a permanent military base there. There had already been a significant change in the island population due to the French ownership of the various plantations there; a 1964 census claimed up to 80% of the populace were contract workers imported from the Seychelles. When talk of a military base resurfaced in the mid-60s, UK sovereignty in the region meant that the territory would remain British, despite any proposed base being a joint enterprise with the USA. Mauritius gaining independence in 1968 caused the UK to relieve the newly-independent former governor of the remote islands in the Chagos Archipelago of its duties, and to set about making plans for the main island's future.

Fifty years ago next month, the British and American Governments signed an agreement that is shortly due to expire, one that allocated the region for military use, nominally under UK control, but essentially an army base for the US. In order to carry out the stipulations of the agreement, the native population was required to be evacuated from Diego Garcia, a task undertaken in virtual secrecy by the Foreign and Commonwealth Office between 1967 and 1973. This depopulation removed most of the island's inhabitants to Mauritius and the Seychelles, though many settled in the unlikely environs of Crawley, West Sussex.

Sneakily skirting around UN rules and regulations on such issues, the British Government claimed the majority of the island's population as it stood when seeking to evict them was 'non-resident', implying most were migrant workers with no historical or emotional attachment to the area. Those who actually contradicted the official view soon found themselves separated from family and friends when attempting to return home from visiting Mauritius, denied entry and suddenly rendered both homeless and jobless.

Perhaps the most despicable method of depopulation came via the cruel and cynical massacre of the island resident's pets. According to veteran journalist John Pilger, upwards of a thousand animals kept as pets, mostly dogs, were taken away from the natives and gassed with exhaust fumes. This barbarous act served as a warning to the population that it was time to pack their bags, and when Labour MP Tam Dalyell received word of what was happening and expressed his intentions to raise the subject in the Commons, the FCO responded with a hastily-compiled excuse to cover their tracks that exposed their compliance with US military interests. By 1971, construction had already begun on establishing an American base on Diego Garcia.

In 1972, compensation payments to natives totalling £650,000 were handed to the Mauritian Government by the British, though it took the best part of five years before these payments reached those evicted from Diego Garcia. When the Washington Post tried to raise public awareness in America in the mid-70s, subsequent US Congressional Committees seeking to look into the matter were brushed off with a 'classified information' clause, whereas successive efforts to return islanders to their home have failed, blocked by endless legal loopholes as the case has been a virtual pass-the-parcel game through various international courts over the last 25 years that the British public has been largely ignorant of.

This week it has been announced that the latest attempt of islanders and their descendents to return home has been rejected by the British Government. FCO Minister Baroness Anelay has said that resettlement was turned down on the grounds of 'feasibility, defence and security interests' as well as 'costs to the British taxpayer', offering £4 million compensation payments spread over the next decade as a means of fobbing off ongoing campaigns to reclaim Diego Garcia from the US military.

Next time the subject of the 'Special Relationship' is raised, it's probably worth examining precisely what that vague description actually means. In the case of the British Indian Ocean Territory, it essentially translates as the British selling their remaining dependencies down the river for the benefit of the American military, something that the upcoming Trump administration would probably wholeheartedly approve of. Nice one, Nigel.

THE REVOLUTION IS OVER
26 November 2016

There's an episode of 'Jason King' in which Kate O'Mara perhaps inevitably plays the obligatory eye candy for the world's most effete novelist-cum-international crime-fighter; in it, Peter Wyngarde's flamboyant alter-ego becomes embroiled in the affairs of a fictitious Latin American country, languidly stumbling into a story as he so often does and used as a pawn by both El Presidente and the revolutionaries seeking to grab power for the people. O'Mara is probably the sexiest revolutionary ever to don the one-size-too-small requisite rebel uniform, but such plotlines were a staple of British and American spy/adventure series throughout the 60s and into the 70s. Late 1950s events in Cuba cast more of a cultural than political shadow in the popular western imagination.

Although he never attained the iconic status of his one-time fellow revolutionary Che Guevara (probably because he lived far too long), the death of Fidel Castro at the age of 90 nevertheless draws a line under an era in which isolated pockets of resistance to global American domination became a beacon for wannabe radicals in student union bars everywhere. Castro's undoubted charisma as a young firebrand whose role in the toppling of a terrible tin-pot dictator made him a worldwide household name continued to exert a powerful hold over outsiders for decades, something that even his dubious human rights record as President couldn't demystify.

Following in the footsteps of other musicians who had flouted the unofficial boycott of Cuban culture by the west, The Manic Street Preachers' 2001 visit to the Caribbean island just 90 miles from the coast of Florida also included a meeting with Castro himself. On the video that documented the encounter, visibly overwhelmed guitarist Nicky Wire turned to the camera and proudly declared 'Noel Gallagher met Tony Blair and we've met Fidel f***ing Castro!' A man who had easily repelled America's clumsy attempt to recapture Cuba forty years previously had by then outlasted eight US Presidents, though the fact this perennial thorn in America's side was still in power in 2001 spoke volumes about the nature of democracy on Cuba. It was, however, always thus.

The country Fidel Alejandro Castro Ruz was born into in 1926 had travelled a familiar colonial path during its lifetime. After 400 years of Spanish rule and several failed attempts to overthrow its imperial masters, Cuba was ceded to the USA following the Spanish-American War of 1898 (along with the Philippines, Guam and Puerto Rico); although America's official role was to oversee the transition of Cuba from a Spanish colony to an independent nation (the Republic of Cuba was founded in 1902), American economic interests in the island rendered genuine independence something of a falsehood. The terms of the Cuban Republic's independence were such that the US remained entitled to intervene in its affairs, which it proceeded to do on numerous occasions as democracy struggled to take hold.

Not until the early 20s did the influx of American tourists and American investment in Cuba serve to transform the island into the decadent playground for foreigners it gradually gained an unsavoury reputation for. Casinos, hotels, restaurants and brothels boomed and the Mafia gained a foothold in the capital Havana that was to last for over thirty years. The contentious figure of Fulgencio Batista first made his mark in Cuban politics during this period, and by the time Batista staged a coup and declared himself President for a second time in 1952, the divisions in Cuban society between rich and poor were glaring, though the island remained an attractive prospect for the worst US imports of crime, corruption and corporate exploitation.

For Fidel Castro, a failed lawyer and active activist whose Marxist political principles were at odds with Batista's increasing anti-Communism (which won him greater US support as the Cold War intensified), the country was in dire need of liberation from a repressive dictatorship bankrolled by America. He formed a guerrilla group called The Movement and embarked upon a series of subversive activities that landed him in prison following a high-profile trial in which he used the platform to expose the rape of his nation to the world. Released early as the result of an amnesty on political prisoners, he emerged from gaol committed to the overthrow of Batista and the expulsion of American companies from Cuba. He plotted this after fleeing to Mexico and recruiting Argentine exile Che Guevara to the cause, eventually returning to Cuba with just 80 other recruits in 1956.

A two-year campaign against Batista's forces was staged from Castro's base in the Sierra Maestra Mountains, picking up the invaluable support of Cuba's peasantry in the process. Sensing which way the wind was blowing, the US slowly began to withdraw its support for Batista at a time when Florida was beginning to overflow with Cubans who had fled the regime and were loudly proclaiming their belief in Castro as the country's saviour. The US imposed an arms embargo on Cuba, weakening Batista's military stranglehold and enabling Castro's much smaller forces to sweep towards Havana on an unstoppable tide of revolutionary fervour that climaxed with Castro's army's triumphant entry into the capital on 2 January 1959 and Batista's flight.

With the extent of Batista's corrupt rule now public knowledge, Castro's achievement was widely welcomed, though events that followed soured initial optimism. The rushed trials and executions of those who had constituted Batista's military, police and secret service seemed no different from the brutal punishments the deposed President had himself overseen, and it began to feel like a case of 'meet the new boss, same as the old boss'. Castro's unashamed Communism did him no favours stateside, nor did his nationalisation of all Cuba's foreign-owned properties. It was inevitable that Castro's rejection by the US would send him into the arms of the opportunistic USSR, and ill-advised efforts to reverse the revolution by America such as the disastrous Bay of Pigs affair, not to mention the CIA's mind-boggling schemes for Castro's assassination, opened the doors for Soviet Premier Nikita Khrushchev to begin shipping missiles to the island. We all know what happened next – or, to be more accurate, what *didn't* happen. If it had, we probably wouldn't be here now.

After the Cuban Missile Crisis of 1962, America's focus shifted to a certain country in South East Asia and Fidel Castro began to implement the educational, agricultural and healthcare reforms for the Cuban people that have often won him the kind of plaudits from those who have not been so favourable towards the methods he employed to hold onto power. Investment from the USSR continued to play a vital part in Cuba's success story, though the collapse of the Soviet Empire in the early 90s dealt a severe blow to the Cuban economy that emphasised the damage of America's long-standing economic embargo.

Fidel Castro finally retired as Cuban President ten years ago; the fact he handed over the reins of power to his brother Raul when doing so emphasised the absence of democracy as the west would recognise it, though whatever means Castro used to assert his authority haven't dimmed his legend as the heroic liberator of Cuba. A regime that has become the blueprint of every revolutionary-turned-President since is not necessarily a legacy anyone with genuine care for human rights would praise, though were he remembered solely for what he achieved in 1958/9, that would be a fitting obituary. Sadly, there's far more to the story than that.

THE COMEDY OF TERRORS
1 December 2016

Like it or not, cities under siege have always been a regular aspect of warfare, from Londonderry in the seventeenth century to Stalingrad and Sarajevo in the twentieth; there are countless other accidental fortresses that could be listed, but if we are to set our time machines for 2016, the city unfortunate enough to be subject to that unenviable status is Aleppo, historically Syria's largest metropolis and one of the world's oldest continually inhabited cities. Archaeological records show that it has been populated since at least the 3rd millennium BC, which makes it all the more sad that one of the goons so dim that he made the other contenders in the US Presidential primaries seem like leading intellectuals didn't even know what Aleppo was.

The constantly shifting geographical changes in the region, such as the advent of the Suez Canal in the late nineteenth century and the encroachment of Turkey into Syria following the collapse of the Ottoman Empire after the First World War, had somewhat isolated Aleppo whilst helping to preserve its numerous antiquities in the process. Being awarded the Islamic Capital of Culture award ten years ago underlined Aleppo's pioneering place at the heart of ancient human civilisation, yet recent events in Syria have turned a jewel in Islam's cultural crown into a charnel house of death and destruction that we probably won't know the true horrific extent of until the shooting has stopped.

Different reports put the death toll of this week's heaviest bombardment of Aleppo somewhere between 25 and 45, and that was on just the one day. Opposing sides in the conflict release contrasting figures in order to suit their own agenda, whereas even independent observers struggle to compile accurate statistics due to the chaos on the ground. Just a couple of months ago, viewers of 'Newsnight' were witness to a remarkable life-saving operation undertaken in an Aleppo hospital basement which was dictated via Skype by a surgeon in London, but even that level of inspired improvisation seems impossible now.

A UN envoy this week declared Aleppo risks becoming 'one giant graveyard' during an emergency meeting of the Security Council, yet the current carnage in Syria once again highlights the impotence and absolute inability of the UN to make any difference to the lives of those caught in the middle of a bloody conflict, just as it has failed to do throughout its seventy-year existence.

When the roll-call of casualties and fatalities in the Syrian Civil War and a comprehensive account of the bloodshed inflicted upon Aleppo are neatly compiled into a book a decade or so from now, the thousands of names lost as a consequence will melt into each other so that only the survivors will recognise them. Buried amongst the tragically anonymous will be the name of Anas al-Basha, whose death as the result of a Russian-sponsored Syrian Government airstrike on Aleppo was announced yesterday.

Anas al-Basha wasn't one of those western gap-year gits who volunteer to work in some of the world's trouble spots solely to add some gravitas to their CVs despite spending the majority of their time there getting pissed and generally doing bugger all to improve the situation. In contrast with some of the jokers dressing as clowns and causing a momentary moral panic both in the UK and US, al-Basha donned the same costume not to scare the shit out of strangers in some overgrown schoolboy prank, but to put a smile on the faces of the children subjected to the relentless pounding the city has received over the last few months – of which there are an estimated 100, 000.

One could be cynical and come to the conclusion that a city without any functioning hospitals and dwindling food supplies doesn't necessarily need a home-grown volunteer clad in clown gear to inject some silliness into a nightmarish scenario; but the fact that al-Basha was prepared to stay put when 25,000 have fled, purely to bring a little cheer into lives without any at all, shows how the human instinct to laugh in the face of extreme adversity cannot even be extinguished by circumstances that would test the funny bone of the most committed comedian. What Anas al-Basha was doing was, to put it as simply as possible, something selfless and rather nice. It would have been easy (not to say understandable) had he joined the exodus from Aleppo when confronted by the kind of pounding few could tolerate on a daily basis, but he saw a way to temporarily alleviate unimaginable anguish and went for it. And now he's dead.

At a time when words such as 'brave' and 'courageous' are severely devalued by being bandied about carelessly to describe pawns in an exploitative game who shed tears on daytime TV when recalling alleged events that took place decades ago, it's worth remembering that in the here and now there are people in the world who are making the ultimate sacrifice just for the sake of raising a smile. They don't beg for sympathy with puppy-dog eyes and they don't give half-a-dozen idle police forces the excuse to spurn current crimes in favour of fishing expeditions to the safe haven of the past; they do what they do because they have a heart and they place the happiness of others above their own selfish concerns. If only the serial protestors could switch their attention to the real issues instead of hysteria over trivia, perhaps Aleppo could figure higher on their radar than it currently does.

Come the Syrian Day of Judgement, one would like to think the guilty will answer for their crimes, even if the example of Nuremburg has been distilled by the slo-mo legalities of The Hague. Chances are the contributions of Anas al-Basha to the pitiful peace process probably won't figure as an antidote to the list of atrocities on both sides, but sometimes it's worth noting those who put their neck on the line because they came face-to-face with man's inhumanity to man and did what they could to neutralise its appalling effect upon the next generation of extremists. We can but hope.

Although I wasn't exactly an avid follower of the news as a ten-year-old, I do remember the murder of Bulgarian dissident Georgi Markov on a London street in 1978. I suppose it was the unusual nature of his death that caught my ear, stabbed in the leg via the poisoned tip of an umbrella by an alleged KGB agent; it sounded like something straight out of an episode of 'The Avengers'. Markov was working for the BBC World Service at the time, broadcasting vociferous critiques of the Soviet satellite state that his country had become; assassinated by such strangely surreal means whilst waiting for a bus, Markov died four days later, his death attributed to the drug ricin.

Echoes of Markov's murder resurfaced almost thirty years later when another 'dissident', Alexander Litvinenko, was also poisoned in London; this time round, the victim was himself a former member of the KGB and its successor the FSB, so he knew all the dirty tricks. That didn't prevent him from sipping tea spiked with polonium-210 in one of the capital's sushi restaurants when meeting up with two other ex-KGB officers, just a couple of weeks after Litvinenko had accused Vladimir Putin of ordering the assassination of Russian journalist and human rights activist Anna Politkovskaya.

The sinister spectre of both these infamously odd, seemingly state-sponsored killings has been revived in recent weeks following the murder of Kim Jong-nam, older half-brother of the North Korean dictator, Kim Jong-un, at Kuala Lumpur Airport on 13 February. Grainy CCTV footage of the incident in which a young woman approached the unfortunate 45-year-old exile from his country and appeared to splash liquid on his face emerged a few days later, though it is far-from conclusive evidence as to what actually happened. Nevertheless, arrests swiftly followed, and two women from Indonesia and Vietnam respectively are to be charged with the murder and could face Malaysia's mandatory death sentence if found guilty.

Although Siti Aisyah and Doan Thi Huong have received the most publicity in the aftermath of the assassination, Malaysian authorities have indicated as many as 10 were involved in the plot, with South Korea claiming at least four of the suspects are spies working for their next-door neighbour. The defence of the two young women poised to be charged is that they thought they were part of a TV prank, paid around £70 to smear the face of a stranger with what they were told was baby oil. It may sound an especially ludicrous explanation, though this story is riddled with bizarre elements.

North Korea is in denial that the Macau-based victim was even their supreme ruler's sibling, though the poison applied to his countenance – toxic nerve agent VX – is not the kind to be found on your average high-street chemist's shelf; it is classified as a weapon of mass destruction by the UN and has been banned by the Chemical Weapons Convention since 1993; its particular rarity means the likelihood of it being in any hands other than that of a government is disputable.

VX is an apparently odourless lethal liquid that assaults the transmission of nerve impulses and Kim Jong-nam died in great pain within 15-20 minutes of the attack, despite informing airport security of what had happened to him immediately thereafter. It was an unimaginably unpleasant way to go, though the half-brother of Kim Jong-un has been on the North Korean hit-list for several years.

He was the first-born son of the late Kim Jong-il and had been earmarked as the former ruler's successor until apprehended trying to enter Japan on a fake passport in 2001. Since then, he has established himself as a vocal critic of the country and of his younger half-brother's regime. Considering the kind of regime Kim Jong-un oversees, it was perhaps inevitable that Kim Jong-nam's life would end in tears.

Other high-profile fugitives from North Korea have gone to ground in the wake of the Kim Jong-nam murder, fearing for their own safety more than ever. So far, North Korea's posturing has been manifested in its periodical nuclear testing, whereas this is a new and scary development for those who have managed to flee the most repressive nation on the planet. The two hapless girls who acted as Kim Jong-nam's assassins would appear to be classic patsies, arriving in Malaysia with high hopes of fame and fortune before ending up working in massage parlours and as gentlemen's escorts. Targeted to carry the can by whoever planned the operation, they are clearly not the masterminds behind the murder yet will still stand trial for it.

When it comes to assassinations of a thorn in a regime's side, an unhinged individual can certainly strike when the mood takes them, but governments supported by a secret service network with a licence to kill are far more effective when it comes to liquidating their enemies. It doesn't matter if it's Obama taking the credit for 'taking out' Bin Laden or that nice Mr Cameron endorsing the murder of two British Jihadist suspects fighting on a foreign field, the end result is the same – as Tsar Vladimir and the crackpot running North Korea know only too well.

The use of chemicals in warfare is almost as old as warfare itself; centuries before scientific advancement was able to produce man-made chemicals on an industrial scale, the Ancient civilisations of China, India and Greece were experimenting with 'organic gases' derived from toxic vegetables with a view to them being weapons. One of the earliest recorded uses of chemical weapons dates from the third century (AD) siege of Dura Europos, when bitumen and sulphur crystals were lit to create lethal sulphur dioxide smoke deployed against the invading Roman army. There's a sad irony to the location of this landmark event – modern-day Syria.

Yesterday's chemical incident in Khan Shiekhoun in the Indlib province of Northern Syria so far has a body count of 52 adults and 20 children; it is the first widely reported example of chemical warfare in Syria since the appalling 2013 massacre in Ghouta, which left hundreds dead. Once again, President Assad denies responsibility; his invaluable ally Russia admitted that Syrian aircraft bombed areas of Khan Shiekhoun, but attributes the deaths to the unintended striking of a rebel chemical weapons factory. Few are buying this story, with one chemical weapons expert rubbishing the idea a nerve gas could have spread in the way it did via an airstrike on a factory producing it.

News footage of those fleeing the attack shows symptoms consistent with exposure to nerve agents, choking and foaming at the mouth; some witnesses also claim the hospitals where the victims were being treated were then targeted by government airstrikes. There's nothing quite like kicking somebody when they're down, is there? The evidence of chemical weapons being used once more in the Syrian conflict is undeniable, though nobody wants to claim responsibility, least of all Assad.

The chemical in question is suspected to be sarin, production and stockpiling of which was outlawed twenty years ago. As a substance, it's so nasty that even a small dose can kill; it's estimated that sarin in its purest form is 26 times more lethal than bloody cyanide. The time it takes to do the business depends on the extent of inhalation, but the average is stated as being between one and ten minutes. Even a non-lethal dose can inflict potentially permanent neurological damage, whereas death by sarin is especially gruesome. After the runny nose, tight chest, inability to breathe, nausea and drooling come vomiting and involuntary defecation and urination, followed by the final comatose condition which ends with suffocation via convulsive spasms – and all within the space of ten minutes. As far as a way to go goes, it's fair to say there are less horrible endings one could endure.

We have the development of modern chemistry in the nineteenth century to thank for chemical warfare as we recognise it today, though it was inevitable any scientific breakthrough would be utilised by man for malignant means. During the Crimean War, the Secretary of the Science and Art Department (yes, there really was one), the wonderfully-named Lyon Playfair, proposed the manufacture of cyanide artillery shells because he seemingly thought it a more humane way of killing the enemy. His proposal was rejected, though the horrific potential of chemical weaponry caused such concern that the Hague Declaration of 1899 attempted to outlaw the use of projectiles 'the sole object of which is the diffusion of asphyxiating or deleterious gases'. All the major powers ratified the declaration except the US.

However, neither the Hague Declaration of 1899 nor the Hague Convention of 1907 prevented the use of chemical weaponry in the First World War. The French initiated the practice, swiftly followed by the Germans; by the end of the Great War, it's estimated around 1.3 million casualties could be attributed to chemical warfare. Between the wars, and despite the damage done by chemical weapons, gas was used to suppress native rebellions in European colonies as well as during the Russian Civil War, though the 1925 Geneva Protocol pledged to never use gas in warfare again. The Western allies upheld this during the Second World War and even Nazi Germany refrained from it, though the Japanese had used it against Chinese forces before 1939.

The fear of gas being used in WWII led to the widespread distribution of gasmasks and it has subsequently been revealed that mustard gas was stockpiled in the event of a German invasion of Britain. It was also intended to be used by RAF Bomber Command should the Germans have resorted to it to repel the D-Day Landings. Thankfully, none of these scenarios arose, though post-war uses of chemical weapons were said to have occurred in the likes of North Yemen, Rhodesia, Vietnam and Angola before its resurgence during the Iran-Iraq War.

The return of chemical warfare in such a high-profile conflict as Syria has shocked the world, though in the aftermath of the Arab Spring, Assad was clearly so desperate to cling onto power that it appeared he would stoop to anything. The support of Russia in this clinging onto power has enabled Assad to stay put; and when he again resorts to tactics that are below the belt even in such a bloody warzone as Syria, Assad knows Putin's backseat driving is his greatest asset.

Russia has the power to veto any resolution on the issue by the UN Security Council, claiming a draft resolution already proposed would pre-empt the results of any investigation into the incident and automatically lay the blame at the door of its Syrian sidekick. Heaven forbid! If, as most outside of Russia believe, Assad is capable of using chemical weapons on his own people, he's hardly unique amongst dictators; a certain sadistic despot in Iraq did likewise a few years ago, after all. But when the world's attention seems permanently focused on Syria, it does seem remarkable that Assad (if indeed he is guilty) can get away with such a crime again; but he got away with it before.

NEIGHBOURS FROM HELL
16 July 2017

The ominous spectre of a totalitarian regime transplanted to a western setting was a regular feature of dystopian post-war fiction for decades, covering everything from 'Nineteen Eighty-Four' through to television dramas like *'1990'* (produced by BBC2 in 1977). The worst development for a democratic society was perceived to be adopting the Eastern Bloc model, though it proved to be a fruitful source of material for dramatists. Watching any new broadcasts from North Korea in 2017 – especially in the last couple of days – one cannot help but shiver at the way in which they appropriate all the clichés from futuristic fiction produced in the late twentieth century and come across as especially toe-curling. Then the viewer remembers that, for North Korean viewers, this is actually the real deal; this is what they see whenever they switch their TV sets on.

The news that North Korea's latest foray into punching above its limited weight has been manifested as the launching of an intercontinental ballistic missile a couple of days ago has added further layers to increasing tensions in the Far East, arguably the world's most prescient powder-keg whilst the planet's eyes remain focused on the *Middle* East. Yes, the pre-inauguration promises of The Donald to 'deal' with the issue of North Korea reflected an awareness of the problem the tiny rogue nation poses to world peace; but it's probably true to say so much attention has been devoted to instability in Middle Eastern hotspots ever since the 2003 invasion of Iraq that Kim Jong-un and his bizarre regime has been allowed to progress to nuclear power status largely unimpeded.

Trump expects China to pull its finger out and lay the law down to North Korea in a way that complements its long-time role as one of the country's few allies; but, to be fair China's real investment in North Korea expired several years ago. Kim Jong-un's kingdom today largely exists on its own terms, without recourse to Beijing. China has too much money and good will invested in western powers (as well as Africa) to fall back on old alliances with archaic Stalinist states that have outlived their usefulness. Prior to Nixon's groundbreaking approaches to Maoist China in the early 70s, Peking's isolation from Moscow had forced it to forge allegiances behind the Bamboo Curtain; today, this no longer applies. It has friends in far higher places. In many respects, North Korea is viewed by China as an embarrassing throwback to old-school Communism that has little relevance to its own free-market interpretation of Marxism.

Since the distant days of Mao and Nixon, China has healed its rifts with Russia, and the Kremlin has exploited American fears of a nuclear arsenal that could reach as far from Pyongyang to Alaska by urging both sides to stop flexing their military muscles. The implicit accusation is that both sides are as bad as each other, and with such an unpredictable character as Trump in the White House, Russia could have a point. Then again, how is the US supposed to react when one of its own states is within the sights of Kim Jong-un's toys? When an even closer nuclear arsenal was spotted on Cuba in 1962, America's response could have had cataclysmic consequences for the world had not Kennedy successfully called Khrushchev's bluff. The thought of Donald Trump being placed in a similar situation is not one guaranteed to ease sleepless nights.

The Russian Foreign Minister Sergei Lavrov said that 'it is perfectly clear to Russia and China that any attempts to justify the use of force by referring to the UN Security Council resolutions are unacceptable, and will lead to unpredictable consequences in this region which borders both the Russian Federation and the People's Republic of China'. Yes, at times, North Korea, with its endless military parades and penchant for showing off its big missiles, is reminiscent of a man constantly stressing how hard he is without actually putting his money where his mouth is; but being able to distinguish between the reality of its threat and the propaganda is difficult when few outsiders can gain access to it.

Fifteen years on from being bracketed along with Iran and Iraq as 'The Axis of Evil', North Korea remains a stubborn sore on the planet's backside, led by a man even more unhinged than his late father. The phrase itself was credited to George W Bush's speechwriter David Frum, and it reeks of old world order certainties, whereby 'rogue states' were headed by unelected dictators redefined as cartoon Bond villains; they ruled over specific landmasses with clearly defined borders that could be found on maps of the world. It's no coincidence that 'Axis of Evil' sounds like a team of Marvel super-villains that can only be defeated by the Fantastic Four or the Avengers. Such terms simplify antiquated concepts of evil and make them palatable to a

western audience raised on Good Vs Evil battles in black &
white terms via the movies and the inherited memories of the
Second World War, when we knew who our friends and
enemies were.

It was telling that Dubya reserved his ire for Iraq above the
other two members of the club, extending the simplicity of his
language to describe the 'Axis' by assuming the problem of
Iraq could be solved simply by invading the country and
removing Saddam Hussein from power. Ironically, the
consequences of Dubya's intervention there have probably
served to dilute his monochrome vision of evil so that what
we have today is the likes of ISIS – a fluid, multi-headed,
stateless organisation that may view itself as a state even if
it's no more a state as we would recognise it than Israel was
before 1948. At least we can still understand North Korea. It
adheres to the traditional template.

President Trump said today 'something will have to be done'
about North Korea in response to its 'very bad behaviour';
what that 'something' is remains to be seen, though America's
recent record when dealing with small, insignificant Asian
countries that stand up to it isn't exactly a blueprint for
success. As the Sun said a few years back in one of its
occasionally inspired front-page headlines, how do you solve
a problem like Korea? It would appear nobody yet has the
answer.

THE (SOUTH) AMERICAN DREAM
30 July 2017

Well, voting is underway today – in Venezuela. The troubled
South American nation hasn't gone to the polls to vote for a
new government, however, but a constituent assembly to
rewrite the country's constitution. A few months ago, when

these proposals were unveiled, an unofficial referendum was held in which seven million Venezuelans voted; 98% of them rejected the proposals, but the proposals are going ahead regardless. And Remoaners think they've got it bad here. The move to convene the constituent assembly followed the decision in March when the Supreme Court announced its intentions to take over the National Assembly, which is run by the opposition. Although the protests that greeted this announcement caused it to be reversed, President Nicolas Maduro was accused by the opposition of attempting to stage a coup, and it is Maduro's determination to carry on regardless that seems to be tearing Venezuela apart, even if problems run much deeper and go back much further.

Venezuela is hardly unique amongst South American countries in experiencing ongoing difficulties when it comes to democracy, but external events have also contributed to its current crisis. With 95% of its export revenues dependent on oil, the diminishing global value of the commodity has hit it hard. Widespread food shortages have been the most devastating manifestation of the economic collapse, with figures estimating almost 75% of the population has lost an average of 8.7 kg in weight in the absence of proper nutrition, whereas only 15% of medicines are readily available. The hyperinflation that has struck the nation as of last year has seen consumer prices rise by a staggering 800% and the annual inflation rate has been estimated at 160%. As if things weren't bad enough, the country also has an appalling murder rate.

Anyone who happens to be a regular listener of Radio 4's wonderfully eye-opening institution, 'From Our Own Correspondent', will be familiar with Venezuela's decline in recent years, though the powder keg atmosphere has finally erupted into violent protest this year and the country now appears to be at breaking point. The portrait of society in a state of collapse that 'From Our Own Correspondent' has documented often seems uncomfortably reminiscent of the chaotic circumstances in Germany after the First World War, the ones that created the conditions for the rise of Nazism.

Nicolas Maduro's predecessor in the Presidential office, the late Hugo Chavez, had written the Venezuelan constitution in 1999 that his successor now seeks to overturn. Chavez used to carry the constitution around in his pocket, the 'little blue book' he was prone to brandishing whenever a camera was on hand. As architect of the so-called Bolivarian Revolution, which had ideological allies in other Socialist South American nations such as Bolivia, Ecuador and Nicaragua, Chavez embodied the classic anti-imperialist revolutionary leader in a Castro vein that has regularly proven popular amongst those opposing the foreign policies of South America's northern neighbour. When the great Socialist experiment invariably runs into a brick wall, blaming US intervention in the country's affairs in remains the default excuse, and Chavez knew how to play that one.

The legacy of Chavez's populist reforms, which were initiated when the Venezuelan economy was riding high on astronomical oil revenues - and included the nationalisation of major industries, excessive public spending, and the establishment of social programmes to improve the health and education of the population - began to reveal themselves in a less benign light at the point when Chavez lost his battle against cancer in 2013. They may have appeared admirable on paper, but Chavez failed to curb endemic corruption in public office and the police force, not to mention lowering the murder rate; a master of propaganda like Hugo Chavez was able to paper-over these cracks in his Socialist vision, but his successor has not been so fortunate. In many respects, Nicolas

Maduro inherited an unenviable economic time-bomb not unlike the poisoned chalice Tony Blair handed over to Gordon Brown in 2007, though one suspects UK-style austerity would seem like affluence to most Venezuelans today.

Nicolas Maduro's response to the crisis has been perceived as the President desperately trying to save his own skin rather than putting the interests of the country first. The aborted attempt to silence the opposition by taking over the National Assembly hasn't deterred his determination to convene a constituent assembly that will have the power to override the democratic institution he failed to seize control of. Over 6,000 candidates are standing for the constituent assembly, none of them from the opposition, which has boycotted it wholesale. But while international condemnation of the election has been summarily ignored, one of Venezuela's prominent neighbours Colombia – only just emerging from its own turbulence – has also refused to recognise the result when it comes.

The President hasn't done himself any favours by cracking-down on more physical opposition to his power; since street protests began in April, upwards of 3,000 protestors have been detained and dozens have been killed. The most high-profile presence on these protests has belonged to 'The Resistance', a masked group claiming to be the protectors of peaceful protestors; they generally head the marches and are prepared to fight fire with fire when confronted by police and security guards. A ban on demonstrations hasn't had much of an impact, with the barricades manned again on streets in the capital Caracas as the government continues to insist the constituent assembly will be the only solution to the anarchy of recent months. But Venezuela has so many more problems than that, and genuine solutions are in short supply.

William Makepeace Thackeray, Rudyard Kipling, George Orwell, Vivien Leigh, Spike Milligan, Engelbert Humperdinck, Cliff Richard, Joanna Lumley, my mate Vicky's dad – all made in India. Considering the British presence in India spanned the best part of 200 years, it's no wonder some of those born in the Subcontinent left their mark on the artistic and pop cultural landscape; though it's ironic that when The Beatles visited India to sit at the feet of the Maharishi in 1968, the one member of the band who had been born there was no longer present - Pete Best. However, by the time the last batch of these household names arrived, the days of British India were numbered, anyway; there were only 500 Brits left in the Indian civil service by 1935 and the posting was no longer viewed as the job for life it had been for generations.

For an exit that was, in the end, perceived by many as ridiculously hasty, there had been warnings for decades that the Raj was unsustainable; but it took the draining impact of the Second World War on the Mother Country for the jewel in the crown to finally slip from the imperial grasp. Some Indian nationalists had expected independence – or at the very least the dominion status afforded Australia and Canada – as a reward for the manpower India supplied in the First World War, where a million Indian troops had served King, Country and Empire; but the failure of the British to concede either fuelled the nationalist movement anew, and saw a fresh figure emerge who recognised the power of enigma.

Like Benjamin Franklin two-hundred years earlier, Gandhi had undergone a transformation from loyal colonial subject to unlikely revolutionary; he had written of his younger self,

'Hardly ever have I known anybody to cherish such loyalty as I did to the British Constitution.' The man who eventually took charge of India upon independence, Jawaharlal Nehru, had been educated at Harrow and Cambridge and had been admitted to the English bar. But both he and the Mahatma were one-time Anglophiles whose previous participation in the traditional cultural exchange between Britain and India didn't affect their desire and demand for independence.

The Raj may have been mythologized in the British imagination since 1947, but it was mythologized during its lifetime. Unlike many of its overseas colonies, India was viewed by Britain in the same way Algeria was viewed by the French, as an extension of home soil; Indian sportsmen from the world of cricket and polo were as familiar a sight in the UK as Maharajas were in London society, and we all shared the same King/Emperor. Even if the beneficiaries of the Raj on both sides tended to be small in relation to those for whom it was either an irrelevance or an encumbrance, the idea of another England thousands of miles away baking beneath a sun that never set was one that embodied all of the vaguely comical grandeur of romantic British pomp and circumstance. Even when the British sensed the sun *was* setting after all, they still anticipated it would take decades after the end of WWII before it happened.

As with the majority of Britain's colonial possessions, the British presence in India had arisen from maritime trading rather than a military invasion. The trailblazers had embraced the nation's religions, taken Indian wives and enjoyed the kind of cross-cultural immersion that was frowned upon following the 1857 Indian Mutiny, when direct rule by the British Crown replaced the corporate rule of the East India Company. From then on, there was a strict divide between colonists and natives; the playing fields of Eton trained the governors, administrators and Viceroys, whereas the civil service was open to any ambitious young Englishman, and many ambitious young Englishmen went for it.

For the generations of Brits who lived, worked and died in India, the standard of living for someone working in the civil service was considerably higher than they could expect back in the UK, and the job was an attractive proposition. Army postings on the Subcontinent were also envied; even the future Duke of Wellington had served his dues in India as a young ensign. In retrospect, it was remarkable that so few Brits were able to govern so many Indians for so many decades and for so long. But the system was stretched on several grim occasions, such as the 1919 Amritsar Massacre or the devastating series of famines in 1876-78, 1896-97, 1899-1900, and 1943-44; the total death toll of the first is estimated to have been in the region of 6.1 to 10.3 million.

The cult of Gandhi and his philosophy of non-violent protest in the 1930s contrasted with the increase in Sectarian violence that the British authorities struggled to keep a lid on. The PR sold back to Britain glossed over the realities of the situation as best it could, but it became harder to attract recruits to the Indian civil service in the years leading up to the Second World War. When British barrister Cyril Radcliffe arrived in India in 1947 to deliver the geographical partition he'd drawn up once India's independence as two nations had been decided, he found the country in a far worse state than he'd been led to believe. Civil war seemed all-but inevitable. In June 1947, the last Viceroy, Earl Mountbatten, announced the date for the end of British India; the remaining Brits had barely two months to get out as the unsatisfactory new map provoked the natives into migration, panic and unprecedented bloodshed.

The shock for the wave of Brits departing the only home they'd ever known upon arriving in Blighty was the jarring comparison with the place they'd left behind. A cold monochrome country, battered by wartime bombing and recovering from a crippling winter was compounded by the sudden diminishing of their social status; from comfortable surroundings complemented by servant staff, most found themselves reduced to living in small, grey homes on small, grey streets and having to accept jobs several notches down from the ones they'd enjoyed back home. It must have been a humbling comedown, and a story rarely told when the end of British India understandably concentrates on the bloody division of the nation the Brits left behind.

A language, an educational system and a legal system are the most visible and valuable legacies of the Raj in India today, surviving and thriving while the statues and monuments to forgotten British figures crumble away with the same slow drift from living memory as those Brits born and raised in the Raj. Not many of those voices have been heard during the media coverage of the 70th anniversary, but this anniversary marks a moment as crucial to the story of Britain as it is to the story of India, Pakistan and Bangladesh. In its own way, 1947 ranks alongside 1066, 1815, 1918 and 1945 as a pivotal turning point in our fortunes.

BEHIND CLOSED DOORS
4 September 2017

Shortwave radio may be the most underused of all the AM wavebands, though its ability to travel far greater distances than either long or medium-wave has enabled it to cross continents, open extended lines of communication between amateur radio hams and provide intelligence services with an invaluable means of both eavesdropping on the enemy and

255

passing instructions on to agents in the field. The clandestine cult of the Numbers Stations (which I have covered in previous posts) has highlighted the indisputable existence of the latter shortwave use, even if governments remain in public denial. The repetitive reading of numbers by an electronically-generated voice, reciting a code indecipherable to the layman, was a vital weapon in the Cold War because shortwave broadcasts can often be untraceable.

The golden age of the Numbers Stations was when the majority of them emanated from behind the Iron Curtain, though they have continued to appear on shortwave long after the so-called Russian Woodpecker over-the-horizon Soviet radar system served as a useful jamming device. Many these days come from the likes of Cuba and China. Shortwave radio is an almost infallible method of secret communication, far more than the easily-hacked and traceable signal from the internet. The notion that a medium dating from the early years of the twentieth century is a safer bet than contemporary technology flies in the face of everything we're led to believe in this techno-savvy age, when the lifespan of mediums means they seem to have a use-by date stamped on them the minute they exit the conveyor belt; but it's true.

It goes without saying that I've no evidence whether or not shortwave is utilised to penetrate the closed world of North Korea, but if it isn't it should be. The global reach of the worldwide web experiences something of an obstacle when confronted by Kim Jong-un's citadel; very few of the great dictator's subjects have internet access, so snooping on the traffic travelling in and out of Pyongyang is a considerably more challenging task than watching westerners wanking over webcam wonders doing rude things in a Belarus bedroom.

That many of the North Korean nuclear testing sites are situated underground has also limited the ability of American satellites to observe the country's rapidly developing nuclear programme. Modern spying techniques that work so well when observing the innocent have proven to be all-but useless whenever the west has attempted to keep an eye on the Far East's most worrisome nation.

North Korea's old sponsor China hasn't seen fit to share what its own intelligence has been able to divulge re recent events, though North Korea's understandably jittery neighbour in the South has claimed more missile launches are being prepared; these would be hot on the heels of the one that flew over Japan last week before splashing down in the Pacific. North Korea has also bragged that it now has the capabilities for attaching a hydrogen bomb onto a long-range missile, after testing out said explosive device at the weekend, one that apparently made the H-bombs that devastated Hiroshima and Nagasaki in 1945 resemble little more than a fart in a curry-house.

The detonation of North Korea's weekend H-bomb could be clearly detected in tremors that were felt in the Chinese city of Yanji, though few who flooded social media with their videos of the aftershocks were initially aware this had been a manmade earthquake. The fact that North Korea chose to test their H-bomb on the same day as Chinese President Xi Jinping was scheduled to give a speech at an international diplomatic shindig perhaps demonstrates its growing detachment from its former ally. Each of the recent publicised North Korean nuclear tests have coincided with major dates in the Chinese President's schedule; the fact that China has backed UN sanctions against the nation it remains one of the few in the world to still trade with clearly grates.

China, however, is still in a position where it could effectively bring North Korea to its knees, being the country's principle supplier of gas and oil as well as laundering billions in its banks; the apparent reason it doesn't seems to stem from Chinese fears over what the collapse of the North Korean regime would do to the region. If North and South were to reunite, with the whole of the nation becoming one giant South Korea, China is concerned that the US would exercise the same influence it already has over the South, turning the reunified Korean Peninsula into another American base in the Pacific akin to Japan. China isn't exactly keen on the thought of US troops stationed on its borders, but how much more is it prepared to tolerate before it exercises its remaining power over its one-time protégé?

China and the USA have a greater influence in the area around North Korea than any other world powers, so they are both better placed than most to change the current situation; but it's equally obvious that they need to work together to bring about a resolution that the UN is incapable of concocting. North Korea has hardly paid much attention to that institution so far. President Trump declaring that America is considering no longer trading with any nation that trades with North Korea seemingly overlooks the fact that China provides the country with 90% of its trade. For the moment, North Korea is essentially dropping its trousers and mooning China, the US and the UN in an act of schoolboy taunting; but China still wields the cane. All it needs to do is use it and maybe the rest of the world can sleep a little sounder as a consequence.

MADMEN
24 September 2017

Well, it takes one to know one. Kim Jong-un referring to Donald Trump as 'mentally deranged' following the US President's characteristically blustering speech at the United Nations this week was at least a diagnosis delivered by someone who recognised the signs. The war of words between Washington and Pyongyang has accelerated again, although on the same day that Iran's response to Trump's criticism of *them* was manifested as defiantly launching a ballistic missile, the American Air Force decided to fly bombers across the fringes of North Korea's east coast – upping the testosterone ante somewhat. There's a lot of muscle-flexing and macho posturing going on at the moment, and though the sanity of the guilty parties is regularly questioned, I think sanity is probably one of the first casualties of power, anyway.

The actions of leaders on the world stage are often engineered to provoke the biggest impact back home, and there are suspicions that one of the ways in which the organised crime dynasty ruling North Korea is retaining its grip on the country is by overstating its global significance. The people of North Korea – or at least those not breaking rocks for the thought crimes of their ancestors – are force-fed propaganda on a daily basis that tells them how important their country is; to the North Korean people, footage of Kim Jong-un viewing missile launches and surveying the troops convey the image of a great statesman leading a great nation; if he has the nerve to repeatedly stick two fingers up at America, Kim Jong-un must be the man the media proclaims him to be.

Twice in the last month, North Korea has flown missiles over Japan, but in the wake of Kim Jong-un's reaction to Trump's UN speech, his foreign minister said that one option open to the great dictator was 'the strongest hydrogen bomb test in the Pacific'. Last time an atmospheric nuclear detonation took place on the planet was in 1980, carried out by China; China's nuclear programme from the 60s onwards had been underestimated by the west just as North Korea's has been, and Kim Jong-un could regard such a potentially devastating test as a means of proving he means business if Trump's confrontational rhetoric is to be taken seriously. Needless to say, the damage to not only marine life, but to the environment as a whole in the Pacific should this happen is scary. Even scarier is the thought of an accident en route. A missile carrying an H-bomb accidentally plummeting down and landing on Japanese soil could have unthinkable ramifications.

A few weeks ago I bumped into an acquaintance of mine who told me she was going away for six months – to Japan. Her son lives there, having married a Japanese woman, and while I wished her well, I couldn't help but think there might be some safer locations in the world to spend the next half-a-year. Going by current standards, though, not many. Mind you, the lady in question has been around long enough to have lived through the Cuban Missile Crisis, so I should imagine she's used up her quota of sleepless nights. The fact she'll be residing in the same geographical neck of the woods as the world's incumbent Public Enemy Number One also probably won't unduly bother her; the alternative was returning home to visit her elderly mother, but as she's American, that prospect doesn't sound too appetising either.

For all the endless foot-stamping, placard-waving protest of Trump's most vocal critics, the fact they live in a country where they can criticise their President without looking forward to ending their days in a labour camp is worth remembering. The ridicule Dubya received during his tenure in the White House looks like gentle leg-pulling in comparison to the treatment meted out to the Donald, though those meting it out are still allowed to do so free from fear of being carted off and never seen again. Faced with persistent provocation from North Korea, Trump is naturally going to respond; but Trump being Trump means this response will inevitably be in the style of an NFL coach bigging up his team on the eve of the Superbowl. Trump gave his adoring supporters exactly what they asked for when he spoke at the UN, whereas those on the other side were understandably appalled by his 'come and have a go if you think you're hard enough' approach. Obama would have done things differently, but Obama hardly left the world a safer place than how he found it by doing things differently.

One positive move amidst the rather tense atmosphere has come from China – still the one country in a real position to cut North Korea down to size without resorting to nuclear options; in response to the latest UN sanctions, China has reduced the amount of oil it supplies to its troublesome trading partner and has also stopped buying North Korean textiles. The latter might not sound much, but many of the clothes that have a 'Made in China' label sown into them emanate from North Korea, and the ban could cost the country upwards of £350m a year. As for the oil, North Korea purchased almost 2.2 million barrels from China last year, so that will hurt it too.

Kim Jong-un has no qualms over murdering members of his own family to ensure he remains in power, so flouting international laws and the authority of the UN probably doesn't cause him any existential angst. And, ironically, there are enough of Trump's own countrymen who regard their President as a dangerous idiot to find themselves in agreement with the Asian Ro-land's opinion of the Donald. As Ray

Davies once said, it's a mixed-up, muddled-up, shook-up world.

A WOMAN SPURNED
13 November 2017

When John Lennon returned his MBE to Her Majesty in 1969, he penned an accompanying, and characteristically flippant, note that defused the potential melodrama of the grand gesture. 'I am returning this MBE in protest against Britain's involvement in the Nigeria-Biafra thing,' he wrote, 'against our support of America in Vietnam; and against Cold Turkey slipping down the charts'. Brenda's reaction was not recorded, though Lennon himself later admitted being a Member of the British Empire was something of an embarrassment re his counter-cultural credentials, even if sending the medal back provoked the ire of his Aunt Mimi, who had proudly displayed it on her mantelpiece for the previous four years.

The award was conferred in 1965, officially as recognition of The Beatles as a Great British Export, though prompted by a canny PM (Harold Wilson) with one eye on a forthcoming General Election he hoped would increase his slender majority. Released from the shackles of the 'mop-top' straitjacket in 1969, Lennon's peace campaigning with Yoko Ono and consequent resurgence of the lifelong anti-establishment sentiments that the Fab Four machine had suppressed earned him the enmity of the ruling class. Mocked and reviled in a manner that may come as a surprise to those who only know the posthumous Lennon as a latter-day Saint (successfully promoted by Yoko herself), Lennon's gesture was the final act of impertinence from the perspective of the set who had enjoyed patting John, Paul, George and Ringo on the head during the Beatlemania era.

What few mentioned at the time of the mortification that greeted Lennon's rebuttal of the State's ultimate Kinder Surprise bestowed upon a 'commoner' was that the initial award of the MBE to The Beatles in 1965 had been received with equal outrage from the same people. Numerous war veterans and distinguished gentlemen who had spent most of their adult lives expecting such an award would come their way themselves returned their precious MBEs in protest at long-haired young men devaluing the honour. Four years later, the politicised youth culture that had superseded Swinging London demanded Lennon nail his colours to the mast; Lennon momentarily appeased them, though the Radical Left continued to be critical of him unless they received an invite to his Ascot mansion. He eventually realised it was impossible to please all of the people all of the time and stopped trying.

Forty-eight years on, another grand gesture has been made by another former pop star, albeit one whose days as such are but a distant memory only upheld by the minority tuning in to BBC4's 'Top of the Pops' reruns. Bob Geldof has announced he will be returning his Freedom of the City of Dublin award in protest over the perceived failure of Aung San Suu Kyi to condemn and prevent what has been labelled ethnic cleansing in her native Burma (or Myanmar, if you prefer). The de facto Burmese PM had the same Irish honour conferred upon her, along with similar pats on the head bestowed by the likes of London, Oxford, Sheffield and Glasgow – three of which she has subsequently been stripped of. A portrait of her has been removed from the Oxford University College she read politics at and there are now calls for the Nobel Peace Prize she was awarded in 1997 to be revoked.

During the long years of her house arrest by the Burmese military (1989 to 2010, on and off), Aung San Suu Kyi was adopted as the poster-girl for political imprisonment and became a beacon around which western virtue signallers rallied in the same way a previous generation had rallied round Nelson Mandela. But the problem with such beacons is that the symbolic halo they acquire blocks out the uncomfortable truth of a warts-and-all human being; she was always a human being, even though the interchangeable nature of such cult figures (from Guevara onwards) means when their feet are exposed as having clay-like qualities, those who turned them into a symbol are as distraught as pubescent girls when they discover their pop idol has got married.

Upon her release, when Aung San Suu Kyi was being feted in the west and the usual suspects were falling over themselves to sing her praises and shower her in awards, the one person from these islands she really wanted to meet was Dave Lee Travis, whose radio shows being broadcast on the World Service had made a difference to her during her house arrest. Yes, DLT – not David Cameron or Theresa May, not even Bob Geldof or bloody Bono or any of the other glorified chuggers emotionally blackmailing the have-nots to donate to endless causes whilst they themselves squirrel their considerable assets away in overseas tax-havens. And now their darling has disappointed them by behaving like the actual politician she is (and in a country where the same military that imprisoned her still carries clout), they've suddenly decided she's up there with Mugabe.

The Mayor of Dublin has responded to Geldof's stunt by pointing out Sir Bob hasn't mentioned dispensing with his honorary knighthood from Britain, a nation whose reputation in Ireland as an imperial power of old doesn't really complement Geldof's principles. Geldof's reason for giving back his honour is Aung San Suu Kyi's indifference to the plight of the persecuted Rohingya people of Myanmar and her failure to act on the refugee crisis as thousands of Rohingya people flee predominantly Buddhist Burma for neighbouring Muslim Bangladesh, even if this isn't the first time it has happened.

For an incredibly complex situation with an extremely long and winding history in the region, the likes of Geldof and others simplifying and reducing it to basic black & white terms of heroes and villains is both condescending to those involved and betrays an ignorance of the far-from straightforward scenario playing out there. Yes, current events in Burma are not remotely pleasant; but Aung San Suu Kyi never asked to be the human rights sweetheart the west manufactured and her actions of late (or lack of them) demonstrate the dangers in projecting western values onto different cultures as much as Dubya imagining American notions of democracy could be imposed upon Iraq.

HELL PRESIDENTE
16 November 2017

Whatever spin the Zimbabwean Army puts on the situation for the benefit of the world's media, it's hard to come to any other conclusion that Robert Mugabe being placed under house arrest by the military is a sure-fire sign that the longest-running elected dictatorship in Africa is effectively over. Unlike Fidel Castro, the President of Zimbabwe wasn't prepared to retire once he reached an advanced age, despite being 93; it seemed the only way he was ever going to leave the Presidential palace was in a box. Now it appears his army has beaten the Grim Reaper to it. Officially, actions that look like a coup in all-but name are being described as a move to protect the President from a coterie of 'criminals' surrounding him; these allegedly include Mrs Mugabe, who was suspected of manoeuvring her way to becoming her husband's

265

successor, especially after his long-term ally, Vice-President Emmerson Mnangagwa was recently sacked.

Like Mugabe, Mnangagwa is a veteran of Zimbabwe's brutal and bloody war of independence that essentially spanned the last fifteen years of the county's previous incarnation as Rhodesia. Therefore, the military hold him in high esteem, for the generation that led the armed struggle against white minority rule – despite the fact the struggle ended almost 40 years ago – is still revered, and its veterans viewed as the founding fathers of the nation. In part, this is why Mugabe has been allowed to maintain his grip on power for so long and why Mnangagwa is regarded as the ideal successor, despite his role in the slaughter of thousands of opponents in the early 80s during his tenure as Security Minister. They can be forgiven for almost anything, with the exception of grooming an ambitious First Lady too young to have participated in the war to take over.

The lowering of the Union Jack in Zimbabwe in 1980 belatedly brought the curtain down on European colonialism in Africa, though it would have happened far sooner if Rhodesian PM Ian Smith hadn't declared UDI in 1965. Harold Wilson had been pressing for Smith to end white minority rule at a time when an economically perilous Britain was seeking to cut costs by severing the remaining ties with Empire, pulling out of Aden and only hanging onto Hong Kong until the 99-year lease was up. Smith saw neighbouring South Africa as the preferable role model for Rhodesia and his blinkered intransigence engineered a climate that ultimately claimed thousands of lives, often in unimaginably savage and barbaric ways. However, the tendency of native rebel groups in Africa to turn to a Marxist blueprint as an alternative to imperialism inspired panic when the Cold War was still in full swing, so even international sanctions against Rhodesia weren't as severe as they could have been when Soviet influence in former colonies remained a potent source of concern for European powers.

Ian Smith shocked both supporters at home and opponents abroad when he proposed the implementation of transition to black majority rule in 1976, but perhaps he could finally sense the guerrilla war he had instigated was a lost cause after a decade of fighting it. What followed was a laborious process of diplomacy between London and Salisbury that climaxed with the Lancaster House talks in 1979, paving the way for Zimbabwean independence a year later. The wonderfully-named Canaan Banana was Zimbabwe's first President, though his role was largely ceremonial; the real power rested with prominent guerrilla figurehead Robert Mugabe, now leader of the ZANU party, who was elected Prime Minister of the new independent nation. In the post-colonial climate, Mugabe was feted by the west and seen as symbolic of a new start for the continent; Stevie Wonder even applauded the birth of Zimbabwe in the lyrics of 1980's 'Master Blaster', though there were a lot of scores to settle.

The African tribal issue, which has been compared to England's class system or the old clan loyalties in pre-Culloden Scotland, didn't disappear with independence; within two years of white minority rule ending, Mugabe suppressed 'dissidents' in the province of Matabeleland by sending in elite troops trained in North Korea; thousands of civilians were massacred in Mugabe's name – estimates of deaths range from 3,750 to 80,000. The majority of those executed supported opposition party ZAPU, led by Joshua Nkomo. With his grip on power solidified, Mugabe's second election victory in 1985 was followed two years later by a pattern familiar to many countries that have been 'liberated' from colonial rule: Mugabe altered the constitution and made himself President – effectively for life. Zimbabwe was now a one-party state.

Mugabe's initial public call for racial reconciliation wasn't helped by the understandable 'white flight' from Zimbabwe to Apartheid South Africa, though those that remained tentatively supported Mugabe until he decided to play the colonial card and demanded 'decolonialisation', a process that resulted in the disastrous seizure of white-owned farms at the turn of the millennium. The economy consequently went into freefall as generations of experienced farmers were displaced by Mugabe cronies who hadn't a clue how to manage the rural economy. The consequences of this were disastrous for a country already being run down, stricken with the HIV epidemic and a pitifully low life-expectancy; hyperinflation followed, with the currency rendered virtually worthless. In the space of just fifteen years, Mugabe had enabled one of the most potentially powerful African nations to become a basket case.

Although opposition grew, Mugabe clung onto power through corruption and electoral fraud, constantly playing upon his war veteran credentials and deflecting international criticism by invoking the 'sour grapes' spirit of the country's former colonial overlords. However, by 2008, international admiration for the great revolutionary had diminished and he was forced to share power with opponent Morgan Tsvangirai, despite the violence he had overseen against his opposite number's supporters. This uneasy arrangement ended with the 2013 elections as Mugabe proved himself yet again to be a canny electioneer, retaining his office with a landslide.

Since then, however, his judgement and standing at home has come into question; the presence of his wife, regarded by many as the incumbent power behind the throne, has destabilised his support amongst the military, and this week's actions appear to have finally called time on a reign that seemed destined to end in death. Whatever happens next, the legacy of Mugabe's rule will take decades to repair, though the enforced installation of another ageing war veteran as President is perhaps not the best way to begin.

THE CHINESE WAY
13 June 2019

Long after most gave up the ghost, my VCR finally collected its retirement clock a year or so ago. It probably won't be replaced, yet I still have hundreds of tapes crammed with off-air recordings, many of which will never see the light of day as commercial releases. Probably due to this fact, I held onto most of them when the pre-recorded VHS movies were bagged and binned – ones I could always purchase again on DVD if need be. The majority of these tapes contain content reflecting my eclectic viewing habits at the time they were recorded; reluctant to waste tape, it's a dead cert any videocassette from the early 90s, for example, will see its last ten or twelve minutes used-up with a TOTP performance, a promo video from 'The Chart Show', and a few clips from 'Prisoner: Cell Block H'.

One tape from 1997 I recall has a characteristically idiosyncratic mix – featuring Radiohead's iconic 'OK Computer' Glastonbury set as broadcast on BBC2, the erotically-charged neo-Noir movie 'The Last Seduction', and highlights of the Hong Kong Handover Ceremony of June 30/July 1 that year. It's only through writing this that I've looked-up the dates and rearranged my somewhat sketchy memory of summer '97 – one in which several substances were consumed and have therefore buggered-up my memory's timeline in the process. I'd thought the Handover

269

Ceremony was closer to something else that happened that summer, something that happened on August 31.

Yes, of course, that summer crashed to its climax with the death of Diana and the month of mourning that plunged the nation into paroxysms of public grief on a scale I was able to view with detachment only because I had always been ambivalent about 'The People's Princess'. Was I alone in finding the final act of the British Empire more moving than the floral display outside Kensington Palace? It certainly felt like it at the time. Odd snippets come back to me now, like wondering how old 'fatty' Chris Patten could have sired two such gorgeous daughters; they were seen on the day China took back control due to the former Tory MP being the last colony's last governor, the consolation prize awarded to him by John Major upon losing his seat at the 1992 General Election. I know it sounds positively 19th century – a man from Westminster dispatched to govern an imperial possession; yet, it was less than 30 years ago.

As a child, I became aware this country had numerous cultural and sentimental tentacles stretching across the globe and that we retained little pockets of British soil a long way from home. There was Gibraltar, and there still *is* Gibraltar; but there was also Hong Kong, which was the one remaining genuinely exotic leftover from Empire – one of the spoils of the Opium Wars that went on to become the Far East's premier economic powerhouse. I remember that early 70s 'mum hunk', the suave Gerald Harper visiting Hong Kong in a couple of episodes of 'Hadleigh'; there was also a BBC documentary series called 'Hong Kong Beat', focusing on the Royal Hong Kong Police Force, with its catchy theme tune even making the charts; and, lest we forget, Bruce Lee made most of his movies there, movies that went on to become staple diets of video rental shops. Yet, as we moved into the

1980s, anything to do with Hong Kong started to centre around Britain's 99-year lease, as if the island was a holiday home owned by the UK that would be inherited by Hong Kong's nearest neighbour once its owner died. Actually, maybe that's how it really was.

For decades, Hong Kong had provided refuge for political dissidents fleeing China, and the prospect of the colony falling under Chinese jurisdiction was understandably worrying for them; their concerns naturally intensified following the Tiananmen Square massacre of 1989. Even though the signing of the Sino-British Joint Declaration in 1984 laid out the 'one country, two systems' concept to allay fears Hong Kong would end up as a suburb of mainland China and be subject to the same repressive rules and regulations governing the People's Republic, it was accompanied by gradual goalpost-moving on the part of the British Government to deliberately limit the potential numbers of Hong Kong natives claiming British citizenship and the right to settle in the mother country. After Tiananmen Square, with the Handover only eight years away, an estimated 10,000 rushed to apply for residency in the UK. Singapore, Canada, Australia and the US proved to be popular alternative destinations, and during its last decade as a Crown Colony, Hong Kong lost almost a million of its citizens who chose to emigrate rather than remain.

Tony Blair had been PM less than two months when he joined his Foreign Secretary Robin Cook, Governor Patten and Prince Charles on the podium to officially cede ownership of the island to China. Brian's unflattering account of the occasion surfaced in the Mail on Sunday a few years later, wherein he compared the Handover Ceremony to a cynically choreographed Soviet-style performance and referred to the event as 'The Great Chinese Takeaway'; the Prince of Wales was of course representing Brenda, as he had 17 years earlier when the Union Jack was lowered in Rhodesia. With Africa long gone by 1997, it was time for the Far East to finally follow suit, and I have to say my memory of watching the Ceremony live on TV isn't one that evokes the heir's cynicism. I was conscious this was something of genuine historical significance, like Churchill's funeral – the belated end of one kind of Britain and (with Blair fittingly present) the beginning of another.

For the people of Hong Kong, there was no sailing off into the sunset on the Royal Yacht Britannia, however; they were left to deal with the realities of the new regime. Their predicament couldn't be compared to the difficulties facing the UK's other ex-colonies following the cutting of imperial apron springs, i.e. being at the mercy of hard-line religious despots or military coups; Hong Kong had not achieved independence, but had merely changed hands. Having a totalitarian super-state on the doorstep is no more a pacifier of anxiety for Hong Kong's citizens than it is for those residing in the former Soviet satellites; the perennial fear that Beijing will slowly implement its own authoritarian agenda on the island by stealth is something that has continued to creep up on the people; and cracking down on public demonstrations of dissatisfaction such as the 'umbrella protests' of five years ago with tough sentencing appeared to suggest their fears were well-founded.

Attempts to introduce a new extradition law, whereby anyone from Hong Kong who invokes the ire of Beijing can be removed to mainland China for trial, has now provoked a fresh outburst of protest. This time, however, it hasn't emanated wholly from the Hong Kong youth born after the Handover, whose view of themselves as international citizens has supplanted the traditional affinity with Britain of previous generations; it has spawned an unlikely alliance of different demographics ordinarily divided by faith, politics and age – united in their opposition at Beijing reneging on aspects of the Sino-British Joint Declaration; this week it has crossed the line from peaceful protest to civil disorder. The island's former colonial overlord, however, can do nothing but issue meek condemnations of China's actions; we absolved ourselves of all responsibility in 1997 – and, besides, China today equates with trade and money. We wouldn't want to upset our friends in Beijing – making one wonder if it was just Hong Kong that was handed over 22 years ago.

5
It Could Be Yewtree

False allegations, fishing parties, witch-hunts
and hysteria

A WARNING FROM HISTORY
22 December 2015

A major celebrity is accused of rape; the media report on the accusation and subsequent trial with sensational relish, exhibiting the worst aspects of what was once called 'yellow journalism' by portraying the accused as a monster and pre-empting a verdict by assuming guilt; puritanical pressure groups call for his execution and colleagues are warned not to speak up on his behalf at the risk of damaging their own popularity and being implicated by association; the prosecutor at the celebrity's trial has ulterior motives, pressurising witnesses to make false statements and concluding the accused is guilty after being fed lurid stories from a convicted fraudster, successfully blackening the accused's character in the process; the end result is a mistrial and the case is drawn out into two further trials, almost as though the powers-that-be are more concerned with establishing guilt than accepting innocence in order to save face; the publicity causes the celebrity's work to be censored and excised from circulation, in some cases destroyed completely; his career is ruined and his reputation permanently tarnished as a consequence, even though eventually cleared of all charges; the legal cost of the three trials forces him to sell his house and places him on the brink of bankruptcy without the means of earning a living from his former career.

Although this sorry story may seem uncomfortably prescient, it actually stems from over ninety years ago and the celebrity in question was silent movie star, Roscoe 'Fatty' Arbuckle. Learning nothing from history seems to be a contemporary curse and in the case of poor old Arbuckle, everything that has become commonplace in courtrooms over the past couple of years already had precedents stretching back to the early 1920s. Oscar Wilde is a name that is frequently evoked when describing some recent show trials involving accusations of historical sex crimes, but the closer one studies the case of Fatty Arbuckle, the closer the parallels with present day miscarriages of justice seem.

A century ago, silent cinema's obvious absence of onscreen dialogue meant that it crossed all language barriers in a way that 'talkies' never have and the stars it produced became international household names with remarkable rapidity at a time when there was no comparable competition in terms of mass media. Someone such as Charlie Chaplin at the peak of his popularity was perhaps the most recognisable man on the planet, enjoying a level of worldwide fame that only The Beatles and Diana, Princess of Wales have experienced in recent decades.

Roscoe 'Fatty' Arbuckle was up there with Chaplin and Keaton in the 1910s, mentoring the former and discovering the latter (as well as giving an early break to a young comedian by the name of Bob Hope). A former child prodigy, ironically famed for his powerful singing voice, Arbuckle's natural comedic talent saw him progress to the Vaudeville circuit whilst still in his teens. As a means of subsidising his stage career, he made extra cash appearing in the nascent Hollywood movie industry's comedy shorts, including the famous Mack Sennett Keystone Cops series. He soon rose through the ranks, as was possible in those early days, to found his own film company and take complete control of his increasingly profitable output. Audiences responded favourably and by the turn of the 20s, 'Fatty' Arbuckle was known and loved across the globe. Then it all came crashing down.

From all accounts, Arbuckle was a kindly gentleman whose shyness around the opposite sex maybe stemmed from his huge bulk; but he made his name in an industry that was attracting the attention of fanatical moral lobbyists that were finding examples of depravity and decadence in all aspects of popular culture, whether jazz, the movies or alcohol; they were already responsible for outlawing the latter and when a sordid story emerged from a San Francisco party in 1921, one at which Arbuckle was present, they viewed it as symptomatic of Hollywood's corrupting influence on the nation. It was just the scandal they, and the newspapers of William Randolph Hurst (the Murdoch of his day), had been waiting for.

A minor actress named Virginia Rappe was also at the said party; when the illicit hooch being served had a dramatic effect on her, the doctor resident at the hotel at which the party was held dispensed morphine to calm her down; what the medical man was unaware of was that Rappe suffered from a condition that alcohol exacerbated. She already had a reputation for drinking too much and then ripping off her clothes when afflicted by the resulting pain and was also in poor physical health due to a series of botched abortions. She wasn't hospitalised until two days after the San Francisco party, by which time it was too late. Rappe died of peritonitis courtesy of a ruptured bladder. Prior to her death, Rappe's friend Bambina Maud Delmont claimed Rappe had been raped by Arbuckle, despite an examination revealing no evidence. The police came to the decision that Rappe's bladder had been ruptured by the weight of Arbuckle and arrested him on charges of rape and manslaughter.

When the case went to trial, the world's media reported it in a manner we'd find all-too familiar today. The prosecutor had ambitions to run for governor and derived most of his accusations against Arbuckle from Bambina Maud Delmont's vivid imagination; that she had a track record of numerous dubious activities of an illegal nature perhaps prevented the prosecutor from allowing her to take the stand, which would have undoubtedly exposed her as an unreliable witness. After two weeks, the jury's indecision was underlined by the presence of a juror connected to the DA's office who had claimed she was determined to find Arbuckle guilty. Unsurprisingly, the jury failed to reach a verdict and a mistrial was declared.

Arbuckle had to endure a second trial whilst fantastically gruesome accounts of him raping Rappe with a bottle circulated in the Hearst press. One of the prosecution witnesses was an ex-studio security guard who it eventually transpired was in the middle of being charged with sexual abuse of a minor, yet even this revelation and the fact that Rappe's history of drunken promiscuity was documented couldn't alter the bias against Arbuckle after months of sensational headlines. The jury was again unable to decide and only after a third trial, by which time Bambina Maud Delmont was touring the country and exploiting her infamy, was Arbuckle finally acquitted.

Arbuckle left court a free man, but the legacy of the trial was something he couldn't shake off. He was temporarily banned from making movies by the man who introduced the notorious Hays Code to clean-up Hollywood and received financial assistance from Buster Keaton until the ban was lifted. The effect of everything he'd been through led to Arbuckle to seek solace in the bottle and the little movie work he could find in the years after the trials couldn't return him to the status he'd enjoyed before them. He died from a heart attack in 1933, aged just 46, unable to live down the scandal that had also resulted in the prints of many of his movies being incinerated, lost forever.

What Roscoe Arbuckle went through almost a hundred years ago has unnerving echoes in the present day. The inconsistencies and holes in the evidence against him, not to mention the unreliability of the witnesses and jurors as well as the ulterior motives of the prosecutor, the influence of moral crusaders, the deliberate destruction of his work and the biased reporting of the press, all appear to constitute a user manual for future witch-hunts. There are many lessons that could have been learned from the fate meted out to Fatty Arbuckle; unfortunately, the wrong side learned them.

AS NATURE OFFENDED
22 May 2016

A paediatrician asks a mother to video her mentally disabled daughter enduring one of her regular spasms in order that he can make an effective diagnosis; a side-effect of her child's condition is that the spasms cause her to rip her clothes off. Upon being told this, the physician whose job it is to tend to the medical needs of children informs the mother he cannot view any such videos. Despite the fact that visual evidence of the spasms will enable him to treat them correctly and possibly ease the girl's suffering, he cannot look at it because he fears possession of such material will result in him being placed on the sex-offender's register. The mother also hesitates at capturing her daughter's spasms on video for fear she will be charged with making offensive images; sending them to the paediatrician could land her with an additional charge of distributing offensive images. Therefore, a woman who gave birth to a child born naked and a man whose profession sometimes requires him to examine children without clothes on both back away from helping a sick child because of fear. This is a true story, told to me by someone who was told it by the mother of the child. What an absolutely ludicrous, not to say tragic, scenario.

This is an extremely smug century. A consensus is afoot that we are sophisticated, liberated and no longer hindered by the repressive sexual pressures that stifled personal freedoms in the past. If the products of this culture have an imagined nemesis, it is the Victorians. Women couldn't vote and were second-class citizens encased in constricting corsets; homosexuals were locked away and broken by the prison system; black people were oppressed colonial cheap labour, barely better off than when they were slaves; the poor lived in squalid hovels with no social safety net other than the workhouse. Weren't the Victorians terrible and aren't we so much better? Are we?

Last year, a BBC documentary on Lewis Carroll aired, in which the 'Alice in Wonderland' author's pioneering photographs received extensive coverage. Carroll – or as he was known beyond Wonderland, Charles Dodgson – specialised in somewhat sentimental portraits of children that enraptured their parents, most of whom were present when Dodgson's elaborate set-pieces were staged and captured on camera. Many of these images featured children unclothed, something that at the time was supposed to emphasise the virtuous innocence of vulnerable cherubs whose lifespan hovered in a permanent state of uncertainty. Sensibilities today see such images rather differently.

One overlong segment of the documentary was devoted to an image of an unidentified naked pre-pubescent girl whose identity was speculated as being that of the real Alice's sister, Lorina Liddell; nobody could even say for certain that Charles Dodgson had actually taken the photograph. But this formed part of the predictable discussion on whether or not Dodgson's penchant for participating in a late nineteenth century vogue for photographing children pointed to him being a paedophile. The squeamish icing on the twenty-first century censorious cake, however, was that the programme-makers wouldn't even let the viewers see the photograph in question. A Victorian photo of a girl who will have been dead for at least fifty years – and that's if she lived to a very ripe old age – couldn't be shown on television in 2015 because it was deemed to be offensive to the sensitive sensibilities of our oh-so superior age.

'Victorian Values' is a wide-sweeping term that is only ever used dismissively; it is supposed to represent everything bad that has gradually been superseded by more enlightened thinking and living. Yet, as hypocritical as the Victorians' attitude to flesh and pleasures thereof allegedly were, they were not terrified of the flesh of children – and they were not expected to see pleasure in it at all, unlike their 'sophisticated' successors over a hundred years on. Of course, there were some adults then who had unnatural sexual desires towards children, just as there were before the Victorians and just as there are today; but the key difference between then and now is that the nineteenth century acknowledged paedophilia as a rare symptom restricted to a minority rather than a commonplace perversion inherent in the majority.

Today, one has to prove the absence of such feelings because their absence is not accepted. It is a given, a presumption that they are in all of us, simply waiting to be exposed. A series of laws introduced over the past decade seem designed to catch us out, to coax these feelings into the open, like some form of thought entrapment; and if they happen not to be in us, they have to be implanted in us because they're supposed to be there. These laws encourage instant suspicion and rushes to judgement, and they persuade people to think the worst of everyone. They negate rationality, provoke paranoia and self-doubt, inspire mob mentality, and more than anything, they generate a primitive brand of pseudo-religious, finger-pointing fear unprecedented in a secular society.

The Victorians were supposedly so averse to the sight of naked flesh that they covered piano legs because they resembled the indecently-exposed legs of ladies. How silly, eh? But they weren't horrified by the sight of children as nature intended; we are. And that's progress.

THE FISHING PARTY
15 November 2016

It's probably true to say Ted Heath was his own worst enemy. Britain's Prime Minister from June 1970 to February 1974 was famed for his cold, brusque aloofness in company, ignoring VIPs, dignitaries and his own MPs at social functions and earning a reputation as a rather pompous and grumpy old so-and-so that won him few friends and cost him support amongst his peers when he needed it. Yet he himself couldn't understand why people found it so hard to warm to him; he always saw everyone else as the problem. He came across as uncomfortable, stiff-necked and ill-at-ease when PM both on television and when speaking in public, a poor communicator struggling to get his message across to the electorate. With the possible exception of Gordon Brown, he remains on paper perhaps the most unsuited man for the job in the post-war era, an unlikely candidate for Downing Street if ever there was one.

Yet, put a baton in his hand and stick him in front of an orchestra or sit him down at a grand piano, and he was in his element. A diffident and difficult man whose shyness was often perceived as straightforward rudeness, Heath relaxed when with those who shared his passions. Music had been the main one from day one, though later in life he applied himself to mastering the art of sailing and this became his other great love. The determination he displayed when it came to learning the latter mirrored his political ambitions. Despite his evident limitations for public office, he wouldn't be swayed and the work he put in was eventually rewarded when he won the contest to succeed Sir Alec Douglas Home as Tory leader in 1965. Five years later he scored a shock win over Labour PM Harold Wilson, a man who had repeatedly dismissed Heath as a lightweight up until polling day in 1970.

We're so used to the nauseating 'family shots' of Prime Minister with spouse and children these days that it seems even more bizarre now to have had a bachelor at No.10 forty-five years ago, let alone one who sought solace of an evening by playing the piano and then took a couple of weeks off from running the country to compete in, and win, a prestigious yachting competition. Heath was certainly his own man, refusing to enter into a marriage solely for PR reasons and brushing off predictable rumours he was an old poof (to use the parlance of the time). Heath became PM just three years after the decriminalisation of homosexuality, though the accusation remained the default insult to aim at the unmarried man; those who were genuinely homosexual during that era tended to marry, such as Liberal leader Jeremy Thorpe, as a means of deflecting accusations, though Heath had no idea how to interact with women in a romantic manner and didn't bother trying just for the sake of his public image.

After innumerable difficulties with bolshie unions and Northern Ireland, as well as antagonism over his pushing of Britain to join the Common Market, the Three Day Week was the final straw for the electorate. After losing two General Elections in 1974 and surrendering No.10 to his nemesis Harold Wilson, Heath's days were numbered. When his unpopularity in his own party gifted Margaret Thatcher the kind of support required to topple Heath as leader in 1975, Heath couldn't fathom why it had happened and for a good year or so was convinced he could regain his position; when Thatcher won the General Election in 1979, her decision not to award a Cabinet post to her still-active predecessor provoked one of the great public sulks in British political history, one that didn't end until Thatcher herself was toppled in 1990.

During half-a-century as a serving MP, Edward Heath made many enemies and wasn't prepared to compromise in order to court popularity. His relatively humble origins for a Conservative leader provoked enmity from the old patrician Tories, who looked down on him as a social inferior, and his obstinacy as PM where the press and public were concerned lingered long after he had left Downing Street. Heath wouldn't play the game and that kind of attitude inspired grudges that have lasted, even more than a decade since his death. Naming and shaming him as a closet gay, though there was no evidence to back up such a claim other than he never married, is no longer a sufficient weapon in our sexually enlightened day and age, so the default insult now is paedophile, a word that embodies all the revulsion once reserved for 'queer'.

The last 16 months has seen 21 presumably thumb-twiddling officers of Wiltshire Police pack their rods for a fishing expedition known as Operation Conifer, a sort-of retarded country cousin of the Met's Operation Midland, in response to unsubstantiated accusations against the deceased PM, and have so far spent £700,000 casting their nets in the vain hope of salvaging confidence in the country's most discredited public service. Heath's name had already been pulled out of the fantasist's hat worn by 'Nick', the anonymous accuser of half-a-dozen VIPs and their alleged part in the Westminster

Paedo Ring that never was, and Wiltshire Police took it upon themselves to pursue additional 'credible and true' accusations even when Operation Midland was rightly recognised as the criminal waste of public money and ruination of reputations it was all along.

This week Operation Conifer was even reduced to 'investigating' (and I use that term loosely) the anti-Common Market incident in 1972, when a protestor threw ink at Heath as he arrived to sign on the dotted line that would enshrine Britain's membership of the EEC. What the hell that has to do with 'paedophilia' is nothing other than the painful sound of a barrel's bottom being desperately scraped. After last week's damning report into Midland, the continuation of Conifer merely confirms the priorities of the police as a time-travelling hit squad whose interest in solving twenty-first century crimes is secondary to rooting around the dirty laundry of the dead and dying on the hearsay of mentally demented finger-pointers fresh out of therapy.

It's no surprise they should single out Heath in a last pathetic throw of the dice. His defiant oddness in Prime Ministerial terms was a gift for them, but each victim of the witch-hunt has been an individual eccentric and square peg, characteristics alien to the consensus of the day. Operation Midland has now been acknowledged as an outrage by the media, yet few have dared to allocate the same condemnation to Operation Yewtree, the granddaddy of them all, and a project responsible for the rotting in gaol of more than one household name as well as the soiled gravestones of many more. Makes you proud to be British, doesn't it? No, me neither.

Just when you thought it was safe to put the Paedo back in the box, the blighter has escaped again. Someone call the cops! Not to worry – cometh the Paedo, cometh the Chief Constable; this time it's the turn of Norfolk's main man, Simon Bailey. The No.1 Bobby from the land of big-eared boys on farms also happens to be 'lead for child protection' of the National Police Chiefs' Council, so he obviously knows his stuff.

Chief Constable Bailey declared on Saturday that there will be a significant increase in numbers coming forward to report historical sexual abuse in sports other than football. Without even heading for the hat-stand in the hallway and reaching for the headgear marked 'cynic', it's hard not to detect the palpable relish in a statement that means we will once again see the nation's individual police forces devoting their resources to investigating alleged crimes committed twenty, thirty or forty years ago rather than coping with the far more difficult task of solving crimes committed in the here and now. It's the crime-fighting equivalent of opting for the cosy familiarity of Radio 2's playlist instead of taking a risk with 6 Music because the memory-laden soundtrack of the past is easier on the ears and easier to deal with than the unpredictability of the contemporary.

In what our law-enforcers know is a tried-and-trusted self-fulfilling prophesy, the announcement by a prominent policeman (at least in his own neck of the woods) that he suspects 'there will be other sporting governing bodies...who will come forward and who will identify the fact that they have similar problems' is guaranteed to unleash the kind of workload the police are evidently in sore need of as well as fuelling this nation's insatiable appetite for the subject it clearly can't get enough of. The words 'credible' and 'true' have yet to be bandied about, but other hackneyed phrases that constitute the lexicon of the historical child abuse narrative have reappeared, just as we all knew they would.

'Brave' and 'Courageous' were employed to describe the sad TV confessions of a group of ex-footballers fulfilling the moral obligation of the moment by providing a voyeuristic public and a salacious media with the most intimate and explicit personal details of their pasts; and, of course, 'other victims coming forward', that other old chestnut, was wheeled out for one more encore. As we are informed that four separate forces are stepping into their customised police boxes for further journeys back in time following last week's high-profile revelations of a former youth coach who has already served time and is recognised as a past offender, the farcical national inquiry into child sex abuse has said it is 'watching events closely', perhaps intending to add football to its itinerary in around three or four years time.

The NSPCC, supposedly a children's charity, has become the unofficial sponsor of the grown men whose miserable childhoods took place decades ago; the usual ambulance-chasing law firms have pricked-up their ears at a development that holds the prospect of fresh exploitation as well as financial salvation; and Crewe Alexandra, the perennial lower-league dwellers who once employed Barry Bennell, the man at the centre of these allegations, are apparently launching their own investigation into the unpleasant affair to boot. The wheels of the industry are being oiled anew and timing, as ever, is everything.

The BBC has given extensive coverage to this story, excitedly rounding-up the ex-pros to spill the beans on Victoria

Derbyshire's coffee-table chinwag in classic Oprah Winfrey fashion; one can't help but suspect the Corporation is rubbing its hands together as it has done on numerous occasions post-Savile, eager to prove it wasn't alone in allowing rampant Paedos to fiddle about to their dark heart's content on their premises in the past. And, of course, the boys in blue, still smarting from the justifiable condemnation they received following the publication of the report into Operation Midland, are desperate to deflect attention away from their own ineptitude and corruption of justice, hoping they can win back the public's trust in them by embarking upon a new mission against the common enemy.

As the most extreme extension of the 'they're all at it' conspiracy theory conviction, the historical child abuse industry has been one of the few post-2008 success stories in the UK over the last five years; and like every booming business, it has a network of individuals and institutions that are financially dependent upon it. What would become of the arms industry, after all, if there were no wars taking place in which the latest weaponry was required?

Likewise, having exhausted the respective worlds of showbiz, politics, academia and various branches of Christianity, this particular industry has spent a great deal of time and energy engaged in a search for the next untapped source of revenue. So far, sport – usually bogged-down with match-fixing or drug-taking scandals – has evaded the shadow of historic abuse. Now, however, its time has arrived.

Like many detached observers witnessing yet another chapter in this saga unfolding, I often ponder on how and why we got here. I sometimes wonder if the obsession of Britain with a rare sexual peccadillo and the belief that every outlet of 'the establishment' has been a haven for its practitioners due to institutionalised blind eyes betrays a deep grievance with this society's social and financial inequality. Intense envy of the rich, the famous and the powerful has grown in line with the dramatic decrease of social mobility; and as economic divisions widen rather than narrow it would appear the only way in which many can deal with the harsh truth that they will die in possible poverty and undoubted obscurity is to take the rich, famous and powerful down with them. Unfortunately, the beneficiaries of this nihilistic approach to a hopeless situation are themselves, if not famous, then increasingly rich and increasingly powerful.

MEMORIES ARE MADE OF THIS
15 December 2016

During the filming of the retrospective Beatles documentary, 'Anthology', in the early 90s, Paul, George and Ringo were largely interviewed individually and it was noticeable on occasion that each recalled certain key incidents thirty years on very differently. It seemed to highlight the difficulties when more than two people recall a particular event at which they were all present; which is the genuine recollection – all or none?

We naturally view the world from our own unique perspective, so it's inevitable that if two or three witness the same event, recalling it in the immediate aftermath will differ slightly, though not as much as when recalled days, weeks, months and years (even decades) on. By then, they are so removed from the moment that each successive recollection is a photocopy of its predecessor, so – as somebody once pointed out – we're not remembering the event, but remembering the last time we remembered it. Distance alters the event in our heads and does so differently for each individual witness. To use just one seemingly trivial example,

291

if we were present at the event with people we still see regularly, in our recollection they don't look exactly as they looked at the time; we see them essentially as they are now, which clearly isn't the same as viewing a photograph or cine-film of the event, when we notice the different hairstyles or clothes that were specific to that era.

Similarly, when we summon up an incident from childhood, rarely do we recall factors that would hit us immediately were we to be suddenly transported back into our prepubescent bodies – i.e. how small we were and how big our surroundings were, not to mention the adults towering above us. Such a sensation is something memory appears to have a problem dealing with, and the physical distinctions between then and now only strike us if we happen to revisit our old infants' school and see how tiny the chairs we sat in were. Our minds reconstruct the event of forty-odd years before to a degree of accuracy, but do so in a context we can relate to in the here and now; it's extremely difficult to envisage something as significant as being several feet smaller than we have been for the entirety of our adult lives.

Our household didn't acquire a colour television until 1976; prior to that, everything I saw on TV at home was in monochrome – yet my vivid memory of Jon Pertwee regenerating into Tom Baker in 1974 is one of sitting by the telly and watching the landmark moment in colour, perhaps because I've subsequently seen the transformation many times since in colour. Another simple example of how memory shouldn't be trusted implicitly comes with the case of a favourite film one has viewed so many times that quoting lines from it just before the actors speak them is second nature; yet the recital is rarely word-perfect. It's only when we watch again that we realise we got the odd word wrong or added a word that isn't actually there in the script. Every time we repeat what we believe to be the quote, we're subconsciously rewriting the lines based on the recollection of what we said last time we recited it.

Taking all of this into account, it's worth noting how much reliance is placed upon remembrance of an event, especially when the police question witnesses to a crime, which is why they're supposed to be trained not to influence the witness during questioning if there's an uncertain pause, hence the tradition of the identity parade rather than the police simply producing a photo of the man they know did it and saying 'Is *this* the man?' The person helping the police with their inquiries may have run through the event in their heads several times before committing it to an official statement, and the natural instinct of memory is to iron out inconsistencies and any illogical elements so that it can be recounted with a cohesive clarity that makes sense when said out loud.

When recalling a visit to the school careers officer during his Sheffield adolescence, Michael Palin once remarked the officer's response to every pupil's career ambitions when asked what they wanted to do was met with a straightforward 'I think it's Pilkington's Glass for you, young man', reflecting his blatant role as a recruiter for one of the city's chief employers.

The psychoanalytical branch of medicine over the last twenty-five years has been taught to make similarly lazy assumptions where memory is concerned, with shrinks resorting to any anxiety their patients express as being rooted in a childhood trauma usually centred on sexual abuse by a family member. And I know this to definitely be the case, for I was pressurised into manufacturing such a memory myself when in therapy. Thankfully, I rejected this because I was convinced had something of that nature happened there was no way I wouldn't have remembered it all my life.

The magician Derren Brown always makes the point that there is no magic involved in his ingenious scams involving members of the public, merely psychological suggestions he knows people are susceptible to. When one considers the shifting sands that constitute memory's flexible foundations, and how vulnerable it can be to such suggestions, it's rather worrying to realise the level of importance that is placed upon it in legal circles these days, condemning men to lengthy prison sentences for crimes that, in many cases, have only the unreliable witness of memory as evidence.

American psychologist Elizabeth Loftus has probably done more research into the untrustworthy nature of memory and the way in which it can be manipulated than anyone else over the last forty years; her work at the Department of Transportation opened her eyes to the variations in separate accounts from those who'd been witness to the same traffic accidents and she realised how easy it was to implant suggestions as to what had happened. She expanded this into a series of experiments that were not a million miles from the mind games of Derren Brown.

Her pioneering work in the field of false memory led to her becoming an expert witness in criminal court cases that rested on eyewitness evidence, some of which had been the result of hypnosis. She remains convinced that a mass moral panic along the lines of the Salem-like 'Satanic Abuse' crazes of the 90s usually has its roots in the manipulation of memory and the dangerous reliance upon it as cast-iron evidence.

More recent events on this side of the Atlantic appear to vindicate Elizabeth Loftus' findings, but we only have to reunite with old friends or family members in a communal trip down Memory Lane to be aware of how our individual recollections change as we age. Could we swear for sure our own memories are the definitive article and everyone else has simply got it wrong when theirs contradict ours? Take that uncertainty into a Court of Law and you're on very rocky ground indeed.

THE FINGER OF SUSPICION
1 February 2017

The granting of effective pardons to deceased men convicted of 'homosexual offences' prior to the decriminalisation of homosexual acts between consenting adults in 1967 may be deemed a Good Thing by those who have long promoted such an event; but when one considers the thousands incarcerated in British prisons on such charges before the long overdue change to the law, it's worth remembering how many of them are still with us. For them, this is little more than an empty gesture. Any amendments to the change to include the living on the list of the exonerated – and the potential minefield of whether a post-1967 conviction for sex with any man under the then-consenting age of 21 could be wiped from the records – were prevented by cynical filibustering. Apparently, one can always apply to the Home Office, but I suppose that august department knows most of those applying will probably be six feet under by the time the paperwork is completed.

Convictions of the non-dead for homosexual offences both before and after 1967 remain on their CVs, and thanks to the advent of CRB (now DBS) checks, the one-time crimes that death would erase the existence of retain the power to prevent the living from working in any profession in which contact with society's 'vulnerable' is paramount. Even the Rehabilitation Offenders Act 1974, which introduced a time

295

limit on a past criminal conviction so that it would cease to be a blot on an individual's future career chances after a specified period of rehabilitation, included numerous caveats in the shape of exemption from it where certain professions are concerned.

However, a system of scrutiny that once only applied to ex-cons now encompasses a far wider section of the population. A criminal check on a prospective employee, as with a credit check by a bank, is regarded by the advocates of the system as a sensible precaution, though many others may see it as an infringement of their civil liberties that places them under unwarranted suspicion, faced with an interminable wait for the process to clear a name that didn't require clearing in the first place. Doctors, nurses, teachers, youth-workers and care-workers (to name just a few) are all under this suspicion until their innocence has been established.

Anybody passing a Disclosure and Barring Service check is awarded with a certificate that essentially proclaims 'I am officially not a Paedo or pervert', confirmation that the individual the system presumes to be guilty is actually innocent. In a Court of Law, the onus is not on the defence to prove the accused didn't commit the crime they've been charged with, but on the prosecution to prove they did – and beyond reasonable doubt. When it comes to a DBS check, the process works the other way round. It temporarily criminalises great swathes of the workforce, marooning them in an unemployable limbo for months, keeping them hanging on for the moment when they receive notification that they are not what they knew they weren't all along.

Following several high-profile cases whereby a genuine rapist/Paedo/murderer slipped through the net and committed their favourite crime again, the restrictions imposed by DBS checks have been tightened to such a degree that the implication for anyone having to endure a DBS check is that these rare occasions are judged to be the rule rather than the exception. Primary schools are struggling to recruit male teachers as a consequence, and it has also had a detrimental effect on organisations like the Girl Guides, who are suffering a shortage of adult volunteers. Who would even want to work with children under such circumstances?

Putting the private business of employers and employees in the hands of an institution as corrupt and untrustworthy as the Police Force was destined to be a recipe for disaster. One may as well hand over the running of social media to the Stasi. Ten years ago, the Home Office revealed almost 3,000 people had been accidentally labelled as criminals following CRB checks, whereas it emerged in 2009 that any minor contact with police, even when there wasn't so much as a caution involved, would be present on an individual's 'Enhanced' CRB or DBS file (the one reserved for those seeking to work with children, the elderly or disabled adults). So, if you once had to give your name and address to a woodentop when he saw you waiting for a taxi and judged you to be loitering before moving you on, it'll be in there.

There is also an immense backlog of checks building up as the net widens to include more professions. Recent statistics exposed the worst performing Force when it came to backlogs; it was – surprise, surprise – the Met; another persistent offender, the South Yorkshire Police Force, was also in the top five. Last year it was reported that as many as 150,000 people with jobs lined-up were prevented from beginning these jobs due to DBS checks taking upwards of four months – and this despite Police Forces being set a target of processing at least 85% of applications over a period of 14 days. Labour blames the delays on Tory cuts, but it would hardly make much difference whoever happened to be running the country. The system itself is the problem.

Mind you, if you've already been through the process and are keen to move to another job in the same sector, it's now possible (for the annual sum of £13) to re-use the same DBS certificate you were awarded last time round; move into another sector, however, and you'll have to go through it all over again.

We have allowed the powers-that-be to criminalise us because we've been gullible enough to swallow the 'it's for your own good and the good of your children' guff, and look where it has left us – suspicious, wary, mistrustful, seeing only the bad in people, encouraged to snoop and snitch, leaving vital professions under-staffed and starved of those who could make a massive difference; but, hey, some dead men convicted of things that were actually illegal at the time can now rest easy in their graves, so we can be proud of our country once again.

THICK AS A BRICK
19 February 2017

Back in the dark days of the Sunday Sport, if the pair of tits decorating the front cover didn't catch the eye from the newsstand, the ludicrous headline alongside said mammaries usually did; long before the term Fake News was even coined, the Sport specialised in the silly and patently untrue. I suppose 'Post-Modern' could be applied to the Sunday Sport if one was inclined to be kind and view it as a parody of a Fleet Street weekend tabloid in the same way that Viz continues to spoof those trashy mags that clog-up the waiting rooms of GP's surgeries with uncanny accuracy. These days, it's often difficult to distinguish between the Real McCoy and the pastiche, particularly when it is the attention-grabbing headline that provokes heated debate, whether or not the causal shopper opts for the paper.

Take yesterday's Mail on Sunday. Emblazoned across its cover was the dramatic announcement – 'POLICE CHIEF: HEATH <u>WAS</u> A PAEDOPHILE'! Those that see nothing beyond that headline therefore have every suspicion confirmed. They may not even notice the 'POLICE CHIEF' prefix; but the headline says a former Prime Minister who never married and was never successfully outed as gay was definitely fond of little boys. There you go, job done. Mr and Mrs Public don't need to pursue the story any further; everything they need to know is there in those four little words uttered by yet another Chief Constable from a nondescript provincial police force desperate to justify the vast expense devoted to grave-pissing. It's there in black-and-white, in print; it's true.

It matters not that the Mail on Sunday has actually exhibited a degree of bravery in its recent efforts at debunking some of the urban myths that have sprouted online wings where the sexual peccadilloes of dead or elderly household names are concerned; with that one crass headline, they would appear to have undone months of hard investigative work that has exposed the stupidity of the police in giving airtime to fantasists from the outer limits of the internet. To most, the word of a Chief Constable means jack shit in 2017; who in possession of half-a-brain would believe anything the police say anymore? They are inherently corrupt and terminally corruptible. Yet, some out there are willing to take the word of Wiltshire Police's Mike Veale as Gospel. Then again, is this an ingenious ruse by the paper to highlight just how dense the men running our police forces really are?

There have evidently been no lessons learnt from the notorious 'credible and true' gaffe when a thick senior officer takes it upon himself to deflect criticisms of police manpower being redirected to fishing parties by making a personal opinion official before the pointless investigation has even been completed. Despite the fantasy of the so-called Westminster Paedophile Ring being utterly trashed, Mike Veale will not let it go; he claims those who have 'come forward' in relation to Ted Heath's alleged hobby have made allegations that are remarkably similar. Fancy that! It's not as though any of these tired old tales haven't been doing the rounds in the cyber kangaroo courts for years, with members of various forums sharing their lurid fantasies and upping the satanic angle with every retelling, is it?

Mike Veale declares he has '120%' conviction about the allegations against the dead PM; but even the language used advertises his level of intelligence. '120%' is the language of the dim, the language of the footballer being interviewed after he's just stepped off the pitch, like saying 'literally' when you don't mean literally. Yet after the Chief Plod issued his '120% conviction' to the press, subsequent PR statements from the Wiltshire Police make a mockery of Veale's comments.

According to a police spokesman, Veale is determined to 'ensure the investigation is proportionate, measured and legal' and the purpose of it all is to 'impartially investigate allegations without fear of favour and go where the evidence takes us. It is not the role of the police to judge the guilt or innocence of people in our criminal justice system'. How does that square with a Chief Constable making his prejudices public in the midst of an ongoing investigation? And are the deceased included amongst those people 'in our criminal justice system'?

Mike Veale's idiocy was apparent from day one, when he launched his force's foray into time-travelling from outside Ted Heath's former home and later denied it was a witch-hunt as the cost began to rise towards £1 million. Investigative officers even turned up at the HQ of Private Eye to peruse back issues of the magazine and see if they could uncover any suspicious references to Heath's unmarried status; yes, I know, this is a development straight out of Private Eye's satirical middle section, but it really happened. Where next? The home of Eric Idle because he wrote a comedy novel in the mid-70s called 'Hello Sailor', which featured a gay Prime Minister? Don't rule it out.

There have been fewer easier targets than Ted Heath when it comes to this kind of posthumous character assassination; as with Jimmy Savile, he had no wife or children to take the accusers and their allies in the police and law firms to task. Also, like Savile, his sexuality was the subject of much hearsay and gossip during his lifetime; and both were disliked by many. Death and the diminishing 'outrage' of homosexuality as a means of ruining a public figure have simply released hounds of an even more malicious nature. And if the prominent can be ripped to shreds with such callous ease it's no wonder the ordinary are so susceptible to the same treatment.

Come the Revolution, as Wolfie Smith used to say, maybe some of our most detestable misery-mongers will find themselves up against the wall for the bop-bop-bop treatment; added to the roll-call of past offenders, we may well see the name Mike Veale. I reckon his presence could be justified, judging by his recent behaviour. *I'm* convinced, anyway...120%.

Hold page 17! Get through coverage of the Budget and you might find the odd reference to the fact that a trio of Scotland Yard officers in the vanguard of the infamous Operation Midland have all been cleared over their handling of the investigation into a nonexistent 'VIP Paedophile Ring' seen in visions by a deluded (though mysteriously unprosecuted) fantasist whom we must still refer to as 'Nick'. Well, fancy that! That august body the Independent Police Complaints Commission has come to an utterly unexpected conclusion. Who could have seen that coming, eh?

Twelve months on from the closure of Operation Midland without a single arrest, charge or conviction, this breathtaking squandering of taxpayers' money achieved nothing other than ruining both the reputations and financial security of those targeted by a bunch of blundering Bobbies whose instructions from on-high to believe the accuser at all costs resulted in the most high-profile case of what has become standard police practice. So standard, in fact, that the current series of hit ITV drama 'Broadchurch' apparently promotes this in-built belief that the accused is guilty and the accuser is innocent long before such an investigation even gets anywhere near a courtroom.

The three who were surprisingly exonerated by the IPCC included Detective Superintendent Kenny McDonald, the dolt who pre-empted any possibility of a fair trial should it have come to that by declaring the accusations of 'Nick' were 'credible and true'. DS McDonald evidently believes his role is not much different from that of Judge Dredd, futuristic super-cop who acts as judge, jury and executioner; and his belief has not been trashed by this judgement. Although the

IPCC hearing, chaired by retired judge Sir Richard Henriques, identified 43 serious failings in the Operation Midland investigation – including stating the bleedin' obvious, that too much faith had been placed in the word of 'Nick' – it still declared the operation was 'extensive and carried out diligently'.

Five Met officers were referred to the IPCC, yet the clearing of three of them suggests the other two haven't got much to worry about. 'There is no evidence to indicate bad faith, malice or dishonesty', says the report, adding 'and no indication any of the officers may have behaved in a manner which would justify disciplinary proceedings'. One other area that gave the IPCC cause for concern was in regards to the detectives involved failing to present all relevant information to the district judge who gave the green light to the search warrants enabling them to kick down the doors of those named by 'Nick'. That three of those whose homes were searched were named and shamed by the media during the investigation is apparently not thought shameful in itself.

Deputy Assistant Commissioner Steve Rodhouse was also cleared of his part in a separate investigation into the involvement of the dying Leon Brittan in the same Paedo Ring, so that draws a line under a parallel farce. Even if the conclusions of the IPCC were utterly predictable and understandably regarded as a whitewash by those who suffered at the hands of the investigation (such as ex-MP Harvey Proctor), in a way one cannot hold the investigating officers wholly responsible for the disaster that was Operation Midland if the instructions they received vindicated the approach they took.

The 'maverick cop', that staple of British TV police dramas from Barlow in 'Z-Cars' and 'Softly Softly' through to Regan in 'The Sweeney' and Tennyson in 'Prime Suspect', no longer exists in the real world. If the police force in this country is inherently bent, it's the natural outcome of the way in which that force is organised from the top on down rather than a Gene Hunt-style rogue cop making up his own rules. The politicised changes in procedure that declare an accused man (and, let's face it, they're basically always men) is guilty till proven innocent means the police have already been trained into making their minds up before an investigation even begins. Should it really come as a great surprise that the likes of Harvey Proctor are engulfed in smoke that couldn't exist without any initial fire in the public perception when the rules have been rewritten to such a damaging degree where ancient British Law is concerned?

I'll be perfectly honest with you. I'm absolutely bloody sick of this subject and part of me resents the fact I feel compelled to pen yet another post on it when so many others online put the work in and do it a hell of a lot better as a consequence. But it continues to represent so much of what has gone wrong with this country over the last fifteen-twenty years that any blog pertaining to deal with the great issues of the day cannot ignore it, however hard the temptation to do so truly is.

The fact is that the small army of bloggers and tweeters who follow the topic with a dedication that is admirable are in the minority. Most people don't even give it much of a thought unless they themselves are on the receiving end of a false allegation and then a door is opened to them that had previously been barely ajar. And these are the people that are denied the platform to air their grievances that Harvey Proctor or Paul Gambaccini can call upon – the genuine silent majority who suffer the most when the finger of suspicion is aimed at them and they are at the mercy of a police force that has been politically remodelled to fit an agenda the police force was not created for. Peel must be turning in his grave.

COMMON SENSE AND SENSIBILITY
13 March 2017

Around ten years ago, my closest female friend – let's, for the sake of this piece, call her Violet – went for a drink with a mutual female friend (who we'll call Pauline) on a Saturday night; after the pair had got into conversation with two unattached guys (as often happens), Pauline abruptly exited the pub, leaving a 'tipsy' Violet in the company of two men about whom she knew absolutely nothing, an action which struck me as remarkably irresponsible. It turned out Violet's newly-single status had caused Pauline to enter that weird feminine phase of competitive bitchiness that makes a mockery of 'the sisterhood'; suddenly seeing Violet as an unattached rival in the pulling game and perhaps perceiving Violet was receiving the kind of attention ordinarily reserved for her, Pauline abandoned Violet when she was in an extremely vulnerable position.

Thankfully, nothing horrible happened, though it could have done as Violet walked half-a-mile home alone in an intoxicated state in the wee small hours of Sunday morning; she only told me of this a few days later. Not only was I angry with Pauline's petty conduct, but I was annoyed that Violet hadn't rung me to accompany her on the journey home; I only lived a short distance from the pub in question and would have gladly joined her simply to ensure she had a safe trip back to base. This wasn't me acting as Sir Galahad; it was me offering to come to a friend's assistance as well as expressing a streetwise awareness of how some men can exploit a young woman when her wits are diluted by alcohol.

I'm pretty certain mothers issue warnings to their teenage daughters about such scenarios; they wouldn't amount to much as mothers if they didn't. It is nothing more than basic common sense. After all, drink can alter behaviour in ways that no other 'legal high' is capable of; it can make us violent and aggressive; it can make us extrovert and hilarious; and it can make us uninhibited to the point whereby situations we'd reject when sober are stripped of their cautionary warning signs.

Back when women wouldn't surrender their virtue without a ring on their finger, some men resorted to plying them with booze in the hope it would loosen more than just their suspender belts; it was a risky business prior to the widespread availability of birth control, but it happened – something that those of us whose parents were rushed into a shotgun wedding are conscious of, even if we ourselves weren't 'courting' at a time when the rules of the game were far more formal than they are now.

The summing-up of Judge Lindsey Kushner when preparing to sentence a convicted rapist in Manchester last week seemed to speak of the changing climate where sexual morals are concerned; she strongly stressed the victim of the convicted man wasn't 'asking for it', but she did emphasise the perils inherent in young women drinking themselves into a stupor when there are men around who seize on the vulnerability drink can engender. She said: 'Girls are perfectly entitled to drink themselves into the ground, but should be aware people who are potential defendants to rape gravitate towards girls who have been drinking. It shouldn't be like that, but it does happen and we see it time and time again.'

Who could possibly dispute the reasonable logic in the words of a judge making her final summary in her final case before retiring? Well, who else but that fanatical and unhinged Police and Crime Commissioner for Northumbria (lucky Northumbria) – the North East's answer to Valerie Solanas, Vera bloody Baird. A bitter and twisted real-life 'Millie Tant' with enough chips on her shoulder to keep an ailing fish shop in business for a good couple of years, Baird's whole shtick is a form of psychological entrapment that is intent on exposing all men as the rapists-in-waiting she believes them to be. A female judge urging her fellow females to not put themselves in a position where *actual* rapists-in-waiting could capitalise on their vulnerability is apparently part of the problem.

Judge Kushner's warnings were (according to Baird) 'victim-blaming'; she accused the judge of implying 'it's your fault for having attracted him in the first place'. One could say Baird had reacted in characteristic knee-jerk fashion without having read the judge's full statement, but Baird probably had her reaction prepared long before, merely waiting for any judge to utter similar sentiments before being able to use it. Her response was utterly predictable if one examines her record.

Thanks to Baird's insistence that virtually every intimate exchange between the sexes constitutes male aggression, the reporting of incidents of sexual assault has risen, though it's worth bearing in mind context. The mentally disturbed resident of a care home can call the police to claim she's been raped, and even though the police are accustomed to receiving such calls on a regular basis and are well aware the caller in question is a deluded fantasist, the call is still registered as a report of a sexual assault. Baird also instigated the committees comprising the usual do-gooders with too much time on their hands that sit-in on rape cases in the North East, issuing severe admonishments to the judiciary should a jury find an accused man innocent. To hand someone with such an extreme and biased agenda the kind of power Baird can call upon is a dangerous state of affairs indeed.

I doubt few parents of young women or anyone with any semblance of common sense could find fault with Judge Kushner's summary; she never hinted girls who drink too much are inviting sexual assault; she simply cautioned them against putting themselves in a place where the kind of men who *do* exploit a drunken woman have free rein to act upon their worst instincts. For the likes of Vera Baird to hijack the summary to slot into her own tunnel-vision viewpoint and present it to the media as an outrage says everything you need to know about that disgraceful individual.

THE PRESUMPTION OF GUILT
19 April 2017

'It was one of those immensely rare and exceptional cases where the decision to prosecute and thereafter to continue the prosecution was an unnecessary or improper act.' So spoke His Honour Judge Martin Edmunds in his official verdict of a case he tried in which a jury cleared a deputy headmaster of raping a 14-year-old female pupil; he came to his conclusion in a written costs ruling that was published in last weekend's Mail on Sunday. It's hard to read the passage quoted without wondering where Judge Edmunds has been lately. 'Immensely rare and exceptional'? *Really?* With an estimated half of cases brought before Crown Courts in England and Wales today being 'sex cases', the case His Honour commented upon seems a microcosm of everything that is wrong with the legal system and the insidious organisation spearheading its abuse known as the Crown Prosecution Service.

If just one case was to be selected as representative of the corruption of the Law and the way in which it is enacted today, the sad story of Kato Harris appears to have it all. And at the dark heart of this sorry saga that left the career and reputation of an innocent man in tatters are (yet again) the toxic twins responsible for a growing trail of injustice and misery that has served to obliterate any lingering shreds of faith in this country's upholders of fair play – the CPS and the Metropolitan Police Force.

The 35-year-old deputy head of the fee-paying St George's School in Ascot, Kato Harris was regarded as an inspirational teacher and a popular one; however, his rapid rise through the ranks ground to a horrific halt when a girl he'd never even taught at his previous school accused him of raping her on three separate occasions. Adhering to the 'she who must be believed' edict issued to all police forces where sexual offence accusations are concerned, the boys in blue demonstrated their noted subtlety by turning up at Mr Harris' school and bundling him away in full view of bemused pupils.

What followed over the next year-and-a-half was a nightmarish ordeal for Kato Harris familiar to hundreds of men in this country who have been at the mercy of a legal system that has overturned the 'innocent till proven guilty' foundation stone upon which English Law was built. Never imagining he'd actually be charged, the moment he *was,* Mr Harris' world collapsed. Suspended from work, barred from his local church and cricket team, publicly named and shamed whilst his accuser enjoyed the luxury of anonymity, Kato Harris became an overnight outcast in the community he had been a prominent member of.

According to a teacher at her school, Mr Harris' accuser (whose parents used to fly her to New York for weekly therapy) was engaged in a competition with a friend as to who could concoct the most audacious story, and it would seem the name of Kato Harris was plucked out of thin air with the nonchalance of a retired footballer extracting balls from the bag during the draw for the Third Round of the FA Cup. What gave her story clout, despite the inaccuracies in her flimsy evidence, were the deep pockets of her parents, who hired Sue Akers, ex-Deputy Assistant Commissioner at Scotland Yard and now working as a private detective. She was recruited via a legal firm known as Mishcon de Reya, along with her partner-in-crime Alison Levitt, who just happened to be a former legal adviser to the CPS.

Sue Akers played her part in the CPS's decision to prosecute by renewing old contacts at the Met, supplying Scotland Yard detectives with a list of tasks that could secure a conviction. Working in tandem with Levitt, she recommended they contact all of Mr Harris' former pupils and that they seize his computer for incriminating evidence (none was found); the relentless pressure from Akers and Levitt even annoyed senior detectives working on the case who were well aware of the gaping holes in the accuser's tall tale; but they carried on lobbying.

When bombarding the CPS and Met with emails, Alison Levitt tellingly stooped to one including a statement from personality-free Labour MP Keir Starmer, her former mentor, who highlighted Levitt's 'findings' in the DPP report into Jimmy Savile. If ever proof were needed to underline Ms Levitt's chilling agenda, this email had it in spades. Yet, still the case went to trial.

Kato Harris was cleared of the charges by a jury in the space of fifteen minutes. Despite this, St George's School declined to resume his employment there. He is currently unemployed and is understandably reluctant to return to teaching in any capacity; why would any man even enter the profession anymore? Judge Edmunds ruled that the CPS decision to prosecute was an 'improper act' and that they should now pay Mr Harris' legal fees, though they have offered a paltry amount so far. The Met, meanwhile, claim that an independent review of their actions by the Greater Manchester Police said no evidence was found that the accuser's representatives 'were inappropriately given any physical access to information concerning the investigation'.

An innocent man on the scrapheap, branded for life and unwilling to re-enter the profession he was apparently extremely good at; a narcissistic fantasist endorsed by wealthy parents and a despicable law firm; legal reforms that encourage such malicious vendettas; the CPS and the Met once more joining forces on an immoral crusade to appease victims lobbyists without a care for those trampled underfoot – none of these factors are unique in 2017.

Kato Harris may not feel it, but he is a lucky man. He's not behind bars for something he didn't do. In the current climate, that in itself is a triumph. The easiest way to ruin anyone today is to simply point the finger and shout 'Paedo!' Job done.

REMAKE/REMODEL (RETRIAL)
20 July 2017

I think I can probably say with a degree of shameful confidence that I was not the only man – or woman, come to that – whose first response upon hearing the bizarre case of Gayle Newland was 'Why didn't she video it?' Okay, so it's not something most would be especially proud of, but as sexual fantasies go it was certainly an original one and would have been a good deal more entertaining than the majority of those that stretch the nation's broadband connections to breaking point in the wee small hours. Beyond the admirable dedication to deception by *both* parties (lest we forget), this particularly strange incident highlights the muddied moral and legal waters physical intimacy has become bogged down in.

For those not in the know, 27-year-old Gayle Newland seduced an allegedly unknowing female friend by entering into a post-'Fifty Shades' fantasy whereby the online (male) identity she had cultivated since the age of 13 arranged to meet with said friend. However, to maintain the mystery that 'Miss X' willingly entered into, somewhat kinky rules were laid down that the lady accepted from the off. We are told 'Miss X' had no idea who the man was that demanded she wear a blindfold even before the pair of them got down and dirty. A woman who only knows someone from (presumably) fruity online chinwags and then crosses the cyber boundary by meeting up with them in person agrees to never actually look the fellow in the eye? A complete stranger she voluntarily puts herself in the hands of with no regards for her personal safety whatsoever? Miss X is either the thickest woman on the planet or her claims of being deceived should've been thrown out of court on day one of the original trial.

Firstly, Gayle Newland must be a remarkable mimic. Some women are gifted with irresistibly sexy husky voices, but even the vocal talents of Joan Greenwood, Tara Fitzgerald or Fenella Fielding at their 40-a-day huskiest could hardly be confused with those of Barry White. There's a world of tonal difference between the two that could only ever fool someone who either wants to be fooled or chooses to ignore the aural evidence. Even if she employed the technical tricks used by the likes of 'Anonymous' in disguising her voice, surely that should have set alarm bells ringing?

Secondly, Miss Newland's elaborate tactics once her 'victim' acquiesced with her mystery man's desire to get his leg over – binding her breasts and donning a strap-on dildo – would have brought Miss X's other senses to the fore. Even if she couldn't see the deception with her own eyes, she must be incredibly inexperienced in carnal matters if she cannot tell the difference between a facsimile penis and the real thing. And despite Newland's best efforts, a woman's body undoubtedly feels and smells different to a man's – not quite as hairy, for one thing, especially at a time when anything pubic is verboten where the young female form is concerned.

So, we have a scenario wherein a woman embarks upon a sexual relationship with an anonymous stranger she initially met online and yet never lays eyes upon him, a sexual relationship that spanned at least ten different rounds of bedroom gymnastics, and yet all the time Miss X unswervingly believed she was being given one by a member of the opposite sex? Do me a favour! The whole assignation was wrapped in knowing fantasy from the moment the inaugural exchanges took place on the internet. This was implicit before the two even met in person, let alone when they did meet, and Miss X was never once allowed to see her seducer. Yet Gayle Newland received an eight–year prison sentence in 2015 and has just received a six-and-a-half year one after a retrial following an appeal.

There was an infamous case around twenty years back when a bunch of sadomasochistic gay guys were done for deliberately inflicting pain upon one another during a private gang-bang – something involving hammers, nails and other DIY tools that Black & Decker didn't specifically design for such an occasion – and the general public's response to the intervention of the police and the judiciary was largely that neither had any business interfering in something the participants entered into with full knowledge of what it would entail.

The Sexual Offences Act of 2003 states that a person agrees to sexual activity 'if she/he agrees by choice, and has the freedom and capacity to make that choice'. Miss X agreed to sexual activity with Gayle Newland in her male alter-ego; granted, she didn't realise she was being rogered by a woman she regarded as a platonic pal; but surely the thrill of the unknown was a key element of the gamble she decided to take when complying with the unconventional circumstances in the first place? After all, the mystery man could've been her father, for all she knew.

Gayle Newland was hardly alone in adopting a persona for online correspondence. Every contributor to this here blog, author and commentator, uses a pseudonym when posting, for example; and there are various long-established sites that take this one step further as nom-de-plumes are expanded into fictitious personas that enter into fantasy affairs with their fellow fantasists. One could argue both are harmless fun in which awareness on both sides invalidates accusations of deception. By transferring this kind of interaction from mobile or monitor to the bedroom, the two participants have to be conscious of what they're doing; and by Miss X acquiescing with Newland's admittedly odd demands, she was preparing to take a risk she ultimately took.

Had Gayle Newland killed Miss X in a hit-and-run accident, the sentence she received could well have been half the length of the original sentence she received in 2015 (as well as the one she received today) for having sex with her; had she inadvertently strangled her during one of their sex sessions, the sentence probably wouldn't have been much longer than eight years. So, one has to ask the question why a consensual act of sexual intercourse – remember, Miss X didn't object – has resulted in a mentally confused young woman addicted to the make-believe realm of cyberspace (hardly unique in 2017) being twice condemned to years behind bars. Is she being punished for what she did or the times in which she did it?

CASTING COUCH POTATOES
16 October 2017

It's less than two years since the Oscars Ceremony presented Lady GaGa's 'Victims Symphony', complete with a chorus line of Survivors™ resplendent in concentration camp chic to tastefully hammer home the metaphor; and it's less than a year since the Golden Globes provided a platform for Meryl Streep to play Meryl Streep by condemning the new tenant of the White House without naming him in a histrionic speech that ticked all the liberal Hollywood boxes. Last autumn, the red carpet residents sided with a woman complicit in covering-up her husband's innumerable infidelities and opposed the election of a man caught on tape bragging about 'pussy' like a teenage boy who'd never been laid. And all the time, they were aware that one of their own was apparently even worse, but said nothing. Dame Meryl had even called him 'God'.

If Meryl Streep's least appealing role is Meryl Streep, nobody quite does Emma Thompson as a simpering-faced identity politician like Emma Thompson; she's been at it this weekend in a video saturating social media, adding her wise-after-the-event voice to the sudden stampede to name and shame Harvey Weinstein now that it's okay to do so. Perhaps the Tinsel Town elite are falling over each other to damn the deposed mogul because his supposedly sleazy activities have reminded the wider world that, for all the PC makeover it has received in recent years, Hollywood is – and always has been

315

– a grubby little corner of California where glorified pimps like Weinstein have free rein to live out their Playboy Mansion fantasies safe in the knowledge that the biz will indulge them as long as the box-office is booming.

I doubt anyone outside of the Hollywood bubble was really surprised at the revelations that have erupted this past week; maybe the only real surprise has been the sheer number of allegations. They only usually happen here if the accused is already six feet under, though the Met must be rubbing its hands together at the thought of being involved in allegations concerning someone in the entertainment firmament who isn't on his deathbed or dead already. But it's not as though what Weinstein has apparently gotten away with throughout his career as a leading producer has no precedence in his seedy neck of the woods.

The casting couch has been a permanent part of the furniture in the American movie business since the silents; Marilyn Monroe allegedly expressed that achieving stardom might hopefully mean that she wouldn't have to suck anymore cocks. Fat, rich powerful men abusing and exploiting wide-eyed wannabe starlets fresh off the Greyhound Bus from Hicksville is a loathsome tradition woven into the foundations of the industry. Indeed, the only voices we aren't hearing at the moment are those of the actresses who got where they are because they submitted to Weinstein's advances.

Lest we forget, however, all we have so far are allegations and accusations, yet it's testament to the times in which we live that Weinstein has been hung, drawn and quartered before any of this has reached a courtroom; mind you, it happened to Bill Cosby quick enough, so Weinstein knew what to expect when disowned by family, friends and the industry in record time. The fate awaiting Dirk Bogarde's character in 'Victim' springs to mind; when his successful early 60s lawyer is threatened with the public exposure of his relationship with another man, he warns his wife that her intention to stand by him no matter what will result in utter social exclusion and the cold shoulders of friends and associates fearful of being tarred by the scandal.

Just as a virtual 'conspiracy of silence' appears to have enabled Weinstein to maintain his dubious lifestyle, the post-outing consensus has been set with remarkable speed. Fashion queen Donna Karan made the mistake of publicly contradicting the sudden about-turn and was forced to issue a hasty apology when swamped by a viciously hostile online reaction which only just stopped short of a mass bonfire of the designer gear Hollywood has clad itself in for decades. James Corden, a man whose comedic talents continue to elude anyone with a sense of humour, has also taken the Karan route of begging forgiveness to salvage his mystifying career following his ill-timed jokes on the subject. Saying nothing was the rule until a week or so ago; now if anything is said at all, it has to constitute absolute condemnation.

The difficulty for those not required to rush to judgement is that, having been subjected to multiple scandals of this nature over the past half-decade, every sensational addition to the roll-call of 'hiding in plain sight' villains inspires instant scepticism in some and utter conviction as to the guilt of the accused in others; we've had so many that it's hard not to fall into a default mode. The pattern is so established now that being bombarded by the latest chapter in this thoroughly modern saga inevitably leads one to react in the same way as one reacted last time round.

As tends to be the case, initial accusations of impropriety swiftly move on to more serious allegations of rape, and one wonders how long it will take before Weinstein is accused of murdering one of the women he supposedly assaulted, let alone being a member of a Beverly Hills Satanic set indulging in ritual abuse and murder. Actually, Alex Jones is probably already bursting his lungs airing that theory on YouTube, thinking about it. The script is becoming as repetitive and predictable as the ones that make up most of the slurry the US film industry churns out these days; but it's box-office dynamite, and that's the currency of the movies. Hollywood, we have a franchise.

HANDS, KNEES AND BUMPS-A-DAISY
1 November 2017

Unfortunately, it's one of the recurring stories of our times and one that it becomes increasingly difficult to say something new about whenever it rears its ugly head; once again, the headlines keep us in a state of permanent déjà-vu and the seriousness of the crime is almost diminished through terrible repetition. Sadly, we're back where we've been so many times before, but there's no way it can be avoided; the grim truth demands our attention. Yes, Damian Green allegedly touched a woman's knee.

In other news, New York experienced a major terror incident when a Jihadist drove a van onto the sidewalk and ploughed down pedestrians and cyclists alike, killing eight of them before being apprehended. Miraculously, he wasn't shot dead by cops and survives to face the music, though the biggest concern for some is inevitably not the bodies cluttering up Manhattan's pavements but an anticipated upsurge in 'Islamophobia'. Anyway, enough of that trivial little domestic business across the pond. Onto more serious matters.

The journalist and broadcaster Julia Hartley-Brewer claimed Defence Secretary Michael Fallon once touched her knee and she made it clear in no uncertain terms what she would do to him if his hand came into contact with said body part again. Fallon withdrew. Fallon is someone who previously edged Philip Hammond in the contest to decide the dullest member of the Cabinet, yet this moment of indiscretion has suddenly and remarkably made the grey man moderately interesting. I doubt few of us would have been surprised had Boris stood accused of such a dastardly deed, but *Michael Fallon?* Lock up your daughters, especially if they happen to be young party activists; just ask Labour.

It's interesting that a professional political class which has unquestionably supported DPP Alison Saunders' cynical crusade to up the rape conviction statistics by broadening the legal definition of sexual assault is now being confronted by the ramifications of this support. The Saunders approach is all fine and dandy if some pleb has the finger of suspicion aimed at him, but the problem with legal definitions is that they're supposed to be egalitarian and don't distinguish between class, wealth and social standing. Granted, the ruthless cuts to legal aid have severely limited Joe Public's ability to defend himself when confronted by an allegation of a sexual nature, but those whose incomes can feather the most exclusive law firm nests probably never imagined they'd be placed in a situation where they'd have to deal with the grim reality of everything they failed to challenge the wisdom of.

William Hague urged caution on Radio 4's 'Today' this morning when it comes to believing the authenticity of every allegation aimed at a public figure, though I don't remember similar caution being advised by Westminster when the Yewtree witch-hunt was rounding up showbiz stalwarts from the 70s and 80s; back then, the 'I believe her' mantra was being recited from every political platform. Operation Midland attracted more criticism in that its targets weren't quite as irrelevant as Yewtree's hapless has-beens, though despite a grovelling after-the-event apology from Sir Bernard Hogan-Howe as the outgoing Met Chief sought to cover his back, the damage done to the likes of Harvey Proctor remains a shameful example of what can happen when the powers-that-be allow our police force to be politicised by an inherently merciless and perennially unsatisfied agenda.

The sudden downfall of a liberal left Hollywood darling like Kevin Spacey shows how when the 'I believe her' (or in Spacey's case, 'him') rule is applied to everyone rather than a select few, it's actually not very nice at all. Holding up a placard or wearing a T-shirt bearing a nifty hash-tag slogan is easy when you imagine you're above the net being cast; when that net is widened and you risk being entangled in it, the experience of thousands of nonentities denied your privileges is brought into extremely sharp focus as the irresponsible gamble of not questioning the placing of a clumsy pass on a level playing field with a brutal rape is writ horrifyingly large. The system that has promoted and repeatedly failed to challenge this fallacy can eject its favoured sons without a second thought if it means the whole system risks being tarnished with the same unsavoury accusations. There must be a lot of leading men in Tinsel Town consulting their lawyers at the moment.

When OJ Simpson was on trial for the murder of his ex-wife way back in 1994/95, the defence shrewdly played the race card, garnering wide African-American support in the process as focus shifted away from the actual crime itself and onto the broader subject of US race relations; their client was rewarded by walking away from court a free man, hailed as the victim of the trial as opposed to the cause of it. One cannot but wonder if Bill Cosby had been accused of murder rather than rape that the voices noticeably silenced in their support for one of the entertainment industry's great black pioneers might have been heard in a way they weren't as, one-by-one, women came forward to accuse him whilst the system that had celebrated him for decades denounced him.

The ruling elite have sat back and allowed this state of affairs to develop unchecked for a long time because they imagined they were immune to it. In their desperate search for votes and eagerness to be seen endorsing various pseudo-'liberal' causes, they have gleefully given the thumbs-up to dubious moral movements without reading the small print; and now they are finally paying the price for their stupidity. Well, more fool them. I should imagine many little men rotting away in a prison cell on the strength of an allegation propelled towards a guilty verdict via a climate fully endorsed by the political class will be short on sympathy; and who could blame them?

THE F**K-IT LIST
5 November 2017

You may recall a post on here last year titled 'Tumbleweed Injunction', all about a story involving a certain *Grande Dame* of British pop music who couldn't be named by the mainstream media on account of a super-injunction and accompanying threat of legal proceedings should a TV programme or newspaper dare to say his moniker out loud when reporting his alleged threesome. This particular case was as good an example as any of how the senior mediums have been rendered redundant by cyberspace when it comes to free speech. Although my piece didn't once say the stage name said musician adopted almost fifty years ago, one would have to be a bit dim not to guess to whom I was referring.

Besides, everybody bloody knew who it was, with or without the trademark platform boot I illustrated the article with.

We now have one more example of how the info is out there and the MSM is powerless to use it whilst the rest of us can choose to access it if we want, finally liberated from having that choice dictated to us by the press or TV. Westminster's uncut 'dodgy dossier' is available via Twitter and the version I've seen is a straightforward photocopy sourced from God-knows-where, with the contents laid bare and not needing a running commentary. My job today is not to repeat that list verbatim; for one thing, there's no point, what with it already having been seen by a potential audience of thousands; for another, it's not my role to be a 'rogue journalist'. A bit of rogue I might be, but I'd never presume to label myself a journalist. Besides, if I were, I'd be even more restricted in what I can or can't say re the names on the list.

It's an odd combination of personal kinkiness, innocuous (and hardly illegal) activities between consenting adults, and genuinely unpleasant lechery. Whoever compiled it clearly collected every snippet of gossip from the frivolous to the serious that had been overheard in the corridors of power and cobbled the lot together in one unsavoury package – not unlike the way in which such behaviour outside of Parliament has been cobbled together in law by a poisonous moral crusade that politicians have endorsed in the belief it would never pierce their sanctimonious bubble. Now it has belatedly encroached upon their own sexual misadventures they're suddenly screaming 'Witch Hunt'! Tough Titty – or should that be *Sugar* Titty?

Like most, I should imagine, there are a great deal of names on the list I've never heard of, but that's no surprise when one considers the sheer volume of parasites sucking on the breast of our democracy. It's a bit like whenever I casually switch on BBC Parliament and catch some moribund late afternoon debate as opposed to the all-star parade that is PMQs. I struggle to recognise the majority of MPs lounging around on the half-empty benches as some anonymous nonentity drones on, and many of them could well be included on this list for all I know. It goes without saying that my eyes took note of names I *did* recognise when perusing it, and there are around a dozen of them. Some have already been safely 'outed', whilst others raised the odd eyebrow. Good Lord, there are even some *women* on there! And here's me thinking this sexual predator thing was a purely male pastime.

One of the women on the list has a very high-profile post indeed, though her crime was having had 'a workplace relationship'; that hardly makes her Rose West. Another female member of the Government with an important day-job is accused of fornicating with a male researcher while a backbench MP – and, yes, fornicating is the somewhat quaint word the compiler of the list uses. One of the mostly male MPs listed is described as being 'handy at parties'; another is 'handy in taxis'. One 'asked a female researcher to do odd things', but we're not told what they were (or what constitutes 'odd' in this context); another 'likes to have intercourse with men who are wearing women's perfume'. One has 'odd sexual penchants' (again – *how* odd?) and is also 'sexual with a fellow MP', who happens to be described as 'a drunk'; another takes the starring role in a video that features him being urinated on by not one, not two, but 'three males'! Whatever turns you on, eh?

However, also included are the likes of one male MP who allegedly impregnated a former researcher and made her have an abortion; another 'paid a female to be quiet' – a right pair of charmers by the sounds of it. At the same time, one MP is damned for taking his personal trainer to the cinema and then to 'private rooms at the Carlton'! I'm sure the personal trainer appreciated the gesture more than the researcher who was cajoled into having an abortion, which makes one wonder why the two actions share the same list. I suppose both are demonstrations of how politicians exercise power over those that work for them – benignly and malignantly; and isn't that what this hoo-hah is really about?

As we have seen, some of the descriptions of behaviour read like stage directions from a sketch on 'The Benny Hill Show', which again underlines the error in throwing the trivial in with the far more worrying allegations; it elevates one to a level it doesn't warrant and diminishes the seriousness of the other. But, as the minor incidents outnumber the major ones on the list, maybe jumbling them all up was the idea; maybe this is a means of enabling those under threat from the list to dismiss it and survive the scandal because the entire dodgy dossier could be discredited as having blown everything out of all proportion. In fact, the leaking of the list could even be viewed as a pre-emptive red herring to derail a proper investigation into the few allegations present that are a bit extreme for your average 'Carry On' movie. But it might just be too late now.

SYMPATHY FOR THE DEVILISH
7 November 2017

Again – yet again – the memorable sketch from 'Not The Nine O'Clock News' springs to mind. Rowan Atkinson and Mel Smith play MPs from opposite sides of the House, engaging in a lively debate chaired by Pamela Stephenson; as their argument reaches fever pitch, Rowan Atkinson keels over and dies of a heart attack. Mel Smith abruptly switches his vitriolic critique of his opponent's stance midsentence and ends it by paying tribute to a Great Parliamentarian. We've seen it one more time today as the death was announced of Labour MP Carl Sargeant, a man who was the Welsh Government's Secretary for Communities and Children until he was sacked last Friday. The reason for his dismissal was related to another allegation of the kind Westminster has been awash with over the past seven days.

It appears Mr Sargeant's death was by his own hand, which is always a painfully sad way to end a life; but it was really only a matter of time before one of the politicians falling under the finger of suspicion took this route out of it. The kind of gushing tributes being paid to Carl Sargeant in the wake of his apparent suicide probably didn't accompany his dismissal and party membership suspension just a few days ago because, as we all know, a man is guilty till proven innocent in 'the Court of Public Opinion', that non-Judicial body vigorously endorsed by every MP confident their own conduct was free from the allegations that have plagued other public bodies since society spinelessly kowtowed to the 'I believe her' mindset.

The Crown Courts of Britain assemble for business each Monday morning with disparate members of the public pulled out of the Jury Service tombola having to put their lives and livelihoods on ice for a fortnight. Whilst the barristers and judges casually stroll into the hallowed environs smug in the knowledge they won't be lumbered with the extortionate parking fees that the potential jurors have to endure if they ignore the condescending advice to use that useless means of getting from A to B known as public transport, the system grinds on at a snail's pace as people without a 'Right Honourable' prefix to their names face the music.

These insignificant plebs have been enduring the allegations Westminster residents are now suddenly confronted by for the last half-decade or so; their pariah status is emphasised by the warnings dished out to the jurors that craving a cigarette break outdoors might entail sharing a smoking space with 'criminals' – the status afforded the accused before their trial has even been graced with a verdict. Of course, the police and the CPS have no politicised agenda at all, and the accused wouldn't even be there if smoke hadn't been sighted before their fire began. Anyone fortunate enough never to have fallen foul of the boys-in-blue nail varnish has absolute faith in their integrity, naturally, and thus a negative opinion of the individual is formed even before the swearing-in ceremony.

Despite the Expenses' Scandal of less than a full decade ago, the elected gravy train freeloaders have continued to recline in their exalted cocoons, convinced their lifestyle choice has rendered them immune from the curse of the false allegation or the taint of an accusation imbued with the power to end a career. How crushing it must be to finally realise they actually have no immunity from a moral crusade that has laid waste to hundreds of less important lives across the country, not to mention showbiz veterans whose advanced years and kitsch celebrity means they don't matter.

Chris Evans and his ginger willy aside, there are no further entertainment icons to pursue, and dead public servants have had their graves so saturated with piss that even their pursuers are now seeking a golden handshake – see Wiltshire Constabulary's Mike Veale. Where else to go to feed the insatiable appetites of Alison Saunders and Vera Baird? Why, Westminster, of course – not forgetting the poor relations of Cardiff and Edinburgh.

It was fine when a dying has-been like Leon Brittan was being shaken out of slumber on his deathbed or a WWII hero like Lord Bramall was having his house turned over on the instructions of a despicable Met chief ironically poised to replace him in the Lords – raised voices were few and far between then. But now we are supposed to be outraged that those who facilitated a climate wherein such events could take place are being bitten by the monster they approved the creation of. Well, sorry for the inconvenience, Westminster 2017; but it serves you right.

Yes, it's sad that a man has to take his own life in the wake of allegations that have yet to be proven; but how many other lives have been taken in similar circumstances – ones that were denied the spotlight Carl Sargeant's suicide has received today? And how many nauseatingly hypocritical tributes were paid to those lives when they were lost? Not many, I suspect. I'm afraid the chickens are coming home to roost now, and it's increasingly hard to summon-up sympathy for the highest profile victims of a witch-hunt that the latest victims of gave the seal of approval to in the belief it would never touch them.

HEADING FOR A SKID, MARK?
6 November 2018

No, the irony will never escape me, but I do have to admit I owe Mark Williams-Thomas a great deal. Deprived of ITV's top investigative reporter rising without a trace in 2012, I certainly wouldn't be writing this and you wouldn't be reading it. Thanks to the tireless efforts of the fearless 'former police detective' and 'child protection expert' in alerting the nation to the scourge of celebrity paedos hiding in plain sight, I have been able to acquire an audience for my ramblings both in this medium and another. In fact, it was the other that enabled MWT to facilitate my first big break; and for that I will always be grateful to my generation's Roger Cook.

The 'Exposure' exposé on Jimmy Savile that aired on October 3 2012 was the career-launching platform MWT had desperately been looking for, following occasional work for 'Newsnight' in a similar vein. It also provided me with something of a platform too. At that point, I'd been uploading videos to YouTube for a good couple of years and had slowly built a small cult following for my redubs, remakes and remodels of largely vintage TV. After watching MWT's sensationalistic hatchet-job on a dead man who was admittedly as loathed as he was loved in his lifetime, my scepticism was superseded by a light-bulb moment. Here was a chance to combine and contrast the old world with the new one. And so Jimmy Savile became Great Uncle Bulgaria.

My first 'Exposure' spoof appeared within 48 hours of its source material being screened and went down well with my regular subscribers as well as helping to pick up a few more along the way. It was fairly short and quite crude – in terms of technical quality; the crudeness of the humour was a given – and I would probably have left it at that had not MWT used his newfound fame to kick-start a bandwagon he was determined to be in the driving seat of. Whilst shocking examples of the real thing were taking place at that very moment (albeit under the radar in faraway northern towns), the media's moral crusader convinced the nation that it had actually all happened in the 1970s and 80s; the rich, the famous and the powerful had been the perpetrators, and their wicked deeds had been securely shielded from the masses by top-level cover-ups, conspiracies and secret societies until MWT had the guts to shine a light on the clandestine network of shame.

The insidious instigation of Operation Yewtree, unleashing the Cromwellian storm-troopers of the police and their allies in the legal profession, spearheaded a Hopkins-esque witch-hunt in which safely unfashionable old celebrities were rounded-up one-by-one, usually thanks to the exhausting efforts of MWT. Yes, it was boom-time for ambulance-chasing law firms, false-memory therapists, and yours truly. By placing The Wombles at the centre of my parallel universe Operation It Could Be Youtree, I was able to expand the roll-call of the guilty (till proven innocent) by substituting each of the aged accused with telly contemporaries of Wimbledon Common's most infamous residents – Bagpuss, Hartley Hare, Mr Benn, Nogbad the Bad *et al* – as well as encompassing the motley crew of Icke disciples, fanatical fantasists and self-appointed paedo-hunters MWT had given the green light to.

Recently revisiting 'Exposure', I was surprised that my version of Mark Williams-Thomas, reborn (almost inevitably) as Mark JOHN-Thomas, doesn't actually appear until right at the very end of the third instalment. However, as MWT became more ubiquitous on-screen whenever Yewtree grabbed a headline, this humourless, pompous individual with a hilarious absence of self-awareness quickly asserted himself as the star of my show thereafter. MWT at that time had his own YT channel and such was his delicious vanity that virtually every appearance he had made on TV was there; I had an unlimited supply of footage I could play with. And I did. By the time I'd taken so much piss out of him that his bladder must have been running on empty, MWT mysteriously removed more or less all the videos I'd pillaged. Coincidence? The fact is my series had taken on a life of its own that went way beyond my usual YT audience, even as far as those directly affected by the events I was satirising.

Whilst I'd been playing my strongest hand to parody the hysteria, others had been playing theirs in different online mediums, and I discovered the 'Exposure' series was being passed around like illicit contraband. Some of its most enthusiastic fans made contact and new doors were opened to me as a consequence. Episodes gradually acquired a little more sophistication both in presentation and in material as I was being fed information I wouldn't otherwise have come across. The mainstream media was sticking rigidly to the MWT manual and no prominent journalist had yet dared to stick their head above the parapet for fear of being labelled a paedo apologist. For a good couple of years, my videos and the more forensic blogs of various determined diggers were the only places where an alternative to the consensus could be heard.

It took until celebrities whose currency hadn't dated along with their dress-sense found themselves caught in the Yewtree net before voices belatedly began to be to be tentatively raised. Gradually, the wider public were made aware of the dubious police tactics and yet we heard little of the non-famous casualties denied access to expensive lawyers, those whose lives had also been devastated by this appalling approach to law and order. Moreover, an #IbelieveHer agenda served to conveniently mute all those women whose men-folk had been whisked away at the crack of dawn by the CPS Stasi – all those wives, girlfriends, mothers, daughters and sisters who were suffering in silence because their stories didn't fit the narrative the MSM had opted for to present events, as ever, in simple black & white terms. Most are suffering still.

I'm lucky. I was able to walk away from the madness when I'd reached the end of the 'Exposure' road with a fourteenth and final episode that retold the tale in the style of Simon Schama's 'A History of Britain' series. I felt I'd extracted every ounce of sap from the Yewtree and there was nothing left to say, for me at least. Firmly established as the resident paedo professor of the daytime TV sofa, Mark Williams-Thomas nevertheless continued to seek out new celebrity scalps even as more questions than ever were being asked about Operation Yewtree and its ramifications, as well as its equally unnecessary successors, Midland and Conifer. And now those questions are bringing the odious role of MWT into the public spotlight at last; prominent papers are actually saying out loud what the rest of us were saying out loud five long years ago, when we were routinely dismissed as beyond-the-pale paedo sympathisers.

Paul Gambaccini's broadcasting clout guarantees him a sympathetic audience and gives him the freedom to openly describe what he went through as well as being critical of the system that exposed him to it, whereas others who experienced the same ordeal remain marginalised by their obscurity and tarnished in their communities. Yes, without Mark Williams-Thomas, there would be no 'Winegum Telegram'; but without Mark Williams-Thomas, there would be far fewer damaged families and far fewer ruined individuals. I'd happily consign this blog to the same great online platform in the sky that the 'Exposure' series now resides in if that pound-shop Titus Oates finally received a taste of his own rancid medicine.

9 781693 363832